Renegade Priest

OF THE
NORTHERN CHEYENNE

The Life and Work
of Father Emmett Hoffmann 1926-

To order books contact:

Soaring Eagle
745 Indian Trail
Billings, MT 59105
(406) 256-8500

Website: www.soaringeagle.org

Renee Sansom Flood

"We have been mistreated in the past
but we can forgive and forget
because God forgives all people."

Dr. John Woodenlegs

First Edition 2003
Second Edition 2005
Third Edition 2007

Printed in the United States of America
Library of Congress #2003114358
ISBN 0-913062-30-8

For Shane, Rachel and Beau Flood
with love and admiration

Acknowledgements

Writing history brings special challenges. Over the past eight years, three computers crashed and burned. Lightning struck my house. That fried computer four. Twice, back-up disks were made and lost, six chapters at a time. It has been an interesting journey.

Throughout the years, friends and colleagues have been particularly helpful in the arduous process. I would like to thank those who assisted by meeting and corresponding with me, by answering questions, or providing just the right photograph or document. Some have asked to remain anonymous and will remain so. Others were so essential to the creation of this book; I must thank them by name.

Clarence "Bisco" Spotted Wolf's friendship has kept me going. He is my mentor extraordinaire. Thank you for putting up with my chocolate crumbs, my tape recorder fumblings and for my know-it-all, non-Indian efforts at understanding the Northern Cheyenne people and their language.

Mark G. Thiel, C.A. at the John P. Raynor, S.J. Library at Marquette University, has helped me with every book I've written for the past 20 years. Mark's latest work, *Indian Way* contains excellent information, including the best Native American bibliography on compact disk.

My Soaring Eagle, a Public Charity colleague, Kim Flagen, has gotten me out of many a mess. Thank you Kim. God bless you.

A special thanks to Tim Boid for believing in me.

I am also indebted to the many people who have shared their experiences and expertise: Cleat Stevenson, Sterling Lord, Jamie and Kimmie Olson, Bula Brey, Dewanda Little Coyote, Chief Jimmie D. Little Coyote, Joe Straub, Gary E. Children, Norbert Jansen, Eloise and Lillian Krautkramer, Marion M. Placke, Catherine Hoffmann Yost, David A. Chang, Mrs. Leo Dohn Sr., Conrad & Ruth Sump, Paul Morigi, Leo Dohn Jr., Viola Campeau, Jon Hauxwell, MD, Gladys Schonenback, Jessie and Eldora Bement, Robert Bement, Fay Ellen Thompson, Dick Fletcher, Patsy Brey, Clifford and Caryl Long Sioux, Delores Little Coyote, Eddie Foote Sr., Joe Fox Sr., Father Larry Abler O.F.M. Cap, Father Chester Poppa O.F.M. Cap, Father Pascal Siler O.F.M. Cap, Father Gilbert Hemauer O.F.M. Cap, Father Dennis Druggan O.F.M. Cap, Father Patrick Berther O.F.M. Cap, Father Kenan Siegel O.F.M. Cap, Lee Eckman, Mary Ann McCullough, Marcus Stevens, Rosaire E. Lemire MD, Mr. Keith Egerton, PhD, the staff of the Marathon Library, Marathon, WI, staff of the Wausau Public Library, Wausau, WI, staff of the Montana State University Library – Billings,

staff of the Henry Malley Memorial Library, Broadus, Montana,
staff of Chief Dull Knife College, Lame Deer, MT, staff of St. Labre Indian School,
Ashland, MT, Ingrid Angel Duke, Irene Duke, Boon Phieng Duke, Dolly Not Afraid,
Dusty Howe, Jamie L. Porter, Jane Talbert Wagner, Richard Tall Bull Jr.,
Jeanne Forester, Reno Charette, Daniel Foote, Larry Amstutz MD, Tom Fenske,
Joseph, Carol Ann, Joe Jr., Justin and Cara George Kunkel, Kirk Green Jr.,
Louie Freiberg, Knud Christiansen, Rubie Sooktis, Butch and Lena Sooktis,
Tiger Stevenson, Mary Jo Fox, Shawn Backbone, Adelle Doughty,
Frank and Alice Huller, Chief Johnny Russell, Teddy Woodenthigh,
Larry Kostelecky, Wayne Leman, Doreen Mundie, Vivienne Wilbur,
Jaylyn, Melanie and Dennis Quaring, Shayla Hagen, Susan Schwartz,
Carolyn Blakemore, Ted and Peggy Fletcher, Sister Phyllis M. Hoffmann S.D.S.,
Dorothy and Joe Karlen, Marilyn Mondrowski, William J. Flood, Cliff Goudelock,
Tony Foote, Sam F. Widdicombe, Mary Jane Robinson, Rick Robinson,
Donald Hollowbreast, Virginia Toews, Gloria Barr, Alice Davis Smith,
Tim Mullette, John G. Crist, Warren Vest, Tom and Barbara Sansom,
Shane, Rachel and Beau Flood, Peter Anthony Figueras MD, Karen, Jacob and Haley,
and Mr. and Mrs. Marlin Johnson.

Contents

CHAPTER
1

Northern Cheyenne Reservation

The temperature was over 100 degrees when the lanky, 27 year-old Capuchin priest stepped off the train at Miles City, Montana. The famous, rowdy frontier town seemed plain and ordinary by 1954.

Two people sitting on a nearby platform bench eyed Father Emmett Hoffmann suspiciously. The man sat straight in his tall, black cowboy hat decorated with a hawk feather, a black silk neck scarf and long, shiny braids. Despite the extreme heat, the woman next to him clutched a faded woolen blanket around her shoulders. She had turned to watch a train pull away from the station when Fr. Emmett stopped in front of the couple and smiled.

"Good morning!" he said cheerfully.

Immediately, the woman disappeared into her blanket like a deer in a sage thicket, her head and eyes covered. The man kept his eyes down and he mumbled something. Surprised at their response and fearing he had insulted them, Father Emmett realized that he had just spoken to the first Northern Cheyenne Indians he had ever seen in his life. Later, he found out that looking down was a mark of respect and that a Cheyenne woman never stared directly into the eyes of a man – especially a white man.

Just then he caught sight of a brown-robed figure coming toward him from the opposite end of the brick platform. His new superior, Father Marion Roessler OFM Cap. [Order of Friars Minor, Capuchin] ran up and pumped his hand.[1] "Welcome Father Emmett! Sorry I'm late!"

The newly ordained friar from Wisconsin had answered a call to help
the ailing Father Marion, whose health was imperiled by the years of
hardship and deprivation he had suffered while running the remote
St. Labre Cheyenne Mission in Montana.

Father Marion wasn't aware that Father Emmett had hoped instead for
a post in Nicaragua, with its steaming jungles and brightly-colored
cottages. Older priests had warned Father Emmett about the perils
of such a journey in the middle of a violent civil war, with guerilla
kidnappings of civilians and priests alike. One priest had actually joined
the guerilla army. "Do you realize that your life could be in danger?"
one of his advisors had asked. Danger? That was exactly what Father
Emmett wanted!

But just days before Father Emmett's dream assignment to Nicaragua,
his Provincial Minister called him into his office to tell the young priest
that he would instead be posted to a small reservation mission in the
western wilderness. Shocked by the news, Father Emmett drew a blank.
He remembered hearing of the Indian Missions in Montana but he
knew nothing about the state except that it was a frigid place in winter
and teemed with rattlesnakes.

When the meeting with his Provincial ended, Father Emmett obediently
knelt down and kissed the hardwood floor, then backed out of the
office. Waves of disappointment poured over him as he shut the door
and leaned against the wall. His dream of going to an exciting far off
place had evaporated. But like a soldier, he was subject to the orders
of his superiors, knowing that his responsibility was to do his best
wherever he was asked to serve.

──────── ⊱◈⊰ ────────

Father Emmett liked Father Marion from their first meeting at the train
depot, but he still felt a twinge of regret when he compared the exciting
jungles of Nicaragua to the barren, dry landscape of Montana. The
Capuchins left the station and drove off on a road trip that would take
all day. By noon Father Emmett remembered how he had cursed the air-
conditioning on the train the night before. For five hours a hot, desert
wind swept through the open windows of the 1953 Chevy Coup, on a
300-mile tour of the Northern Cheyenne Reservation and surrounding
areas.

After passing an occasional ranch, all vestiges of white civilization disappeared. Smooth sandstone rocks, the color of ripe wheat, pocked with empty, wind-sculpted caves and fantastic red outcrops, rose skyward a hundred feet from what had once been ancient sea beds. Father Marion pointed out the high, jagged rim rocks where "Cheyennes," as he called them, had buried their dead in times past, but empty now that looters had desecrated them for saleable artifacts.

As they continued on, the arid wilderness gave way to vast, open spaces. Giant tumbleweeds blew across the road in the hot wind and small whirlwinds appeared and disappeared among sagebrush, yucca and well-armed prickly pear cactus. Father Emmett tasted dirt in his mouth. Always fastidious about his appearance, he dressed in clean clothes everyday. He cringed as sweat trickled down his face, back and arms and a fine, red dust covered his robe. Bumping along the dirt road, it became increasingly clear that in Montana, Father Emmett couldn't be as picky about cleanliness.

Dying of thirst during the long trip, Fr. Emmett listened as Father Marion talked about the Northern Cheyenne people and the local ranchers. Hearing that the tribe had endured 78 years of mistreatment, disease and broken government promises, he wondered aloud if the Cheyennes would ever trust a white man. Father Marion said they had always treated him well, but in his private conversations with the chiefs, they had told him they were still being persecuted by the government because of their victory over George Armstrong Custer at the Battle of the Little Bighorn in 1876. From his own observations, Father Marion believed this to be true.[2]

The chiefs explained what had happened to the tribe after the defeat of Custer's 7th Cavalry. Within a year after the battle, the U.S. military had caught the Cheyennes. They herded them to Oklahoma, where many sickened and died in the hot, humid environment, so different from their homeland in Montana, with cool streams and pine-covered meadows.

Their principal chiefs, Dull Knife and Little Wolf, escaped from the Oklahoma agency with their bands, pursued by military and civilian forces. The chiefs then split up, Little Wolf and his people going over the mountains in the dead of winter to reach Montana, while Dull Knife and his band walked towards Nebraska.

After many hardships, Little Wolf's group made it home, but Dull Knife's people were caught in a blizzard by soldiers and taken to Fort Robinson, Nebraska.[3]

At first they were treated well with feasting and Indian dances. During the entertainment, the fort commander, Captain Wessells, made advances to one of Dull Knife's daughters but she rebuffed him. He tried several more times to court her and each time she refused. Angered, he tried to force the band to return to Oklahoma. When they did not comply, he locked the Cheyennes in a log building for eight days without water, heat, food, fuel or light in January 1879.

Among the Indians were pregnant women and elderly people who began to starve. Deciding to die fighting rather than to starve to death, the band broke out of the stockade in temperatures of 40 degrees below zero and ran for their lives. Soldiers slaughtered men, women and children. Fathers dug holes to protect their wives and children, but soldiers fired down into the holes killing everyone without mercy.

One young woman carried her little sister on her back. She was shot in the head and when she fell, she told the child, "You know where they went. Run and don't look back! Run!" The toddler ran off into the night. Not many escaped alive, among them Chief Dull Knife and part of his family, who were taken in by the Lakota in South Dakota.[4]

This torturous event became known as a stain of dishonor in the annuals of American history. It divided the Northern Cheyenne tribe, but in 1883, General Nelson Miles, who had treated them humanely, allowed the tribe to return to their homelands in Montana.

A young Catholic soldier at Ft. Keogh, Montana, Pvt. George Yoakam, persuaded the Vicar Apostolic of Nebraska, Rev. James O'Connor, to help the tribe settle around land on which St. Benedict Joseph Labre Mission and school would be built. The chiefs and headmen of the tribe signed an agreement with the Catholics, stating that the land could be used in perpetuity as long as it was being used as a school and church.[5]

The Mission began when five Ursuline Sisters from Toledo, Ohio, led by the kind Mother Amadeus Dunne, and a couple of priests arrived to occupy an old log shack with mud roof and plank floor. Pvt. Yoakam helped the Cheyennes move near the Mission, while he stayed with his friend, Father Barcelo.[6]

One night the Sisters were terrified when five ranchers, their faces covered with black cloth, grabbed Father Barcelo and put a gun to his stomach. They were looking for Yoakam, who they blamed for bringing Indians into territory where ranchmen had been "squatting" for years. After roughing up Barcelo, the men found Yoakam, tied him to a tree and beat him severely. Before he blacked out, they told him that if he ever returned, they would kill him.[7]

Father Barcelo's health deteriorated after the incident and he left the Mission. Despite attacks from ranchers, harsh weather and poor health, the fearless Ursulines persevered at their school, but priests came and went. For the next fifteen years, cattlemen waged a bitter and sometimes violent campaign to force the Cheyennes from their homeland.[8] In the late 1890s, ranchers were finally forced to move off reservation land. Since the establishment of the reservation, the tribe continued to suffer from disease, near starvation and medical neglect.[9]

———— ⣿◇⣿ ————

As they drove along, Father Marion explained to Father Emmett that ranchers were still sometimes brutal in their treatment of the Cheyennes. "If I understand their past, maybe I can help them to see a more hopeful future," Father Emmett told him. Just then, the priests reached Blessed Sacrament Church in Lame Deer at the Northern Cheyenne Agency. "You'll be driving this route every Sunday," Fr. Marion quipped cheerfully. Father Emmett shot him a surprised look as they pulled up in front of the church. His throat felt like sand paper.

Fr. Christopher Hafner saw the car and came out to meet them. "You must be thirsty! Let me fix you something." He served them delicious chocolate milkshakes in sanctuary lamp glasses. As he drank the best milkshake he'd ever had, in the back of his mind Fr. Emmett could hear his uncle, Father Herbert Hoffmann, saying: "I told you not to become a Capuchin, Buddy. You're completely unprepared for that kind of life!"

Father Emmett thought the worst was over. When the sun slipped beneath the horizon of pine-covered hills along the Tongue River, they arrived at St. Labre Mission, on the eastern boundary of the reservation. As they parked in front of an old, two-story stucco friary, Fr. Emmett looked through dust-streaked windows at half a dozen yellow lights hanging inside the main recreation room. He followed Father Marion up on the porch but then suddenly froze. His worst pet peeve – flying insects – hundreds of large, hairy moths filled the room, attracted by the lights.

Once inside, he couldn't stand it. He jumped, whacked and smashed the gray-white moths with intense determination. Within minutes, the floor was littered with squirming insects. Seven silent Capuchin priests watched the newly ordained priest's reaction to the moths they had learned to ignore. All of the solemn, bearded friars in identical brown robes, sat in identical, green upholstered recliners, smoking identical pipes. Watching the young man's frantic attacks was far more entertaining than listening to the scratchy reception on their General Electric Short Wave Radio.

In the middle of the recreation room sat a proud, old fireplace made of native fieldstone and all around the room were stacks of newspapers, cardboard boxes and religious magazines. After Fr. Emmett swept up the slaughtered moths, he made a mental note to clean up the junky room as soon as he got the time. Two other walls held bookshelves full of faded, green German sermon books. The old books definitely had to go.

After evening prayers he went up to bed in his small, dingy room, bare except for a desk, chair and a single bed, a crucifix and two wooden pegs, one to hold the robe he had worn to bed and the other for his brown woolen robe with cowl for every day wear. Exhausted and hungry, Father couldn't sleep. His thoughts turned to what needed to be done at the friary – the dirt and the dust, the rickety stairs, the dirty windows with frames that didn't fit and the floors that sagged. And that mess downstairs! He decided to start throwing out litter the next day. Listening to the mournful howling of coyotes, Father Emmett fell into a deep sleep.

Morning prayers started at 5:15 a.m., Mass at 6 a.m., then a 15-minute breakfast of oatmeal so hard he put a spoon in it and lifted the bowl upside down. After neatness, Fr. Emmett's second compulsion was time. He perpetually checked his watch, perhaps a carry-over from strict seminary training. Upstairs, he unpacked his two small suitcases. One contained all of his notes from the seminary on theology and his clothes, underwear and shoes. The second held a family photograph album with snapshots taken at his First Mass and a small stack of Nicaraguan brochures. He leafed through the brochures for a few minutes, then bounded downstairs to make himself useful. He never wasted time.

He gathered up all the papers and boxes on the floor and stuffed them into the fireplace. The room sweltered, even before he set the blaze. With his sleeves rolled up and sweat pouring down his neck, Father finished by sweeping and mopping the masonite floor. He felt proud of himself as he surveyed the spotless room.

Suddenly, he heard a stern voice behind him: "What did you do?" Father Marion stood in the doorway with his hands on his hips. Bewildered, the superior scanned the vast, empty room.

"Thought I'd clean up the place," Father Emmett said with an air of accomplishment.

"That," Father Marion said with painful emphasis, "was our entire winter fuel supply!"

And so Father Emmett had nowhere to go but up. Ashamed of himself, he walked around the barn and then up the hill above the Mission, where he sat down and prayed. He remembered the peace and pleasure of the Wisconsin woods; the sweet, ripe alfalfa, thin bands of lemony sunlight on timothy hay swaying in the wind, the coolness of cranberry bogs beneath his feet. From that morning on, he ticked off the days until he could leave St. Labre. He only had 364 more to go.

Father's first months at St. Labre were difficult because he knew nothing about the Cheyennes. He listened to all the old priests, some with obvious religious prejudices against Indians.[10] Others, like Fr. Marion, loved them unconditionally and believed that Cheyenne language and culture should be preserved at all costs. Inherently shy, Fr. Emmett was exceptionally so during Mass, when he knew that Fr. Patrick Berther half-jokingly rated his performance in church on a scale from one to ten.[11] The tally usually turned out closer to one – the lowest score.

The young, time-conscious priest was still dreaming about Nicaragua when Christmas, his favorite holiday, rolled around. On Christmas morning 1954, Father made his rounds to offer Mass at all of the Indian churches on his long route. When he left the Mission, the temperature had dropped to 25-degrees below zero.

He pulled into the Muddy Creek reservation community in time to see a Cheyenne family coming down the hill in a wagon pulled by skeletal horses, snorting steam from ice-clogged nostrils. At Mass the children sat beside their parents on cold, wooden benches, wrapped in their mother's blanket. He watched their breaths rising to the ceiling, while the children shivered. None had on overshoes and their coats hung thin and ragged. Father had to put the holy water bottle in his pocket to keep it from freezing.

Pity swept over him. He knew these poor people didn't understand Latin, let alone much English. He asked himself how he could teach the word of God to humans suffering from hunger and cold. As they knelt at the altar to receive Holy Communion, he glanced down at a tiny girl named Teresa, hiding beneath her mother's shawl. She peeked up at him with doe-brown eyes and smiled.

After Mass, Father drove 28 miles back to St. Labre, ate a quick lunch of venison (In urgent need, Father Marion had poached a deer.) and immediately started gathering Christmas gifts, handmade by the School Sisters of St. Francis; dolls, caps, mittens, boots, socks, and wool coats. Remembering thin, little Teresa, the child he had seen at Mass, he wrapped each gift, along with a special treat, hard ribbon candy. He would return to the Indian camp on Muddy Creek to celebrate Christmas with Teresa's family.

While he loaded the gifts into the trunk of the car, Father's long, brown habit whipped around his body. He walked sideways to the wind as he made his last trip out to the car. If he didn't hurry, darkness might overtake him on the dangerous, frozen roads. Father Emmett drove out of the Mission past the old tents and dilapidated log cabins of the Ashland Indian camp along the frozen Tongue River, edged by tall, bare cottonwoods that swayed like naked, ghostly figures in the wind. He passed the bottom land on the river where hundreds of U.S. Cavalry soldiers had camped just 56 years before, to prevent a threatened battle between the Cheyennes and hostile ranchers.[12]

Since then, main roads had not been paved, which had helped protect the tribe over the years from tourists, truckers and traveling salesmen. In the distance, Father caught a glimpse of the snow-capped Big Horn Mountains and nearby, the dark, multi-layered hills. He started up the winding, narrow path of the notorious "Divide," or "Death Road," as many called the road, over which many a team and wagon had fallen over the steep sides, down into the dark, pine forests below. On top of the divide it was always snowing. The closest trees rose like dark giants, yet fifty feet in the distance, they faded away into fog covered forests of tall Ponderosa pines, only their tops showing up the mountain sides.

Fr. Marion had warned him not to go. The weather could change in minutes – he might get stuck in the middle of a sudden snowstorm on a lonely reservation road. But fear held no power over Fr. Emmett. This weather was nothing compared to the 3 feet of snow he'd shoveled to make an alley to the barn on his parent's dairy farm in Wisconsin. Nothing was going to stop the eager, young priest from delivering Christmas presents.

Father sang as he drove around the uphill curves. Finally, he reached the top of the Divide and then started down the long hill to the picturesque agency town of Lame Deer, nestled between red buttes. Few cars were in sight, no signs, a trader's store, a few cabins here and there and Indians on horseback. Then five miles further into the hills and Father neared Muddy Creek.

Suddenly, the sky turned sickly gray, the unmistakable color of a snowstorm. Ahead, the road had already drifted over with snow. Undaunted, he tried to plow through the snowdrift, a mistake he would remember for a long time. After spinning his wheels, Father got out and shoveled until his gloved fingers were numb and every breath seared his lungs. That morning, one of the priests had asked him: "Why punish yourself Emmett? You will suffer enough in this wilderness without taking on more than you can handle." Now here he was, floundering in frozen drifts, a blizzard about to set in.

Carrying two large bags of gifts, Father trudged through snow banks as a bitter wind turned a few snowflakes into heavy snow in a matter of minutes. He struggled on, snow biting his nose and cheeks like sharp needle pricks. But Christmas tidings permeated his soul and nothing gave Father Emmett greater pleasure than giving gifts to celebrate the birth of Christ.

In the distance he saw a darkened cabin on the side of a hill. A wisp of chimney smoke rose up into the dreary sky. His toes felt numb as he climbed up the hill to the dilapidated log home. Dogs snarled nearby as he stomped his massive boots to remove the snow. He set his bags down and knocked on the door. Long moments of silence passed and finally, the door opened a crack. An emaciated Cheyenne peered out; elbows stuck out of his stained brown coat, his feet wrapped with gunny sacks, newspapers and rag twine. The Indian was shocked to see the tall, blond priest standing on his front porch.

With a cheery "Merry Christmas everyone!" Father Emmett entered the log cabin through a door so low he had to crouch to get inside. The dark, damp, room had no ventilation. He could make out 9 figures huddled around a wood stove in the middle of the dirt floor. "Merry Christmas!" he blurted out once again. His exclamation of cheer met with dismal looks from the adults and five frightened children buried their heads in the folds of their mother's faded calico dress, held at the waist by a wide leather belt and a butcher knife in a studded sheath. The mother gave no indication that she had company.

Father Emmett's face, neck and ears turned suddenly red and he felt foolish as he saw the looks of despair, the sad, gaunt eyes and the emaciated baby sleeping in a shawl on his mother's back. The mother and children coughed at intervals and spit into a can on the floor. "Rubies and pearls" they called it. If the spit was bloody, "Rubies" meant tuberculosis. "Pearls" was just plain spit.

A fragile girl with stringy hair glanced up at Father Emmett and he saw the sweet look of the child who had smiled up at him in church. He glanced beyond her to the butcher paper and odd pieces of cardboard nailed to the log walls to keep out the freezing wind and snow. Not far above his head, a long, peeled willow pole hung horizontally from the ceiling beams. Two thin pieces of dried meat hung on the pole where mice couldn't get them.

Father felt he had stepped back in time – no electricity, no Christmas lights or decorated tree, no gifts and no happiness on the day Jesus was born in Bethlehem. Instantly, Father Emmett experienced a hopeless feeling of government betrayal as he transcended into the misery and suffering of the silent figures around him. He felt that these wretched human beings, once the bravest warriors and greatest horsemen of the Northern Plains, had been neglected by the American Government, an entity that Father had always been taught to honor and respect.

A tight anger welled up in his chest and throat and stinging tears of utter disappointment filled his eyes. "This can't be America," he mumbled. The little girl now shyly left her mother's dress, appeared behind her father's legs and then made her quiet way to Father's side. She reached out and took his enormous white hand in her little brown one.

"Well, here you are Teresa!" Father said. "I've come to give you some Christmas presents. Tell me which present you'd like; a dolly, a warm coat, some candy?"

Teresa looked down and said nothing for a full minute. She covered her head in her shawl and wouldn't look him in the eyes. "Anything," she whispered.

Her pitiful response stabbed Father's heart and the girl's father caught the hurt look. The solemn, ragged Cheyenne and the Catholic priest looked deeply into each other's eyes for only a few seconds but it was long enough to have communicated on a spiritual level deeper than words. Suddenly, the man's quiet demeanor changed as he began a beseeching prayer in the old way, tears streaming down his face. He prayed to Maheo, Creator God, mesmerizing the young priest, who could not understand one word – yet he understood everything. This was the true Cheyenne nature, thankful, prayerful, humble, crying out to God. Tears came to Father's eyes as he saw the man transformed into the warrior of old, both arms uplifted, begging God to help his family. This was the Cheyenne soul.

The intense prayer lasted for six or seven minutes, a stunning agony to watch and just as quickly, the Cheyenne, beautiful in his state of Grace, now turned away in his tattered clothing, back to his silent nature. To Father Emmett, it had been an epiphany, an intuitive perception of the truth. The Cheyennes had been trampled, their self-esteem and manhood beaten down by poverty, disease and persecution. But on the inside – nothing had changed. Prayer meant everything to them, an ongoing, never ceasing closeness to "The One Above." When the prayer ended, Father felt cleansed, his second Sacrament of Holy Communion in one day.

Then, one by one, each child inched toward Father and he passed out the dolls, coats, warm mittens, and other clothing. None of the adults in the one-room cabin offered to speak English, but Teresa had been to school for three years and she tried to interpret. That became unnecessary when her father suddenly began to speak to Fr. Emmett in broken English, comfortably, with no fear. A wooden chair – the only chair in the room – appeared and Father sat down and accepted a tin cup of strong, hot coffee, made he knew, from Muddy Creek water. Everyone stood and watched as Father drank the coffee. Next, he accepted a cracked tin bowl of thin soup with a wild turnip and a piece of bush rabbit bobbing up and down in it. He ate the soup with relish. Soon everyone had a bowl of soup and the stoicism changed to hilarity. Father realized that humor was also part of the Cheyenne nature. This simple meal with genuine, good people meant more to him than any fine Christmas feast he had ever eaten.

When he got up to leave, Father insisted that the children should not accompany him out into the bitter cold, but the older boys escorted him anyway, all the way to the Mission car. It was still snowing when they pushed the Chevy out of the drift. For the rest of the afternoon Father visited other families with names that he loved: Yellow Robe, Hard Ground, Red Robe, Crazy Mule, Walks Nice, and Old Bull. Most of the families were living in wall tents and log huts in dismal poverty. By nightfall, the relentless snowstorm had done its worst, but Father Emmett pushed on to St. Labre. The predicted blizzard had not turned treacherous as predicted.

When Father got back to the friary he was too mentally exhausted to eat. After evening prayers, he tossed in his bed, unable to sleep. Saddened, disillusioned and angry at the country of his birth, he remembered the sound of the children coughing and he watched in his mind as the frail Cheyenne mother spit "Rubies" that he knew meant tuberculosis and death.

A twinge of homesickness filled Father's heart as he remembered his youth on his parent's dairy farm. He had always thought that his folks lived one step from the poor house. Now he realized that although they had family problems like everyone else, and they didn't have much, his plate had always been filled with delicious food, especially at Christmas, the most exciting time of the year.

Devout Catholics, his parents kept the Christmas tree locked in the parlor, away from the children's eyes until Christmas Eve.[13] That night, Ed and Regina Hoffmann trimmed the tall tree and decorated it with common objects transformed to uncommonly enchanting ornaments; holly, hawthorn, mistletoe and evergreen boughs. Gingerbread cookies and glowing lights, streaming ribbons, every dazzling trim of tinfoil and hand-painted, twinkling glass ornaments from Germany wrapped the children in holiday magic. On the top of the tree sat the Angel Gabriel and near the lower branches, a manger scene surrounded by white candles that reflected off glass like stars to signify the birth of Christ.

After a merry and delicious Christmas meal, amid cheers and clapping, the door to the parlor flew open, the lights went on and the entire Hoffmann family gathered around the tree to sing "Silent Night" and "O Tannenbaum." The gifts were distributed, to the children's great delight, and then off they went to midnight Mass at St. Mary's Church in a horse drawn sleigh. After Mass the children ate Christmas Stollen coffee cake filled with dried fruit, raisins and covered with powdered sugar. With tummies filled, they went to bed with happy hearts.

The contrast between Father Emmett's secure childhood and that of Cheyenne poverty brought the priest back to reality as he sat up in bed. "What can I possibly do for these people?" he thought. There was only one answer that came to him – the only answer he could live with. The Cheyennes needed him much more than the people of Nicaragua. They were proud Americans – real Americans. How could he have been so blind? He got out of bed and went down on his knees, vowing before God to give Cheyenne children the finest education and care he could possibly provide. He would make sure these Cheyenne youngsters and their families got a chance to succeed in life, not merely to survive with nothing to hope for. He prayed for most of an hour, affirming his promise, God willing, that he would be allowed to sacrifice his life for them. Completely genuine but naïve to the core, the Wisconsin country boy had no way of knowing that 50 years of strife, hardship and emotional struggle lay before him.

CHAPTER
2

Escape to America

F ather Emmett's grandfather, George Hoffmann Sr., was the first rebel in the family to seek his fortune in America. Like thousands of young Germans, he escaped military service in Keiser Wilhelm's army after his father secreted him away to Belgium. George landed at the Port of New York on November 9, 1883, after a two-week voyage on the steamer Pennland.

The robust teenager chose as his destination the state of Wisconsin, a place as much like the old country as he could find, with 36 million acres of land and 14,000 lakes. George's first harvest in Wisconsin was a paradise of vegetation and wildlife. Writer Hamlin Garland described his beloved Wisconsin best:

> The corn fields, dark green and sweet-smelling, ripple like a sea . . . Waves of dusk and green and yellow circled across the level fields . . . The trees were in heavy leaf, insect life was at its height, and the air was filled with buzzing, dancing forms and . . . bobolinks sailed and sang in the sensuous air, now sinking, now rising, their exquisite notes ringing, filling the air like the chimes of tiny silver bells . . .[14]

George liked Marathon City, a small village in the upper midlands of Wisconsin, founded by a hardy group called "The Pittsburgh German Homestead Society." For many years, German immigrants had cut through dense forests of maple, white pine, birch, ash, oak, bass-wood and butternut to build a log cabin community. Thick, dark woodlands discouraged other farmers from settling in the area, but German pioneers joined together to clear the land, a back-breaking task.

George labored in logging camps, saw mills, and as an extra hand during harvest on farms already established, his pay taken in cattle. It normally took years of hard work before a man established his own farm and these were years of sacrifice and struggle despite severe hardships, accidents and illnesses. George found the land he wanted to buy, land that two succeeding generations would call home, but he didn't obtain citizenship overnight. It took thirteen years before he became an American citizen and three more years before he received title to his farm in 1899. His was a hard-earned "American Dream."

George met and married Anna Margaret Ament while she was a cook in the Butternut logging camp. Catherine, their youngest daughter later recalled: "Mother always saw him walking and eating alone and she took pity on him. She thought he needed looking after." Anna was still a teenager when they married. During the next two decades she bore her husband twelve children and all but one lived to adulthood. With no money for medical help and no running water or electricity, Anna's feat of devotion and perseverance equaled George's determined work to clear and prove up the farm.

Daughter Catherine also remembered that her father was strict with all of his children: "He forced every child in our family to hoe corn and carry stones from the fields from the time we were five years-old. When I got tired and hot, I complained. I didn't think it was fair making a girl work like a boy. He told me more than once and I heard him tell the others, that he had come to this country alone with only the clothes on his back, and had worked in a logging camp to save his money when he was hardly a man. "'You will work like the rest of us!'" he'd tell us."[15]

George may have missed his parents and the land of his birth, but early on he had steeled himself against feeling emotional pain by a never-ending cycle of hard labor. In his determination to gain economic security, George lost a father's gentleness. His sons were his priority. "His coldness towards me was the one great sadness of my life," Catherine remembered.[16]

Mother Anna, constantly pregnant, sickly and in pain, became an irritable mother who wanted things done her way or no way at all. Perhaps due to her husband's high ideals, she later viewed outsiders, including her in-laws, with a nose slightly elevated. Her demanding husband's favorite saying was: "Everything has to be perfect."[17]

Anna and George had neither time nor money to build a house, but their large barn stood as a wonder of craftsmanship. They lived in the granary, which served as their home for years until they had time to build a house. Washing and mending for eleven children, their underwear, work clothes, towels, washcloths, shirts, trousers, and coats, not to mention the linens, would have exhausted any woman, especially with no running water. Bath time for eleven youngsters and two adults must have been a daunting experience for a mother always pregnant and in ill health.

A few lucky citizens in Marathon took their first photographs with a Kodak Camera, a one-dollar purchase through the popular Sears & Roebuck Catalogue. Automobiles, telephones, airplanes, and electric sewing machines made life a lot easier and more fun, if people could afford such luxuries. America boasted that it was "the greatest country on earth," and in small towns, where sixty-percent of all Americans lived, the title seemed appropriate. They were proud, honest people and whether they worked as businessmen, tailors, grocers, or farmers, they sought out the company of other men in taverns and barbershops. By custom, German-Americans found camaraderie in the tavern after hard labor in the fields. George often brought his son Edward along and the young man soon learned to "drink like a man."

As he aged, George Hoffmann Sr. wondered who would inherit his farm. Five of his children went to college. Edward, the only boy who did not go, stayed home to help his father farm so that Felix, George Jr., Herbert and Louis could attend seminaries in preparation for the priesthood. Two eventually became Catholic priests, while Edward sadly laid aside his dream of becoming a doctor.

Herbert, always the serious, reliable boy, could always be counted on, while Ed the good-humored, accident-prone prankster was the exact opposite of his father. But Felix was the "renegade' in his generation. Catherine recalled that her brother Felix "thought differently. We were all too conservative for his blood. He took too many risks." For years Felix had been saying that he was going to become a priest, but he wanted to go back to the old country to study in a German seminary.

His father didn't like the idea, but Felix had already made up his mind.[18]

At this point, George Sr. realized that he had forfeited his youth, his life with his parents and kinfolk in Germany and had suffered many years of struggle and worries over the farm – and for what? Not one of his healthy, energetic sons wanted to farm.

George never understood why his handsome son Felix wanted to return to the very place from which he had risked his life to escape the Keiser's army. George had jumped on board a ship bound for America and now Felix was returning to the old country the same way.

George Sr. had read about the rumors of war in Germany. He asked his son to reconsider, but Felix ignored his father's warnings. He left home to enter a seminary in Munster, near Dusseldorf, Germany, and was still in the seminary in 1914, when Germany invaded Belgium, France and Russia. When newspapers in Wisconsin reported the danger, George cabled his son in Germany and Felix responded with a wire asking his father for money to leave the country. The Hoffmanns immediately sent their life savings. That was the last communication they had with Felix.

The family waited through 1915 and 1916, until finally, America entered the war in 1917. The mistreatment of American prisoners of war was common knowledge and they prayed that Felix was still alive. Worry and stress took a heavy toll on George, who couldn't eat and became ill. Edward then took on more farm responsibilities for his father. When America declared war on Germany, Ed shocked his parents by enlisting for active duty. They were horrified to think that yet another son might be lost. As luck would have it, Ed and other recruits were on a train headed for a Milwaukee boot camp on November 11, 1918, when the Armistice was signed ending World War I. The passengers whooped and danced for joy but Ed may not have been as thrilled as the others. He had missed his chance to leave the farm.

Another year passed without word from Felix. Anna was sure her son had been killed. George insisted that Ed return to the family farm and he obliged his father. But in 1919, Ed had another interest as well. He had fallen in love with Regina Mary Richart, the daughter of railroad worker, Ludwig and his devoutly religious wife, Katherine Becker Richart, immigrants from Nunkirchen, Germany. Ed first saw Regina in church during choir practice and later met her again while she was working as a housekeeper for a physician in Marathon. Ed came for

Regina in the evenings and he often had to sit on the porch until the doctor, his family and housekeeper finished saying the rosary on their knees in the parlor.

Regina's father was a rough man who did not believe in spending money for medical bills. His grandchildren remembered him standing in the summer kitchen in front of a mirror. He had broken a tooth and instead of going to the dentist, he filed the tooth smooth. When the youngsters giggled behind him, he whirled around with the file in his uplifted hand and yelled, "Ruh!" (Quiet!) The children jumped up and ran away. When Ludwig had to have surgery to remove a cancerous tumor in his neck, the physician made an incision from under his ear, all the way down to his trachea. Ludwig refused anesthetic during the operation because he didn't trust the doctor.

The first automobile purchased by a Marathon citizen chugged into town in 1908. Ed Hoffmann and his brothers pooled their money and bought the second car, possibly because Ed wanted to court Regina. She was attracted to the young man in the twenty-two horsepower invention. Ludwig, however, did not approve of his daughter riding around in the "contraption" because he thought they'd get killed. But Regina, called "Ray" by her friends, had a mind of her own.

Regina and Ed dated during the Prohibition years and they secretly made home brew together. Ed filled brown, earthenware jugs, corked them and tied the heavy cargo to the running board of his car. The couple took a few wild rides to sell "moonshine" and the cops couldn't catch them. When the police met them at the edge of a village, Ed waved jubilantly and the cops followed the pair all the way through town to make sure Ed didn't stop. They drove from Wausau to LaCrosse, many hours of travel on gravel roads. The hot, dusty trips soon dulled the thrill, although outwitting the police had been fun. The two sweethearts were never caught, but bad roads and flat tires put an end to their "moonshine" nights. Grandma Anna also became locally known for her delicious bathtub beer. After Prohibition ended, Marathon was known as the town with 13 bars but no alcoholics.

German American men looked for wives who possessed traits of endurance, persistence and cleanliness. A woman had to have strength and energy and a certain contempt for those who shied away from rigorous labor. Edward saw all of these qualities in Regina. They were married on May 27, 1921, in a small family ceremony at St. Mary's

Church. Regina was still cooking chicken for the wedding dinner when the first guests arrived. Their wedding was especially memorable for another reason. Father Felix Hoffmann arrived home safe from Germany in time for the ceremony! During the war, he had been hidden in Germany by friends after it became too dangerous to walk the streets. With help from fellow classmates, Father Felix continued his studies in the seminary and was ordained a priest in 1917. Now, after a long absence, the rebel priest returned to America to marry his brother to Regina Richart. George and Anna rejoiced, but their happiness was short-lived.

On July 5, 1921, their 17-year-old son Louis, a seminarian at Mt. Calvary, went swimming with his classmates. Louis was another "high strung" Hoffmann boy who took risks. He loved to swim and after seeing how reckless he was in the water, Anna repeatedly begged him not to take chances. "Oh, Mother!" he laughed. "Stop worrying about me!" Horsing around as usual one day, he hit his head on a rock and drowned before a priest could pull him out of the water.

Death continued to stalk the family. On December 10, 1921, Ed's 31-year-old brother, George Jr., took his two sons, 7-year-old Andrew and 9-year-old Aloysius, Christmas shopping. When they were finished, they took the street car and then walked toward St. Michael's Orphanage, where George and Anna were living temporarily with their son, Father Herbert, the reliable, newly-ordained priest.

The trio held hands, one child on either side of their "Papa," when Aloysius turned and saw a speeding car coming from behind. He shouted to his father and jumped back off the road, but the warning came too late. A "death car" smashed into them at great speed. There was a loud crack and then a terrible silence.[19]

An eyewitness tried to hold Aloysius from going to his father, who had died instantly, but he broke away, saw that his father was horribly mangled and then ran screaming to his younger brother. Little Andrew had been thrown thirty feet across the road, but he was still alive and moaning. Aloysius rushed to the orphanage and burst into the cottage where his grandparents were seated at the kitchen table. "Andrew and Papa are killed!" he gasped and collapsed in his grandmother's arms.

Fr. Herbert ran to the scene and found his brother's body, then Andrew, who was still breathing. He held his dying nephew in his arms while a police car rushed them to the hospital. Father Herbert was kneeling beside the child's bed when the little boy died thirty hours later. After an extensive search, police found the driver of the "death car" – a respected businessman in a neighboring community.

After his sons died, George never farmed again. His hair turned white and he seemed to have lost the will to live. Anna changed into a bitter, domineering woman who was increasingly harder to get along with and for some reason, she seemed to focus her bitterness on Ed's wife, Regina.

Over time, Regina became especially sensitive about Anna's whispered remarks aimed at her family. Ed was in the middle of it. It often seemed that the two families – the Hoffmanns and the Richarts – were in competition with each other. Whether he liked it or not, Ed represented his family and he was the one who had to listen to complaints from his wife, as well as his mother. Early in his marriage, Ed learned to remain quiet during these conflicts. It wasn't his way to bully anyone. It took kindness, patience and strength to remain calm and busy, despite his unfortunate position as middleman.

In 1920, women won the right to vote, they bobbed their hair and became "flappers" By stark contrast, Regina was no flapper, nor did she wear short skirts and go to wild parties. Her marriage to a dairy farmer meant practiced teamwork of feeding and milking 20 Jersey cows twice a day, with no help from a milking machine. She also went to work in the fields and back to the wood stove for hours preparing meals. Her first child, a sweet baby girl she named Dorothy, was born on October 6, 1923. Regina gave birth in her own bed with help from the midwife, Mrs. Opperman.

George Sr. sold his farm to Ed and Regina in the early 1920s, just as hard times befell farmers all over the country. From the start, Ed's mortgage payments to the elder Hoffmanns were seldom paid. This created an even greater chasm between Anna and Regina, although Regina was hardly to blame for the state of the national economy. A sense of helplessness in the face of overwhelming debt gripped farmers across the nation. Ed and Regina were better off on the farm than most city dwellers because they lived self-sufficiently by butchering a hog or a chicken, but they rarely saw cash. Ed smoked and cured pork in his smokehouse and stored beef and veal in two-quart jars in the cellar. The Hoffmanns were not malnourished, but contrary to what Anna thought, they did not live in an extravagant manner.

In late spring and early summer of 1926, Regina spent more time than usual on her knees every evening saying the rosary. She prayed for the safe arrival of her second child, due in late July. "God grant us a boy," she prayed, "and God, we want a boy who will become a priest."

The weather in July was hot and sticky, with temperatures in the 90s. Wisconsin farmers found their pastures burnt and the price of feed expensive. Dangerous thunderstorms brought high winds and hail. Scores of farm buildings blew down and fields of grain were destroyed. On July 26, a violent thunderstorm cooled the temperature to 60 degrees as the evening wore on. Regina tried to keep cool throughout the night but the unmistakable pains became hard waves right before dawn on the 27th.

When she felt her delivery coming, Regina decided against having Mrs. Opperman, the midwife. Instead, she sent Ed to town to pick up Dr. Frenzel. This pregnancy had been different. Regina thought she was carrying a boy and she wasn't taking any chances. By the time Dr. Frenzel arrived, Regina was in the last hard pains of labor. Ed sat in the kitchen and heard the loud, yet reverent prayer in the bedroom: "Please God, give us a son!"

Just at sunset, the rain stopped. Thunder growled in deep, low tones and was lost as the darkness passed away. A moist breeze cooled the earth and everything seemed new-washed and fresh. Ed was bending over the wood stove stirring the boiling towels when he heard the rooster crow. At 7:50 a.m., Ed glanced up from his work after he heard a second cry. This wasn't a rooster, but it was definitely an "early bird." Regina's prayers had been answered with a big, healthy baby boy. They named their son George after his grandfather, but they nicknamed him "Buddy." From that day on, Regina set her sights on the priesthood for her newborn son.

CHAPTER 3

The Barnyard Priest

E d Hoffmann didn't like farming. He bought the farm from his dad because it would have killed the old man to see it sold to another family. Ed still dreamed of going to medical school, but he knew that his married happiness depended on his ability to keep the farm. He got into the habit of spending an afternoon or two every week at the local tavern, joined by many of his neighbors, there to console one another and renew kindred ties and troubles. Men didn't want to worry their wives with talk of dwindling farm prices. Instead, over a few beers and a couple hours of good camaraderie, they drowned their economic concerns at the tavern, which stood as a warm beacon of good will.

Regina drowned her troubles in fervent prayers and laundry soap. She saved and strained beef tallow after butchering, then mixed it with lye and water in a kettle. This she simmered with frequent stirring, until it felt like jelly. After cooling the soap, she poured it into box molds, then cut it and left it to harden. Regina's parents had been poor immigrants and she had done without most of her life. Before she and Ed bought their Maytag Washing Machine on time payments, they had carried hard water in pails from the well, filled a large copper boiler and heated it on the wood stove. She boiled the clothes and then fished them out with a stick. Then she scrubbed the work clothes by hand on a washboard and wrung them out through a hand-cranked wringer. The clothes were then rinsed in another tub of warm water, then a tub of cold, with bluing added to whiten the clothes. The load went through the wringer again to squeeze out the water. Regina carried load after load to the clothesline. The Maytag was a true blessing, especially now that Regina had another child on the way. Phyllis Marie was born on

March 31, 1929, followed by Rita Florence on August 22, 1933, and finally the baby, Marilyn Regina, on December 3, 1935.

Buddy, a happy, "high strung" boy like his father, moved from chore to chore, with an insatiable appetite for yet another job to do. Every morning he propped open the barn doors to let in the breeze and shoveled cow manure out of the barn. Framed in the doorway, four or five miles to the east, rose a single, high crest called Rib Mountain, one of the highest points in Wisconsin.

Surrounding the "Rib" in all directions were the fertile, rolling hills that George Hoffmann had first seen when he arrived nearly fifty years before. Perhaps his grandson Buddy would take over the 160-acre farm and the two-story farmhouse that George and his sons had built, each red brick made by hand. The hip-roofed barn had been grandpa George's special accomplishment, 40 feet wide and 80 feet long, with horse stalls and many cow stations. The sturdy, red barn still stands today, over one hundred years later, as an example of fine craftsmanship learned in the old country.

Grandpa turned 70 in 1933. After the Stock Market crash on Black Friday, October 14, 1929, dairy farmers were some of the first to feel the weight of the Great Depression, one of the hardest economic decades in American history. Perhaps the distressing news – that almost 300,000 families had lost their homes and one quarter of the country's banks had closed – had something to do with George's depression and final illness.[20] The day before George died, Ed received word of his father's worsening condition. Despite a dangerous, stormy night for travel, Ed was determined to be with him. As stern as George had been with his sons, they were all around him on their knees at his deathbed, a moving tribute to their father's courage and sacrifice to provide for his large family.

Before Ed left to make his farewell trip to his father's deathbed, he went to the bedrooms where his children lay sleeping. As was his custom every night, he sprinkled Holy Water on each child, then blessed and kissed them. That night, Phyllis Marie woke up and felt the Holy Water on her forehead. When Ed bent down to kiss her goodnight, she reached up and put her arms around his neck. Seventy years later, Phyllis remembered that she had taken her father's gentle kindness and loving devotion for granted because she thought all fathers were the same.[21]

During George's funeral service, Ed, his brothers and sisters sat in their old familiar pews in St. Mary's Church, some dry-eyed. Often, their father had been tough with them, but occasionally, Ed had seen the real man and it was that man who had earned his lasting respect. Ed must have known that if he couldn't make a go of it on the land, at least his father wouldn't live long enough to see the loss of the farm.

Of all the times in the world Regina wanted her children to behave perfectly, it was during her father-in-law's funeral, but that was not to be. Regina heard a ruckus and caught Buddy pretending he was the Green Hornet under the coffin. She caught him by the seat of his pants and hauled him out for "disgracing the dead." Later she found that her children had gone on a childish rampage, spilling shoe polish on the bed. Grandma Anna afterwards hinted that Regina could not control her children, but the truth was that Regina was controlling them too much.

Regina's need for perfection at any cost often made life hard for her children. Dorothy, the oldest daughter, felt the brunt of her mother's inflexibility at a young age. Washing and waxing the kitchen floor was one of Dorothy's many chores. The girl did her best but if Regina saw one streak on the hardwood floor, Dorothy had to get down on her knees again and again to repeat the process. In striving for impossibly high standards, Regina carried perfectionism to the extreme. Years later, Regina's children expressed the sentiment: "Nothing was ever good enough for her."[22]

Despite her rough edges, Regina also taught her children the basic, decent qualities that would someday make them all good citizens; honesty, integrity, love of God and country. Regina was often unhappy and disappointed because she couldn't stop her husband's drinking habit. She couldn't make him a perfect husband. In the early years, Ed wasn't a constant drinker but he had his "toot" once in awhile. Regina went to great pains to cover this up from everyone, even from her children and from Ed's brothers. Buddy knew that his father took a "nip" from the whiskey bottle in the barn once in awhile, but it didn't seem to interfere with the farm work or in the positive attention he gave his children. Regina felt that she might have bought her kids new clothes, paid bills and had a nicer home if Ed hadn't spent what he earned in the tavern. Like Ed's mother, Regina never let him forget it.

The children were usually playing in the washroom when shouting arguments over money started in the kitchen. Grandma Anna's constant threats and demands for farm payments added considerable stress to the household. Even behind a closed door, the yelling could be heard plain enough: "You spent all that money!" Regina yelled at her husband. "Versoffen luf!" (Drunken no good!) Years later, Buddy recalled: "I was caught in between. I tried to love them both but I felt bad for each one. If I stuck up for either side, I was wrong." Ed would usually end up apologizing. He told his wife that he worked like a slave all day in the fields and he didn't see any harm in having a few drinks in a tavern with the neighbors. When they started calling each other hurtful names, Buddy crawled to his favorite warm place behind the wood stove and the kitchen wall. He liked the warmth but he was also used to the cold.

Upstairs, there was only one heat register and that was in the girls' room over the kitchen. Buddy's bedroom under the attic was without heat even in winter when temperatures reached 40 degrees below zero. He slept on a mattress made of corn husks and on many winter mornings when he woke up, frost covered his bedroom walls.

Regina was just as frustrated raising five children during the Depression as many mothers were at the time. Children might not have taken much notice of the hard times, but parents scrimped and saved. Although the Hoffmann kids found their mother picky about cleanliness and often critical, they also remembered that she loved to sing while she worked. One time a census taker came to the door and he said he'd never heard such a musical family. Regina was singing in the kitchen, Dorothy was on the piano in the living room, Phyllis was listening to music on the radio, while Ed and Buddy sang and whistled in the barn. Life's disappointments got in the way sometimes, but Ed managed to keep an outwardly optimistic, jovial attitude, despite the private battles. As in most families, there were problems, but this family prayed together, sang together and stayed together. Given the circumstances, the Hoffmanns overcame obstacles that might have destroyed most families.

Ed spent hours reading to his youngsters and helping them to study. Winter and summer, his doting children greeted their father at the back door every evening. They hung on him until he sat down, then one brought in a pan full of warm water. A short fight usually broke out over who would get to wash daddy's feet. The lucky winner lovingly washed away the weariness of long hours walking behind the horses and the plow. Another child slowly combed his hair, parted it, combed it back and then forward, instantly relaxing him. Another gently dried his feet with a towel.[23]

Once when Buddy had gotten into trouble for playing hooky from school to go fishing in the creek, Regina said, "Just wait till daddy gets home!" Sure enough, when Ed came in the back door, she told him about Buddy's transgression. Throughout the harangue, Buddy stood stone-faced, ready for his punishment, which he knew meant the belt. Ed solemnly took off his belt and led the frightened boy into the bedroom, closing the door behind him. The girls ran to the door to hear the beating. Ed whispered to his son, "You yell like crazy every time I hit my knee with this belt." On each wallop, Buddy gave a convincing howl. "That's good son. Did you catch any fish? I used to do the same thing myself," Ed told his errant son. The ruse worked. The two culprits came out of the bedroom and Buddy went out to the fields with his father close behind him. They had tricked Mother again and it became a standing joke between father and son. Dad whistled cowboy songs while he plowed, songs like, "He was just a lonely cowboy," and "Whispering Hope." They talked while they worked with Buddy asking many questions about life and the priesthood.

An aggressive churchgoer, Regina Hoffmann was called "the Pope of the Parish" by her relatives. The priests listened to her advice, especially after she became head of the Wisconsin Deanery. Although devoutly religious, Regina was not a person to hug or give physical comfort. Dorothy recalled that her mother, "was a hothead. She had a big ego, and her ego got satisfied. When she wasn't mad, she was funny and we all laughed. She was good at everything she did. Those who didn't live with her got along fine. Dad was lenient, too lenient sometimes, but he was a good father."[24]

Ed's brothers, Father Felix and Father Herbert often came to dinner to savor the best cooking in the county. A main-course table heaped with succulent pork roasts, hearty home-made bread, aged cheese, squash roasted with maple syrup, potatoes and gravy, bubbling hot. Regina's servings were not small, exquisitely arranged, quiltless desserts, but generous helpings of spicy puddings, savory pumpkin pies and German chocolate cake to die for.

The smell of exuberant foodstuffs lured Buddy from completing his chores. It was a given in his family that nothing was too good for his uncles. At an early age the boy made a value judgment that would change the future course of his life. Priests were feted to the best, always arrived in a shiny, new car and one or the other slipped Buddy a nickel or a quarter when he walked them out to the car. With his nickel, Buddy bought five-penny candies or he saved it all. He thought they lived a pretty good life. Priests drove new parish cars, they didn't have to wash or iron their clothes, they didn't have to cook or pay for their meals, they always wore nice, black suits and they never had to worry about bills. Buddy thought they had the inside edge with God. From then on, Buddy "played priest" for his parishioners, made up of his sisters and all the farm animals that wandered by. His altar was an orange crate covered with a large, clean rag, and a cross nailed on the shed over the altar served as the Crucifix. Father Buddy's robe was an old tablecloth that he dragged around while raising his hands in benediction to the Lord. He gave the homily, the Our Father and Holy Communion consisted of dry bread crusts and juice. There wasn't a chicken, a dog, or a pig on the farm that wasn't baptized and confirmed. This went on until Regina caught them in the act and scolded Buddy: "I can't believe you do that! Poking fun of religion!"

As soon as Regina was out of sight, the children broke into giggles. Later in the house, the kids played together with much teasing, punching and tickling. Regina got annoyed at the roughhousing. When they tickled her, she got mad. The girls knew that if Buddy got angry, he would fume and his face turned as red as a Sheboygan tomato. At that point, they grappled him to the floor and tickled him until he laughed so hard, he cried. Overpowered, Buddy had to give up. The team effort controlled him. Just to see them coming would discourage him from getting his own way.

Buddy sat by the radio in the evenings with his family listening to "Captain Courageous" and "Tarzan of the Apes," good guys who exuded virtue and clean living. Since Buddy didn't go many places, the barn became his world of adventure when he got bored. His imagination often got the best of him. One morning after he had propped open the barn door to rake hay, a whirlwind formed in the middle of the field. He'd seen many of these exciting mini-tornados whipping up dirt, tearing in circles through a field of grain and he'd always wondered what it would be like to stand in the middle of one, perhaps lifted up into the air by a force unknown. Here was his chance! Buddy ran out into the field and right into the swirling mass of dirt, grass and flying pebbles. Immediately, his adventure turned into a cruel mistake. Face, arms and neck felt the prick of a thousand sharp-edged sticks and rocks, his eyes and open mouth filled with dirt and instead of becoming airborne, Captain Courageous fell to his knees bruised and bleeding as the whirlwind sped on toward other adventures.

Occasionally, Capt. Courageous sneaked out to the barn in the evening to light one of the Camel cigarettes that lay hidden under a loose, weathered board in the loft. One night when the Captain looked for a better place to hide his cigarettes, he found a half empty bottle of whiskey that some other hero must have left behind. He threw back his head and took a big swig, grimaced and put it back. It was awhile before Buddy figured out that his dad drank whiskey in the barn. Buddy never mentioned his father's hidden booze and Ed never mentioned Buddy's cigarettes stashed in the loft.

Many homeless people were on the move during the Depression. Foreclosed farmers, migratory field hands, entire families headed to California on foot or in broken down cars. Just as Buddy learned how to care for tools and work with wood from his dad, he learned about caring for others by watching his mother. Regina was the epitome of the Good Samaritan.

Hobos rode the rails between towns and jumped off Chicago & Northwestern rail cars near the Hoffmann farm.[25] They followed the chalk marks on telephone poles or trees, marks in the shape of a black cat, which meant that nearby lived a woman who was a good cook and had a kind heart. Sometimes tiny pencil marks on door facings or mailboxes and gates served as a guide to anyone who knew the code. An upside down "Y" meant run away quick and a cross meant that church talk would get you a free meal. Most folks were afraid of hobos, although most were good-natured men down on their luck.

But sometimes dangerous young men robbed people and stole from stores and townspeople. Farmers didn't allow their wives to open doors to strangers. They kept mean dogs by their back doors and loaded rifles in case a ragged drifter showed up. Many hobos, among them Art Linkletter, Jack London, Carl Sandburg, William O. Douglas and Jack Kerouac may have been honest, but communities through which they passed connected them with every theft, murder and crime. Anxiety about vagrants ran high.

Regina couldn't bear to see a man who had lost his job, someone sick, injured, homeless and hungry. When a hobo knocked at the door, she told him to wash up at the well and to sit down on the back porch. She may have preached a bit to the poor soul, but she made sure he had a nourishing, hot meal, with home-made bread and butter, probably the best meal he'd had in months. Regina's sympathy for the homeless and hungry was a lesson of her religious faith. She believed that generosity was a sign of God's presence. Regina taught her son generosity by her own example and it was a lesson that Buddy remembered all of his life.

On Friday evenings the Hoffmann family went to town like everybody else and Regina made Ed wear a starched shirt and tie, even when the temperature was over 100 degrees. After praying for an hour at St. James Church, in Wausau, they stopped at the Fair Store, a general mercantile where they traded thirty dozen eggs for staples such as sugar, flour, matches and kerosene for house lamps. No money was exchanged. Just at a child's eye level, the round, built-in glass cases provided a perfect view of the most incredible array of candies to tempt the little ones. There were jaw-breakers, jelly beans in assorted colors, candy corn and licorice, chocolate drops and raisins.

Harry & Ott's Deli-Bar was the next stop. The Hoffmann kids knew that it was the egg money that bought the treats. Fresh eggs were a cash crop and there was always an old hen for making soup. They'd buy a slab of Limburger cheese wrapped in heavy wax paper, a couple of brown glass bottles of "Little Willies Beer" and soda crackers. Sometimes Ed bought homemade root beer for them. The Limburger smelled rotten but it tasted great.

There were times when Buddy had occasion to feel the sting of poverty. When Regina was pregnant with her last child, she sometimes had to stay in bed. On Saturday she couldn't bake as usual so she sent Buddy to Webber's Store in town to buy an 8-cent loaf. When he got to the counter with the bread, Buddy held out the 8 cents to the clerk. The tired owner folded his arms and frowned in disapproval at the boy. "Bread has gone up to nine cents!" he barked. "If you want bread, you'll have to charge the extra cent and pay for it mighty quick!" Embarrassed in front of the other customers, Buddy made a promise to himself that he would never charge anything again.

Ed was one of many dairy farmers in the Marathon area who was having a hard time. In February, 1933, dairymen all over the state struck against dairy companies, withholding milk or dumping it on the ground in protest. On the outskirts of Marathon, Ed Hoffmann joined other farmers in preventing milk trucks from reaching town. At first they picketed, but when they saw the dairy trucks ignoring them, the men resorted to other tactics. In surrounding towns hundreds of strikers routed sheriff's forces, demolished milk trucks and threatened to burn down dairies and creameries. National Guard units were called out to the scenes of violence. Fifteen hundred dairy farmers gathered in Marathon to hear union organizers call for a strong, united front. One striker, a local doctor, told the crowd that if they didn't band together, " . . . they will take your homes from you!"[26]

The strike then took a more aggressive turn with arrests and tactics that included beatings, threats of arson and bombs. "Massive battles among farmers, dealers and guards hired to protect plants and trucks" brought troops armed with machine guns. Retaliation from farmers came in the form of sniper gunfire, a dairy was burned and another bombed. One of the dairy truckers was stopped and beaten by men he had known all his life. Days later, his brother found his lifeless body hanging from the shed rafters.[27]

Buddy and his sister Dorothy were too young to understand exactly what was going on, but they heard their parents talking about Aunt Mame, Regina's sister, who lived with her husband and children in Marathon. Aunt Mame had a large family, two of her children had disabilities and she needed milk for them. When Buddy and Dorothy walked the five mile round trip to school, they watched the crowds of angry pickets placing rows of rubber strips, studded with nails across the road, in case a trucker tried to break through. Their father told them never to stop and watch. "Keep out of their way," he warned.

Finally, Regina's sister became desperate for milk and Ed knew that something had to be done. If anything drove Regina crazy, it was seeing little children going without nutritious food, especially her own nieces and nephews. One evening Ed sat his children down and they had a talk about the strike. Ed told Buddy, "There is something important I want you to do for Aunt Mame and your cousins." The next morning, Ed handed Buddy two pails, but instead of lunch, the pails contained milk. Ed took his son by the shoulders and looked him in the eyes. "You walk by the men as if you are innocent. Don't look at them – just keep walking. I'll be standing right there with them when you walk by. It's up to you son. You have to get that milk to Aunt Mame." Then he winked at Buddy and said, "Machts gut!" (Make it good!)

The next morning Buddy walked tall. He now understood his family needed his help. He knew what a strike meant and he knew how dangerous it was to break a strike. If he got caught, the men might attack his father or burn their farm down. The morning was cool and the meadowlarks sang their familiar songs along the country road. Dorothy and Buddy started off as usual and Buddy felt the heavier weight of the pails. When they got close to the noisy crowd of men, Buddy kept on going and never looked at them, although he later admitted that he got a little worried. It seemed an eternity until the children passed by the unruly crowd. Buddy breathed a sigh of relief when he neared his aunt's house in Marathon. The tears and grateful look on Aunt Mame's face was all that he needed to continue breaking the strike. Years later, when asked about his childhood, nearly everything Buddy remembered began that first day he broke the milk strike during the Great Depression. His parents had planted the rebel seed with loving hands.

CHAPTER
4

Becoming a Man

"If Hoover won't get out of the White House, I'll have to go in there and throw him out on his rear!" Ed growled. The Hoffmann children blinked and stopped eating. Ed and his family had been eating breakfast at the kitchen table in March, 1933, when Franklin Delano Roosevelt's winning presidential election returns were announced over the radio.

Ed chuckled and they all burst out laughing. A liberal Democrat, Ed Hoffmann felt that Roosevelt was the only hope for a nation in despair. He joined with many farmers who believed FDR and his New Deal would lead the country to better times.

But Regina did not agree. Every week without fail, Ed and Regina Hoffmann listened to a radio broadcast from The Shrine of the Little Flower in Royal Oak, Michigan. Reverend Charles Edward Coughlin led the National Union for Social Justice. He used his radio show to denounce political leaders, laws and countries he didn't like, namely Roosevelt and the Jews. He called Roosevelt a "dictator" but it was his anti-Semitic views that landed him in hot water. It wasn't long before Father Coughlin announced his withdrawal from radio and the suspension of the National Union. This was not the first time, nor the last – that a Pope in Rome muzzled a controversial American priest.[28]

After Father Coughlin lost his program, he continued to attract devoted followers to the Shrine. Among his visitors were Ed and Regina Hoffmann. Since Ed was a wholehearted Roosevelt supporter, it must have been Regina who avidly supported Coughlin's views. Ed had never spoken ill of anyone besides Hoover, but Regina was well-known for her biased views. Her children remember that like many farm wives, she was uncomfortable with anyone who wasn't white and of German origin. She didn't like Poles, Asians, Blacks or Jews.

Regina's sister Elizabeth worked for a wealthy Jewish family in Chicago. The family had a boy two years older than Buddy and when the lad out grew his clothes, his mother generously gave them to Elizabeth, who sent them on to Regina. The only really good clothes that Buddy wore throughout his childhood came from the kindness of Jews. But Elizabeth was unhappy in her job. She bitterly complained that the family misused her by throwing extravagant, spur-of-the-moment parties, expecting her to drop her free Sunday activities to serve as waitress. It angered her to such an extent that one day she made a special delicacy for the party guests, to which she added an unusual ingredient. Half way through the party, she began to enjoy herself as she "watched the guests run to the bathroom for the rest of the evening."

Ed remained a Roosevelt man despite Reverend Coughlin's radio speeches and Buddy continued to wear the best leather shoes, woolen coats and tailored pants that money could buy, while other farm children were wearing less stylish hand-me-downs. Along with her favorite Rev. Coughlin program, Regina never missed Eddie Cantor and Jack Benny on the radio. She probably didn't realize that both comedians were Jewish.

Small town bigotry also existed among people of various Christian religions in Wisconsin. Religion and background divided villages until well into the 1970s. Rigid barriers existed against intermarriage between Polish Catholics and German Catholics. Norwegians thought themselves better all the way around. Few families broke the religious barriers, like the Gresens, who lived near the Hoffmanns. Although they were Lutherans, (German Lutherans) they were well liked and they decided to ignore prejudice. On the other hand, if the Gresens had been Polish, well . . . that might have been another story.

The Roman Catholic religion stood as a foundation of hope for the Hoffmann family during the Depression. Despite all the disappointments, sacrifices, and losses, Ed and Regina taught their children religion with the same zeal that had sustained Buddy's grandfather as he hung out over the side of a huge ship, retching into the Atlantic Ocean on his voyage to America. George Hoffmann Sr. had been a stern taskmaster, an aloof, no-nonsense individual, a total perfectionist who bowed to no man. But in front of his sons and daughters, in front of neighbors and friends, George Hoffmann had easily knelt down on his knees before God. Ed and Regina did likewise, teaching their children to say the rosary every evening after supper.

They knelt on the varnished maple kitchen floor using chairs as kneelers. The floor was tough on the knees and leaning on a chair relieved some of the pressure. Most of the time Buddy knelt next to his dad, or between mother and dad. The girls knelt on the right side of their mother. Sometimes the chair served as a pillow when Buddy leaned over and fell asleep after The Apostles' Creed. Regina never failed to say the prayer closest to her heart – that her son would someday become a priest.

The Hoffmann children were taught to do their homework and to treat teachers and school property with respect. Phyllis was especially observant of school rules, but by the time Buddy got to the 3rd grade, he detested school. The boy could not keep still. When his body wasn't racing, his mouth was. On the first day of school in third grade, Sister Anastasia, a Franciscan nun of the Sisters of Perpetual Adoration, called out the student roll from her desk. The stern, heavy-set nun went down the list and crossed off the name after each child answered, "Present." The names continued until she called out: "George Hoffmann." No one said a word.

"George Hoffmann!" the Sister repeated. Everyone looked around. Children in the back row giggled. Angered, Sister Anastasia placed her heavy hands on the desk and rose like a giant crow from her chair. "I SAID GEORGE HOFFMANN!"

Nobody moved. Buddy looked right and left for another kid named Hoffmann. He thought he was related to every Hoffmann in town. Suddenly, the black image hovered directly above him. "You are George Hoffmann, aren't you?" she demanded. Buddy cringed, but he didn't lower his eyes in submission as the Sister may have expected him to. Instead, he glanced over at his pal, Joe Micklic. Joe's usual lopsided grin had changed to a look of terror.

"No, Sister. My name's Buddy Hoffmann," Buddy whispered from what seemed like a far off place. He tried to duck when Sister grabbed his left ear and lifted him out of his chair. She twisted his ear until he cried out in pain. Then, she dragged him across the room, opened the closet door and shoved him inside.

Confused and hurt, Buddy sat on the closet floor and held his throbbing ear. He sat there all morning, wondering why he had been punished for another boy's crime. Later when he went home, he found out that his real name wasn't Buddy after all. Ed Hoffmann had named his son "George" after his father. A milk inspector had visited the Hoffmann farm when George was not yet two years-old. As the man walked up to the barn, George ran out to greet him with a big smile and a handshake. "Well, hello little buddy," the man had said, laughing. After that, everybody in the family called him "Buddy." But the painful 3rd grade experience changed the boy, starting with his name.

It seemed to "George" that Sister Anastasia singled him out for special ridicule from the first day of school. He spent 3 days out of 5 in the closet and learned almost nothing in the 3rd grade. Worst of all, his disrespect turned to a deep loathing for nuns. Sister wouldn't tolerate misbehavior in her otherwise quiet and well-behaved classroom. George, tall and strong for his age, seemed older. Incessantly restless, noisy and bored, he either made sarcastic remarks, (a lifelong habit) joked or daydreamed, and he was often the class clown. The minute Sister's head turned, George would be somewhere he shouldn't have been, on an unpredictable pursuit of something new and exciting. Much like the other male members of the Hoffmann family, his unorthodox uncle Felix, his reckless uncle Louis and finally, his father Ed, an accident-prone, highly energetic man who loved action – men who were always on the run, the first to take dares and the last to back down. They were born with an inability to slow down and a reluctance to gauge dangerous risks. George had inherited the family trait.

Sister Anastasia had no patience with a child who would not conform to her rigid standards. She had attended Catholic schools all of her life and unbending rules were the norm. The only way she knew how to cope was to break George's rebellious spirit. Unfortunately for the "Big Bitch," as George called the nun in private, he had a lot of quiet time in the closet to plan his revenge.

The struggle between George and the hated Sister escalated. George went out of his way to annoy Sister. One of his all-time favorite tricks involved taking a friend far out on the playground on a rainy, muddy day. The boys caused a commotion in order to create a crowd. They yelled and hit wildly at each other for a few minutes, swearing and pretending to fight – long enough for Sister Anastasia to see them. Running toward them with lifted habit, screeching as she jumped mud puddles, Sister always got there too late. Laughing, the boys had scattered in different directions. George knew he would be thrown in the closet each time that he angered her, but as long as she was made the fool in front of the other children, it was worth it.

Finally, the day of reckoning came. Sister hit George one too many times. George looked down at the bruised knuckle on his left hand and something snapped. He reached over and picked up his inkwell. Ink splashed on the classroom floor and it speckled the two little girls sitting nearby. Sister lost all composure, threw up her hands and ran out of the room. It was a miracle that George wasn't expelled from school. Perhaps his mother's excellent reputation in the Wisconsin Deanery had something to do with it. This would not be George's last altercation with a nun.

At home George helped his father and walked to school with his sisters and his friends, Jack Seibert and Claude Bauman. Every morning, they passed St. Anthony's Friary, a large, red brick Capuchin Monastery, set back among dark pines. A high fieldstone wall in front prevented people from watching the friars. Occasionally, the children caught a glimpse of a long, single-file procession of dirty-robed friars, white cords swinging from their waists, hooded cowls, arms folded in front of them. The youngsters were told never to stare at the processions of silent, strange men. George stared anyway. He thought they looked dirty and he detested their straggly beards. He would have had a good laugh if someone had told him that St. Anthony's Friary would someday play an important role in his life.

As much as he disliked school, George loved Church. He became an acolyte at the age of eight and helped to serve Mass at St. Mary's Church. Father Ott, a young priest who loved and understood children, became an enduring inspiration to all the youngsters in the parish. George followed him around like a puppy. A kindly priest's patient example was one of the most powerful factors influencing boys to become priests.

When George stepped up to the altar to assist the priest during Mass, he experienced a certain trance or reverie. A fervent, yet mystical feeling came over him. "I feel different near the altar," he told his mother. "I rise above life, above myself." George felt humbled in the presence of God. Years later a relative said, "The family loaded the priesthood on him," and that may have been true, but George didn't really need to be pushed. Despite his hard feelings toward nuns, he knew all along that he would become a priest.

He also knew there had to an easier way of making a living than farming. He saw his uncles, Fr. Herbert and Fr. Felix, as successful men. It seemed to the boy that priests had it a lot easier than his parents and other relatives. They went on vacations and met interesting people and they had things his parents didn't. Comparing his dad to his uncles, George said, "All dad ever did was work, work, work!"

In 1932, secular priests like Father Felix and Father Herbert earned about $800 a year, on top of free room and board, use of the parish car, gasoline and vacations every year. True, teachers made higher salaries. A doctor earned $3,400 a year and a bus driver, $1,373.[29] Clean living, helping the poor and the sick, these were virtues George learned at home by seeing his uncles and their good works and by watching his father's largeness of spirit and his mother's generosity to the poor. They all had their faults, but the Hoffmann family had one, all abiding, comforting belief in God. No matter how many misfortunes the hard times brought them, no matter how angry they got at each other, they could always pray and be comforted by a Spirit greater than themselves.

The Catholic Church was a refuge of beauty amidst the difficulties of everyday life. Beautiful churches built around the country testified to the faith of the common people. During the Depression, people of other faiths questioned the need for elegant Church architecture. They didn't understand that the beauty and mystery of the Church played an important role in the lives of people who had nothing else. Parish leaders often raised the money to build chapels and cathedrals. The Church succeeded in blending opposing groups into a real community. Everything that happened in the parish was important and a priest's presence was an assurance of help.

"Father" was an important title in small towns. Priests worked at the center of the Catholic community. A good priest was an inspiration. They were sometimes rigid and narrow-minded in their beliefs and some held themselves in very high regard, but for the most part, priests taught discipline, got things done and stood as positive role models.

A parishioner with a family problem found comfort kneeling beside stained-glass windows and hope in the glow of sanctuary candles.

A priest was usually a man of action, always looking out for his flock and concerned with helping the poor, people out of work and those with family problems. Perhaps the German communities made a priest so holy by ordination and held such high ideals for him that he couldn't measure up, but at least there was a respect and admiration for him.

At the same time, a priest had no worries about paying food bills and his hands were not thick and cracked from hard labor. Fr. Felix, and Fr. Herbert had running water and indoor plumbing. George imagined the priesthood as a life of service and a step up from shoveling manure and worrying about frost, hail and never-ending bills. To him, the Church meant Easter lilies around the altar, old Latin hymns, ornamented prayer books, votive lamps, and holy cards stamped in gold and decorated with flowered wreaths and a saint's picture. From the moment he was born he was surrounded by people who didn't look at Catholicism as a ritual doctrine but as a symbol of beauty, goodness and comfort in a world of hard manual labor in the fields.

But George understood and enjoyed hard work. Besides his regular farm chores, he labored with his father in the logging camps as soon as he could work alongside the men. He cut logs for the sawmill before the days of chain saws. One man on each side felled trees and cut dimensions. The logs and pulpwood were hauled on bobsleds and horses were used for skidding logs. Once, while cutting wood on a cold day, George saw a man chop off his own finger. The man was so cold, he didn't notice until he saw his blood splattered across the snow.

Americans began to worry about war with Germany in the late 1930s and Ed Hoffmann read with disgust about Adolph Hitler's rise to power. But the old country was far away. To take their minds off international problems, German Americans grabbed a violin, cleared off a space in the barn, brought in homemade beer and danced to polkas and waltzes. At local dance halls, two or three hundred people gathered for wedding dances. A bar ran the full length of the hall and local bands came to play. George danced right along with his sisters and the neighborhood girls. He felt awkward, but he liked to dance and have fun.

When George turned thirteen, Ed enrolled him in Marathon Public High School, knowing that if the boy found new friends and started having fun at high school events, his plans of becoming a priest might change. This seemed a good way to find out. George's ideals and values clashed from the first with a school curriculum designed for children interested in agriculture. He wanted to learn more Latin, while most of the kids talked about crops and livestock. Discouraged, George complained to his parents that he wasn't learning anything that would help him become a priest. One night, he got angry and told his dad: "I'll never be a farmer!" Ed listened but urged his son to continue in school. After all, he might feel differently as time went on.

George decided to give school another chance; but only because he got to sit next to Agnes Beyer, the Lutheran minister's pretty daughter. He developed a crush on Agnes, and if it hadn't been for a certain agriculture class, he might have become a farmer after all. The teacher began a course in husbandry and George was picked to help the instructor demonstrate how to castrate a pig. This was the finishing touch. With revulsion, he performed the castration on several hogs. That evening he blew up again. "I'm wasting my time!" he told his parents. "Priests don't castrate hogs!" It was that and the dirty magazines in the boys' bathroom that finally got to him. He told his dad that he was dropping out and that was the end of it. Ed wasn't surprised and he didn't oppose his son's plan. Anyway, Ed was happy to have his help on the farm during the winter cutting logs in the woods. After the castration incident, Ed gave up trying to make him go to school and George gave no further thought to Agnes Beyer.

News of Germany's bloody assaults overseas were followed in radio broadcasts in America. Most Americans felt that Hitler had to be stopped. Although Ed didn't talk much about Hitler with George, he often stopped into the local tavern to discuss events in Europe with his friends. One afternoon, George sat in his father's Chevy while Ed went into the bar for a drink, saying he would only be a minute. An hour later, the 13 year-old boy got bored and went in to persuade his dad to come home. As he walked up to the bar, a crowd of men surrounded him. They all raised their glasses for a toast. "This boy's almost a man, Ed Hoffmann," one man said. "Give the boy a drink! We'll make a man of him!"

Soon cries of "Give him a drink!" echoed throughout the tavern and a shot of whiskey and a chaser of beer landed in front of the boy. "Drink up, son," Ed told him. George took a big gulp of whiskey. It burned going down and then it warmed his throat and he drank the chaser of beer after it. The whole tavern erupted in cheers. "He's a man, the boy's a man now!" they yelled. "Let's hear it for Buddy!" The men applauded, whistled and clapped him on the back. Ed left the bar with his arm around George's shoulders. His boy had passed the ritual with the belief that only real men could drink. Later in life, George learned the hard way that it wasn't alcohol that would make him a man.

CHAPTER
5

Breaking the Rules

"You're full of s…!" George snapped at the shocked nun. Sister Elizabeth had blamed him for yet another infraction. After dropping out of school in Marathon, George had surprised his parents by agreeing to enter Aquinas High School in La Crosse, Wisconsin. He boarded with his Aunt Catherine, but his reputation had arrived in La Crosse before him.

The first day of school in Sister Elizabeth's English class, she found out George Hoffmann's name and she singled him out with the cutting remark: "So you are the boy who caused my sister Theonela to have a nervous breakdown in Marathon!" George hadn't thought about Sister Theonela in years.

Back in the sixth grade in Marathon, Sister Theonela had suffered a nervous collapse in the middle of the school year and had to be institutionalized. The Hoffmann family thought she had "gone nuts" because the school had burned down. Classes were held in a small house with little room and too many students. George had nothing to do with the fire, but apparently Sister Theonela had blamed George for her anxiety and subsequent hospitalization.

Toward the end of the year in La Crosse, George felt that he had finally taken enough from Sister Elizabeth and he made the disrespectful excrement comment in front of the class. By all accounts George probably should have been suspended from school. But in the Principal's office, Father Pretzel listened to George tell how he had always been blamed for everything because Sister Elizabeth was intentionally persecuting him on account of her sister's mental break down. Father Pretzel believed him and sent the boy back to class without punishment. George's uncles, Father Felix and Father Herbert were respected priests in the Dioceses of La Crosse and this may have influenced his decision. He also knew the boy wanted to become a priest and a school suspension on his record could have been embarrassing when he tried to enter a seminary.

While World War II raged on, the Hoffmann family saved enough money to send George to the seminary of his choice. He chose St. Lawrence Seminary at Mt. Calvary, Wisconsin, a place referred to as, "The poor boy's seminary." George stayed home a year and worked in a pea vine factory and for neighbors to help fund his tuition.

In the fall of 1942, Regina and Ed drove their son to the minor seminary at Mt. Calvary, 125 miles from Marathon. As they neared their destination, the enormity of losing their only son hit them hard. George had mixed feelings as well. His father was losing his best helper and companion and George's childhood was coming to an end. He gulped back a tear as he watched his dad's reactions. As they neared Mt. Calvary, Ed betrayed his confusion with a sudden loss of direction. He took a wrong turn on a country road and it wasn't until he saw the church steeple in his rear view mirror that he realized he was going in the wrong direction.

They finally arrived at Mt. Calvary, parked the Chevy and walked George into the administration building to help him register. Ed hadn't slept much the night before and now George was having second thoughts. He had made the commitment but he didn't know if he could survive in the austere atmosphere of the seminary. Considering his past school performance, he knew that if he dropped out now, he'd be "the black sheep" forever.

George walked his parents back out to their car, hugged them and said goodbye. He didn't cry because "men didn't cry," but when Ed hugged his son, he held him for just a few seconds longer and both had to hold back the tears. Ed composed himself and got back into the car while George kissed his mother. As he waved goodbye to them, George saw his father point upward as if to say, "Make it good!"

To the naïve, country boy, Mt. Calvary seemed like a forbidding fortress. He hesitated, then walked up the steps and entered the enormous, gray brick building. Suddenly, his eyes widened. Everything seemed so modern! That night George put his hands under warm running water and had his first shower. "Boy, this is living!" he wrote home. Built in 1872, the seminary had been renovated with central heating, a gym and basketball court and a theatre for stage plays and a library. On Sunday evenings the boys got to watch movies.

George had 25 classmates at Mt. Calvary and because he had dropped out of school, he was a year older than most of them. "Chet," one of George's new friends (Father Chester Poppa), recalled that at first George "found it difficult to study as much as he had to."[30] But the constant reminder that he would end up a black sheep if he dropped out, kept George going. And he didn't want to waste the money his parents had saved for his education. Room, board and tuition came to $250 a year, an enormous amount of money for a farm family to provide.

Mt. Calvary was impressive but the areas of most interest to the teenage boys were the kitchen and the cafeteria. The food didn't compare to Regina's delicious home-cooking. George wrote home telling his folks that Sunday dinner consisted of "sliders, fish eyes and belly wash. Sliders is a macaroni dish with oil added to keep it from sticking to the pan, served with ring bologna and rye bread. Fish eyes is tapioca, or dessert, and we call coffee "belly wash." Regina thought it was terrible that her son had to eat gravy made from a box. George had taken her tasty cooking for granted, but not any longer. To boys of German ancestry who loved fresh baked bread and home-made noodles, pies and cakes, seminary food took a lot of getting used to.

A sick joke went around the dorm that if somebody died, the students had hash for lunch on the day of the funeral. George watched the pattern and remarked in a letter, "There isn't much meat unless there is a funeral." From then on, Regina sent chocolate chip and peanut butter cookies back with George's weekly laundry. Dirty clothes were shipped home once a week in a laundry case and sent back clean.

Mt. Calvary activities began at 6 a.m. when Father Gerald Walker looked out of his dorm room and rang a bell. At the same time, the boys heard the bell tower chimes. They hurried to clean up, hurried to morning prayers and hurried to Mass. After church, a fifteen minute breakfast of oatmeal, a short walk, then off to classes: Geometry, Latin, Greek, German, History, Science and English. The Geometry instructor was also the Rector or school disciplinarian. Father Alexis Gore was a stare-you-down taskmaster and nobody crossed him. George went to the blackboard one day wearing the U.S. Navy jacket his cousin Eddie had sent to him from Pearl Harbor. Father Alexis grabbed George's jacket and jerked the boy right up to his face. "What in hell do you have on?" he roared. George sputtered something about his cousin surviving the Pearl Harbor attack, but his explanation trailed off when the priest reprimanded him. He had ignored his mother when she nagged and wouldn't listen to a Sister but George lived in fear of Father Alexis and never again wore or said anything out of the ordinary in the Rector's class. Father Alexis had a bulldog named, "Jiggs" that followed him around – the perfect dog for the grouchy old priest who leaned against the wall and watched as the boys came out of the cafeteria from lunch. He caught each student's eyes and stared, slowly pushing his goatee back and forth with one finger. No funny business occurred at Mt. Calvary as long as the "evil eye" was upon them.

Father Alexis died suddenly in the middle of George's first year in the seminary. Students ate hash on the day he was buried and there were a few snickers in the cafeteria. Father Gerald Walker took his place and no two priests could have been as different. A kind man, Fr. Gerald was almost apologetic if he hurt someone's feelings. As soon as George and the rest of the guys figured out his routine, it was no problem to sneak out back of the handball court for a cigarette, something they wouldn't have done when Father Alexis was alive. Playing hooky wasn't too hard. As "Chet" recalled, "If there was a rule against it, we'd try to do it."[31]

Lights went out at 9 p.m. and George felt a twinge of homesickness, but it soon wore off. He didn't expect a phone call from home. The Hoffmann family had an oak crank phone on the farm but it was only used in case of a medical emergency. George had his appendix removed that year, which meant a call home, but for the next eleven years, he never received a phone call. In a way, the minor seminary at Mt. Calvary was the hardest. It may have been the difficult subjects he wasn't ready for, or perhaps he wasn't sure of what the future held, but it took George awhile to catch up with the other students.

He spent Christmas and Easter vacations working at home on the farm but by the fall of 1943, changes were in the works. Ed and Regina had saved the farm through the difficult Depression years, when many farmers had given up. They had raised their children and provided their son with a seminary education. Now, George's pretty sister, 14 year-old

Phyllis, entered St. Mary's Convent in Milwaukee. She had joined the Sisters of the Divine Savior with a happy heart.

While George was home on vacation, Ed told his son, "If you don't want the farm, I'm getting rid of it." Regina evidently felt the same way. They were getting older and the work was too much without hired help, which they couldn't afford. In the end, the Hoffmann dairy farm was auctioned off for $4,000. Ed and Regina then moved to Wausau, where Ed held two jobs at the Silvernagel Company and at Stuber Dairy. When Father Herbert found out the farm had been sold for so little, he was dumbfounded. "If I'd known it would go for that, I'd have bought it myself!" he told his sister Catherine.[32] But the sad truth was that nobody in the family had the time or the money to run the family farm.

By then, George had settled into the steady routine at Mt. Calvary. On Saturday nights during evening study hall, the Priest Prefect allowed the boys to listen to the Bell Telephone Hour on the radio. Other than this program, they didn't have access to a radio. Radios were only for the solemnly professed, ordained members of the community. Students didn't hear news reports and they didn't read newspapers or magazines.

As a child, George had been repulsed by the bearded, dirty-robed Capuchin seminarians he saw as he walked past St. Anthony's Friary on his way to school. At Mt. Calvary he met Capuchins who were just the opposite; men with an avid interest in music, traveling and missionary work. Above all, they were excellent teachers. George began thinking of the Capuchin life. He decided to make the decision before he saw his folks at Christmas.

Regina was totally unprepared for her son's socially unacceptable announcement that he wanted to become a Capuchin priest. She let him know that he was about to "waste his education." His parents' negative reaction didn't change George's mind. The discussion ended abruptly when George told them: "If I can't be a Capuchin, I won't become a priest!" That settled it.

George had been away from home for three years when his parents sold the farm. Regina got a job as a cook at St. Mary's School and with two salaries coming in, the Hoffmanns built a new house in Marathon. Regina's work was meaningful to her, but Ed wasn't as lucky. He was over 50 and he had to live with the stigma that he had let the family farm go. With his wife happily working outside the home, he may have lost confidence without his dairy business. Now began the hardest years in the Hoffmann marriage, with life changes that neither spouse had expected. With no dairy cows and no crops to put in, Ed's drinking got worse. For the first time in their marriage, Regina knew they had a stable income, a nice home and money to pay the bills, but Ed went to the bar more often. Regina considered a separation, but she changed her mind after Father Herbert sat down with them. Their fights would continue for years, some confrontations much worse than others, but Regina knew that despite her husband's drinking, he was a good father and their children adored him. A divorce would have destroyed the family and broken their hearts. They had worked too hard over the years to let that happen.

On February 20, 1945, George Hoffmann graduated from Mt. Calvary. He then set off by train for Milwaukee to join nineteen other young men on their way to the Novitiate or novice year at St. Felix Friary in Huntington, Indiana. During this year of spiritual reflection and meditation, priests would scrutinize them and vote on those who should remain and those who shouldn't. At least one of the young men eventually had a nervous breakdown and ended up in a mental institution. Others seriously questioned themselves as to whether or not they really wanted to give up marriage and children to become priests. Yet another – the "high strung" young man who could never keep still and drove his teachers wild by drumming on his chair with a pencil during lectures – that young man would thoroughly relish the whole experience.

On the stop-over in Milwaukee, four of the guys stayed at Danny Zach's home. That night they celebrated a few hours of freedom by drinking beer. Did they have the "guts to stick it out?" Were there going to be uncomfortable surprises? George hated surprises. The guys drank, played cards and talked all night. They knew that smoking and drinking weren't allowed in the seminary and most felt that this was their last party. The next day, George and Danny Zach were exhausted, excited and "somewhat apprehensive" at the same time. But when they arrived at St. Felix Friary, George thought the building looked like a mansion in a brochure. Built in the classic Spanish style, it reminded him of photographs he had seen of a European monastery with red-tiled roofs and cream-colored brick. The courtyards were filled with flower gardens, peach and grape orchards.

The seminarians were immediately placed in seclusion for eight days.

They couldn't talk to priests or to one another. Absolute silence was not George's favorite atmosphere. During the days of meditation they prayed and reflected on their personal lives. The older friars, one year ahead of him, were out playing volleyball and talking. That made it more difficult still because they were his old friends and he wanted to joke around. Hard as he tried to remain silent, he slipped up a few times.

Novices were invested by Provincial Father Clement Neubauer on March 2, 1945. They received their brown robes and after services, they were instructed to stand outside Fr. Clement's office. It was time for them to receive new names. George dreaded this moment. Earlier, a few of the guys had gone to the Novice Master to suggest names they preferred, but George was too shy to request a name. He had prepared his mother by teasing her that he might "get some weird name like Popnucious." By preparing her for the worst, he hoped the name they gave him wouldn't shock her.

The door opened and one by one the men lined up and knelt down in the Provincial's office. George was fifth in line when Father Clement began to bestow the names. The first was "Severin." Well, that wasn't too bad. The second was "Baldwin," then "Dunston." George was glad he didn't get that one. Then came "Ewald." George was squirming. "Oh, my God – it's going to be a terrible name," he thought. "I know it!" Kneeling with bowed head and eyes closed, he waited for "Popnucious."

Finally, it was his turn. Fr. Clement stood over George and gave him the name he would have for the rest of his life – "Emmett." "Lord, what a relief!" he later recalled. The restless farm boy named Buddy and the mischievous schoolboy named George had now become brother or frater Emmett and he liked his new name.

Although frater Emmett was very serious about the priesthood and used the next year to meditate and deepen his commitment to God, he rapidly sized up his situation and knew what he had to do to survive:

> If it had been real, I would have followed the rules, but the whole Catholic seminary system was a game. You played their game and you were okay. You were either a sinner or a "scroop," a scrupulous religious person. I didn't go for the "Holier than Thou" mentality. But whatever they wanted, I gave it to them.[33]

His new name didn't keep frater Emmett from feeling out of touch with reality. He felt the so-called "vow or poverty" was a sham. It looked to him like the poverty vow meant living in a palatial mansion and having all his needs met. The Novitiate was a time-out, when a man learned about religious life, but for Emmett, living in a beautiful home like Huntington was not living in poverty – it was pure luxury compared to the farm.

President Franklin D. Roosevelt suffered a cerebral hemorrhage and died on April 12, 1945. Less than a month later, on May 7th, Germany surrendered and the war in Europe ended after 2,076 days of suffering and more than 55 million deaths. Japan would fight on in the Pacific until the United States dropped two atomic bombs on Hiroshima and Nagasaki on the 5th of August, 1945. Late that evening the novitiates were told of the day's event. Frater Emmett's first cousin Eddy had seen the slaughter in the Pacific first hand. Never a pacifist, Emmett would have gone to war if his country had called him to active duty. But on August 14, 1945, Japan surrendered.[34]

While dramatic events occupied the world, life as a novice friar went on as before, quiet and studious on the outside, but extremely stressful behind the scenes. The friars were constantly observed by an irritable Novice Master, Father Raymond De Mers, a tense, exhausted priest trying to control fifty young men who had suddenly lost their adolescence. George stayed out of his way as much as possible but his friend, Danny Zach, had trouble adapting to the rigid atmosphere. One morning in Spiritual Life class, Emmett glanced over at Danny after he heard strange mutterings. Danny was having a conversation with himself. He had a nervous breakdown in front of his friends. He asked strange questions, sputtered, giggled and couldn't focus his thoughts. The Novice Master hurried him out of class and Danny was admitted to a mental hospital. The stress of being evaluated 24 hours a day weeded out the men who were not emotionally strong enough to become priests. Frater Emmett was upset about his friend but he understood what had happened. The priests voted three times a year on each novice. If a young man didn't pass scrutiny, he was out. The fraters had to act as perfect as possible – beyond human. The only way Emmett could reach that goal was to put on a good act. Unfortunately, Danny couldn't act.

As soon as frater Emmett learned what he had to do, things got easier. Looking around to find something to keep his hands and mind busy, he "found" a broken-down lawn mower in an old shed. Emmett had never taken apart a gas engine, buy he knew that he could fix almost anything.

He took the lawn mower apart, cleaned up the pistons, put it all back together and it ran like new. After this accomplishment, he had even more fun with an old abandoned truck that he "found" in the machine shed. Emmett and another novice, frater Eugene Roessler, took the engine apart and cleaned it. The truck consisted of a frame with wheels, a steering wheel and an old engine. Emmett put a couple of boards across the frame and that's all it took.

Off they went on their first joy ride. This went on for a week until one day they rounded a corner and drove right past the shocked Novice Master! Caught red-handed, both men were scolded but Emmett found that he didn't feel too badly about the incident after all, in fact, he felt great about it. From this enlightening experience Emmett learned that his little adventure had entertained the priests. He really hadn't gotten into much trouble and he thought he saw a twinkle in the Novice Master's eyes. From that day on, he knew that being a priest wasn't going to be nearly as difficult as he had originally thought. The Novitiate encouraged docility, yet the Novice Master had been amused by the rebel with the useful talent, a young man who did not have it in him to fake a docile heart.

One morning, Emmett and "Breezy," (frater Baldwin Beyer) sneaked down to the bakery to see if "Sonny," (brother Philip Schwartz) had some fresh baked bread or warm rolls. The Novice Master must have suspected Emmett was up to something because he came into the bakery unexpected. Not seeing anything, yet suspicious, Father Raymond engaged brother Philip in a long conversation. When they first heard Fr. Raymond's voice, the two young fraters, dressed as usual in their woolen robes, had crawled into a tight space behind the red-hot oven. If there was one thing that Emmett couldn't stand, it was having to sit still for long periods of time – the feeling of not being able to move. Both novices were tall men and now Emmett found himself squeezed on all fours between a scorching wall and a hot stove. To make matters worse, the two culprits had been munching on raisin pie. The fast-acting diarrheic effects, coupled with the hot, stifling environment, now began to do its dirty work on Breezy and Emmett. Father Raymond finally left the bakery and the two novices fell out from behind the wood-burning oven, their faces reddish brown and shiny like fresh-baked loaves splashed with butter topping. With no time to go to the bathroom before their first class with Father Raymond, they barely made it. When the uncomfortable hour ended, they ran for the bathroom.

During the eighteen months at Huntington, longer than usual because of the war, Emmett took his simple, three-year vows on March 3, 1946. The first of these vows was the vow of poverty. Since Emmett was living in luxury, the vow of poverty seemed ridiculous. The vow of chastity wasn't difficult either, but the vow of obedience proved a little tricky. He breathed a sigh of relief when he found out that the professed friars had voted to allow him to stay. The voting process, an ancient rite, consisted of a choice between black and white beans. The priests passed a bowl around. If they liked the novice, they placed a white bean in the bowl, if not, the unfortunate novice got a black bean and he was out. Miraculously, frater Emmett's beans were all white. He had passed basic training.

Each young frater was then issued a black suit and a white collar for the train trip to their next seminary assignment, the House of Philosophy at Mary Immaculate Friary, located on the Hudson River at Garrison, New York. On the trip, Emmett learned that when he wore a white collar, drunks latched on to him. He ran into one who had to confess all of his sins. It was messy. Emmett heard all of the man's problems and sins in a loud voice and finally the slurred words, "Hey Father! I'm a good Catholic!"

Mary Immaculate Friary, an elegant mansion surrounded by manicured lawns four hundred feet above the Hudson River, had once been the Hamilton Fish estate, where politicians and high society matrons gathered in the indoor greenhouse to walk among exotic plants all year round. Emmett had never seen anything like it. His life of poverty was getting richer and more luxurious all the time.

The Garrison years meant rigorous study in Logic, Biology, World History, Empirical Psychology, Hebrew, Latin, Metaphysics, Church History and Philosophy. Emmett was stimulated as never before, but he skimmed through the subjects that he thought he wouldn't need in the priesthood. He relished Philosophy and the teachings of St. Thomas of Aquinas, known as Thomastic Philosophy.

Some said that the study of philosophy was dangerous because it led young men to deceit and subversive acts. In Emmett's case, there was no need to worry – subversive acts were his specialty. For example, he was adept at studying patterns. Where were the priests on Saturday nights? Where were the goodies best hidden and by whom? On Saturday nights, the faculty left and only the older priests who went to bed early stayed around, a perfect set-up for parties. The clerics, led by the craftiest of them all, gathered in the kitchen pantry and bribed the cook for altar wine and cheddar cheese, fruit and home-made bread. What a heavenly feast! Ten to fifteen guys drank a gallon jug of wine. The cook, brother Dan Brady, stashed his private booze in the bakery. On special occasions, like Christmas, he brought out the whiskey. After a couple of drinks, the men enjoyed the Irishman's heavy brogue lectures about "those damn clerics."

As soon as Emmett knew everybody's pattern, he began to push authority. If something was missing or suspicious, the older priests suspected him, with good reason. Emmett had developed an interesting sideline business in the carpentry shop. The novices from New York had regular visits from their parents and siblings. After each visit, extra cigarettes floated around – and Emmett liked to smoke. For the next couple of years, Emmett manufactured a most ingenious, custom-made typing table, so creative in fact, twenty novices put in special orders. Each table had a drawer for typing paper. The drawer also contained a secret compartment, ideal for hiding forbidden cigarettes. In exchange for one of Emmett's desks, he got all the cigarettes he wanted to smoke at parties and in the woods behind the friary.

In June, 1950, Emmett graduated from Mary Immaculate with a B.A. in Philosophy. He then came full circle when he returned to his home town of Marathon, to the House of Theology at St. Anthony's Friary, the mysterious monastery he had passed every day on his way to elementary school. He became one of the men in long brown robes who walked single file on daily sojourns around the grounds. The truth was that he had become one, but he didn't look like them. First, he figured out how to get rid of the beard. He "found" a razor and every week he trimmed his beard. The sandals didn't last a month. He got a physician's order that because his feet were flat, he had to have more support and that meant shoes. Emmett had entered St. Anthony's with a host of old friends. Now in his eighth year of study for the priesthood, he was just four years short of his ordination as a Capuchin priest. The friars and the Capuchin superiors had accepted the renegade in their midst.

Meanwhile, the world outside the seminary walls had changed

dramatically. After World War II ended, an era of unprecedented wealth belied the ever-increasing tensions and potential dangers of the "Cold War." The Soviet Union lowered an "Iron Curtain" across the center of Europe and President Harry S. Truman declared that the United States would protect any nation threatened by a Communist takeover. The two most powerful nations in the world dominated international affairs for many years to come. In January 1950, North Korean Communist troops attacked South Korea, and the U.S. condemned the invasion. The resulting war cost America and Korea 2 million lives.[35]

The men cloistered at St. Anthony's Friary in Marathon had not seen television, and most had never turned on a transistor radio. During his third year at St. Anthony's Emmett took a required course in human sexual behavior called "De Sexto." Fr. Basil Gummerman taught the Moral Theology class and part of the course covered moral and immoral acts and how to deal with the sins that priests would hear about in the confessionals. Fr. Basil enjoyed shocking his students. When he described a particular immoral act, he lowered his balding head, covered with wisps of hair, slid his round glasses down on his hooked nose, winked and chuckled. He made snide remarks, which amused his students. He was also a pastorally-oriented person who could sympathize with the problems of ordinary people.

During his last year at St. Anthony's, Emmett began thinking of becoming a missionary in Nicaragua. He learned that Nicaragua was a frightening place to live, a country teaming with alligators and dangerous guerilla fighters. People had been held hostage by the notorious dictator, General Anastasio Somoza. Emmett felt that the poor needed homes and bridges repaired and new schools; peace instead of hatred. He thought it was a challenge for a priest who thrived on finding solutions, an initiator of new ideas, a man with an active mind in constant motion. Better yet, Nicaragua was an exciting place – a far cry from the quiet streets of Marathon.

On August 27, 1953, Emmett was ordained a priest at St. Mary's Church. Bishop William O'Conner D.D. (Emmett called him "Wild Bill" because he was from Chicago.) poured the consecrated oils over Father Emmett Hoffmann's fingers and tied his hands together with a long, white, narrow cloth called the maneturgium; the symbol of his indelible bond to Jesus Christ. From that moment on, the priest's hands were no longer considered the hands of an ordinary man because he could absolve people of sin. The Bishop held Father Emmett's bound hands in his and said in Latin: "Do you promise obedience and loyalty to the Church?" Father responded, "I promise." Then the Bishop put his hands on the young priest's head and said, "Thou art a priest forever . . ."

Father Emmett's entire family attended the ceremony. His uncle, Father Herbert, looked fine in his vestments and he was hugely proud of his nephew, although he never thought Emmett would make it through the seminary. Anna, his frail grandmother, sat with his parents, who both watched with tears in their eyes. At that incredible moment, Regina's prayers had been answered – her son was now a priest and she was no longer his mother. He now belonged to God.

Regina made the arrangements for Father Emmett's celebration of First Solemn High Mass and the banquet to follow. If he had been ordained a secular priest, Father would now be counting his gift money with plans to buy an automobile. Instead, he rejoiced with plans for a ministry in Nicaragua. Two or three hundred people attended the First Mass and Father Herbert delivered the homily. Although a rebel and prankster, Father Emmett was secretly insecure and timid. He was glad to get the whole thing over with because he didn't like people making a fuss over him.

After his first High Mass, Regina Hoffmann was extremely disappointed when she heard that Father Emmett had been posted to St. Labre Mission in Montana, instead of to Nicaragua. His Provincial had assigned him to the dilapidated Cheyenne mission because it was on the verge of closing due to lack of funding. The Father Superior at the mission was ailing and needed help.

Likewise, Father Emmett's uncles were not impressed. When he saw their reaction, a twinge of regret shot through him. Perhaps he should have listened to his mother in the first place. Despite the fact that he was now an ordained priest, he felt guilty that he had not lived up to his mother's high expectations. In July, 1954, he packed and made ready for his Montana assignment with a heavy heart.

CHAPTER 6

St. Labre Mission

A week after Father Emmett arrived at St. Labre, a Cheyenne employee died from a sunstroke while irrigating the Mission fields. It was not the Cheyenne custom at that time to embalm the dead. Family friends immediately dug the man's grave in the Mission cemetery and Father Emmett was chosen to hold the service at the gravesite. After Mass, the sad procession walked slowly up the hill to the cemetery and Father began the solemn service.

Father was a little apprehensive as this was his first Cheyenne funeral. After the mourners lowered the rough pine coffin into the grave with ropes, he leaned over and sprinkled holy water on the coffin saying: "In the name of the Father, Son and the Holy . . . BAM! A loud rifle blast startled him, his left foot slid part way into the grave and the Ritual Book slipped out of his hands and fell with a thump on the pine coffin. Father barely managed to keep from falling into the grave, although every time he tried to get up, his robe caught under his shoe. He finally regained his composure and scrambled to his feet, looking sheepishly right and left for the sniper.

"Uh . . . who are they shooting at?" Father mumbled to the Cheyenne standing next to him. Not one of them had pulled out a gun, nor flinched when they heard the shot. Clarence "Bisco" Spotted Wolf, grandson of old Chief Spotted Wolf of Bighorn Battle fame, explained to Father that the dead man's favorite horse had been shot according to Cheyenne custom, so that its spirit would accompany his master to the spirit land. Father was relieved that he hadn't been the intended victim and that he hadn't tumbled into the grave like a flying squirrel that had missed a branch. While it was a strange way to strike up an acquaintance, Bisco, a rancher and rodeo team-roper, remained Father Emmett's loyal friend.[36]

Father also had difficulty accepting his duties at the Mission. He was surprised when Father Marion lined up the regular daily chores. First, he was to mend fences! Father Marion didn't realize the weight of his words as he casually described the Mission farm operation; the crops, cleaning out chicken coups, herding cattle and castrating hogs! Disgusted, Father Emmett immediately complained.

He had come to St. Labre to teach Latin and religion classes. There had been no mention of chickens and hogs. He wanted to become a priest to help people, not to work on a farm. While shoveling cow manure, Father told another priest: "I didn't spend 12 years in the seminary just to castrate hogs. I could have stayed in Wisconsin to do that!"

Understanding the Cheyenne people was no easy task for a white man. Father Marion loved the Cheyennes unconditionally and had stressed to Father Emmett how important it was for them to preserve their language and culture. Otherwise he didn't think they could survive. Other priests at the Mission scoffed at Indian traditions. Their only interest was to convert them to Catholicism. This rigid view meant that when a Cheyenne did not forsake his culture, language and traditional religion and convert to Catholicism, he was considered a "heathen," or "pagan." Much to Father Marion's credit, he and several other Capuchin Fathers were not as narrow-minded. He taught Father Emmett to appreciate and value the Cheyennes for their culture, generosity, humor, and most of all, for their humble, yet profound spiritual understanding of "Maheo," the Creator.

Father hadn't been at the Mission long before he experienced Cheyenne spirituality first hand. One night, he went to bed early. At 2 a.m., the friary doorbell rang. A light sleeper, Father Emmett woke up and listened. When nobody got up to answer the door, he ran barefoot down the squeaking stairs in his night robe. He switched on the light, and there on the front porch stood a bedraggled woman in torn clothes, her hair cut in different lengths, with ashes smeared over her face. It was the dead man's widow. "My husband's spirit is restless, Father," she told the astonished priest. "Can I have some holy water?" He didn't understand the unusual request, but he ran back upstairs to change into his robe and then returned to accompany the woman to the Mission chapel. He carefully handed her the holy water and watched as the grieving widow, bathed in eerie moonlight, walked back up to the cemetery to bless her husband's grave. Father stood there awhile and listened to the mournful wailing of the devoted wife. He had never heard anything so dreadful, yet so full of love. News of Father Emmett's willingness to help people, no matter the time of day or night, soon spread across the Northern Cheyenne Reservation.

Another first experience at St. Labre was much more humbling. During the first of his Sunday Masses, Father Emmett noticed the nuns sitting in the front row with their hands folded. Many tribal elders were also present. Acutely shy, Fr. Emmett always worried about verbal errors or slips of the tongue, especially in Church. He didn't yet know that the Cheyennes were just as shy about making mistakes. They often pretended not to speak English at all for fear they would make grammatical errors and look foolish. On that particular morning, Fr. Emmett promised himself that it would not happen. The service began and he rose to make his way to the altar, head bowed in reverence, hands held prayerfully in front of him. He began to pray.

Suddenly he heard a baby cry out and he glanced up. A Cheyenne mother was nursing her baby in church. Having never seen this before, he was momentarily stunned, scrambled what he was saying and the whole world fell apart right in front of him. Terribly nervous, he started to laugh.

The laugh did not explode in howls. It was a seizing up of his entire body, a grimace very funny to see – so funny that it tickled everyone, or almost everyone. The Sisters in the front row were not amused. Embarrassment hunched Father's shoulders up to his reddened neck and ear lobes and he convulsed in gasping giggles. He removed his glasses and wiped his eyes. At this point, the slightest grin on any face caused a repeat explosion of giggles, uncontrollable for several hilarious moments. He tried to read again and now the entire Cheyenne congregation, including the little children and elderly, waited with great expectation for the next giggle. Everyone laughed and all bad thoughts melted away. A spiritual cleansing had taken place. From then on, the Cheyennes felt closer to Father Emmett, the priest who like themselves, sometimes made mistakes and got embarrassed. To see that he was a human being, a shy person who could lose decorum and laugh at himself, endeared him to the grandsons and daughters of the warriors who had fought and won the Battle of the Little Bighorn.

Edward and Regina Hoffman on their Wedding Day. – May 27, 1921

Grandpa George and Grandma Anna Hoffman with their children. – 1910

Back row standing, left to right: Henry, George, Felix, Mary, Herbert, Edward, Andrew
Front row, left to right: Ann, Grandpa George, Louis, Grandma Anna and Catherine

George "Buddy" Hoffmann – 1928

Edward and Regina Hoffmann and their son "Buddy" on his First Communion Day. – 1933

Young seminarians on their way to the novitiate having their last beer and cigarettes. George Hoffmann is third from the left. – February 20, 1945

Friars relaxing at Mary Immaculate Seminary, Garrison, New York.
Friar Emmett is seated at left (the only one wearing shoes).

St. Anthony Friary – Marathon, Wisconsin

First Solemn High Mass
St. Mary's Church, Marathon, Wisconsin, August 30, 1953

Father Marion, O.F.M., Cap.

The Edward and Regina Hoffmann family. – 1953
Back row: Dorothy, Father Emmett, Sister Phyllis and Rita
Front row: Edward, Marilyn and Regina

Ursuline Sisters at St. Labre Mission. – 1880s

Father Emmett climbed the hill above St. Labre for his first look at the Mission. – 1954

Mary McGarvey holds Cooky, her new foster daughter. – 1956

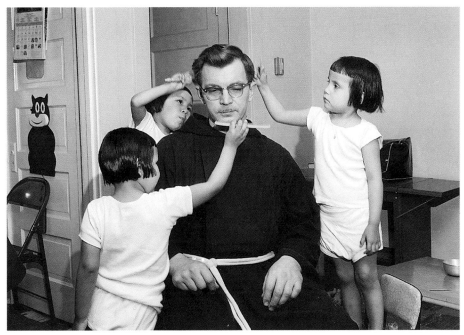

Dolly, Doreen and Cooky comb Fr. Emmett's hair. – 1950s

Father Emmett with Cooky – 1957

William Yellow Robe, last surviving Cheyenne Scout for Gen. Nelson Miles and an unidentified Capuchin priest. – 1950s

Father Emmett wrecked the Mission car in 1954.

Sitting at right, smiling: Mr. Leo Dohn Sr., St. Labre benefactor
Standing left: Louie Congro, long-time employee of
Guild Arts & Crafts – 1950s

Clarence "Bisco" Spotted Wolf, grandson of old Chief Spotted Wolf of Bighorn fame. Father Emmett calls Bisco his "guiding light." – 1950s

John Wooden Legs and Albert Tall Bull perform the ceremony
making Father Emmett an Honorary Chief of the Northern Cheyenne
Council of 44 in 1961.

Ashland Guild Arts & Crafts Factory
Left to right: Sylvia Yellow Fox, Katy Three Fingers,
Josephine Sooktis. – 1962

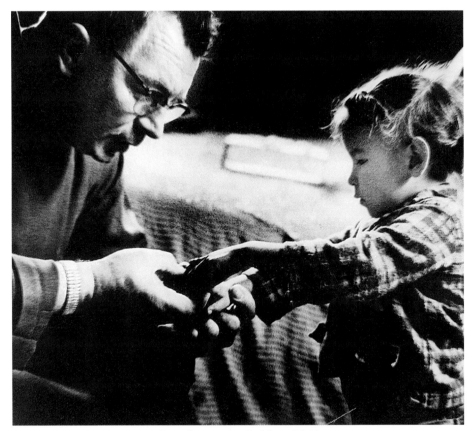

Comforting a child. – 1963

Mary McGarvey serves lunch to Doreen, Dolly and Cooky. – 1957

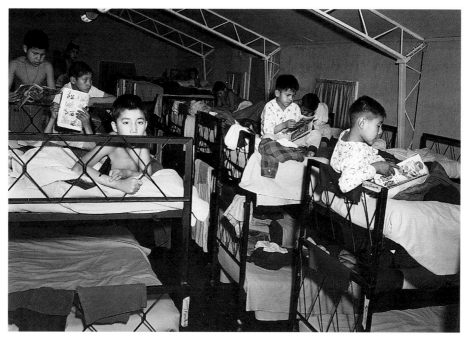

Little boy's dorm at St. Labre. – 1960s

Brother Berthold, the "Candy Man" – 1957

Dr. John Wooden Legs,
Cheyenne Visionary

Housing conditions on the reservation. – 1960s

Dried meat hung on ceiling poles in nearly every home.
This family had a good supply.

Reservation living conditions. – early 1960s.
Walls made of cardboard kept the wind out.

Mrs. Albert Foote with
Father Emmett. – 1960

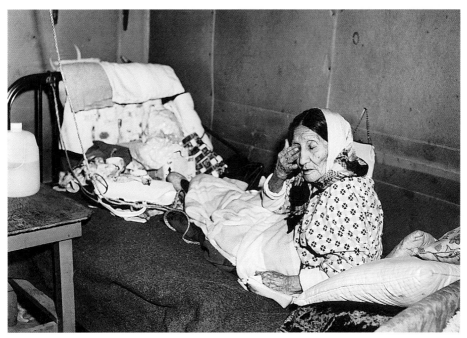

Mae Medicine Bird – 1965

Father Emmett and Connie Sump with a student at St. Labre. – 1970

Northern Cheyenne employees of Guild Arts & Crafts. – 1970s

*One too many at a friary
celebration. – 1976*

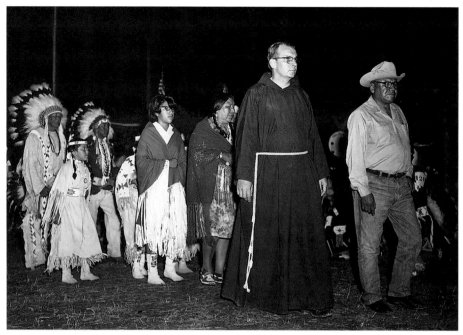

Father Emmett and Harry Little Bird lead an honor dance. – 1960s

Cooky visits with Regina Hoffmann. – 1971

*Nurse Viola Campeau with her dog
Charmin. – 1980*

Joseph and Carol Ann Kunkel on their wedding day. – August 29, 1980

St. Labre Indian School with new buildings. – 1971

St. Labre Mission Church

Father Emmett greets Pope John Paul II
on an American tour in the 1980s.

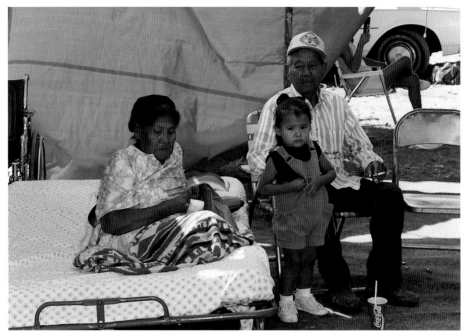

Eddie and Regina Foote with their granddaughter. – 1980s

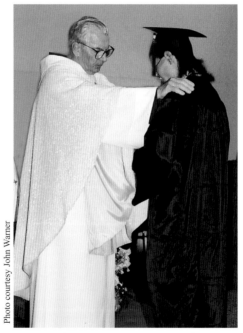

*Father Emmett prays with a
St. Labre graduate. – 1990s*

St. Labre Indian School – 1992

St. Labre Indian School – 1954

One winter night Father Emmett's old friend, Harold Fisher, froze to death when he went outside to start his car.

A little Cheyenne grass dancer. – 1990s

Clarence "Bisco" Spotted Wolf, Chief of the Northern Cheyenne Council of 44. – 2001

Austin Two Moons and Father Emmett at the St. Labre
Soaring Eagle Gym Dedication. – 1992

Montana Chapter, National Society of Fund Raising Executives Award 1993
Standing left to right: Conrad Sump, Father Emmett,
Dewanda Little Coyote, Adele Doughty, Ruth Sump and Mary Jo Fox

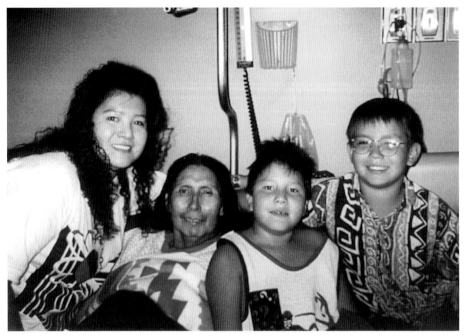

*Chief Jimmie D. Little Coyote with daughter Dewanda and grandsons
Shawn and Cordell James. – 1995*

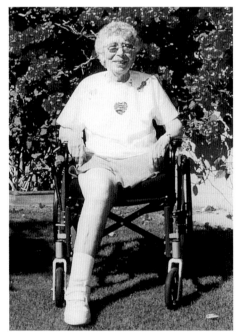

*Viola Campeau during her
recovery. – 2001*

Father Emmett joins Northern Cheyenne chiefs at the Heritage Living Center ground breaking ceremony in June 2001.

Heritage Living Center Dedication Day – August 30, 2002
Left to right: Conrad Sump Sr., Paul Morigi and Fr. Emmett

Heritage Living Center, Lobby – 2002

Heritage Living Center – 2002

When Father first came to the reservation, the Cheyenne people still lived in wall tents and shacks made with tar paper and cardboard, most with dirt floors. Other homes were made of boards with a tent canvas laid over to keep out the wind. Many log cabins had a single, small window that didn't open and when it rained, the dirt floor dampened where the roof leaked. During the summer, no matter how hard a woman tried to keep out the flies, it was impossible, because without ventilation, the door had to be kept open during the day, so women cooked outside in warm weather. Mothers threw water on the earthern floors when it was hot outside to keep the inside of the cabins cool.

Inside each cabin sat a wood stove, sometimes made from a galvanized washtub with a hole cut in it for the stovepipe. If that didn't work, an old, automobile gas tank set up on bricks with a hole for the pipe would do. One way or another, the result was a hot, stuffy atmosphere inside the cabins during the winter months. Anyone who got sick quickly infected the rest of the family, sometimes twelve people lived in one or two rooms.

Father had studied the poverty in Nicaragua, but what he found on the reservation did not exist in history books. Nothing he had ever experienced prepared him for ministering to a people living without the basic necessities of life, without clean water, proper shelter, food and in many ways, people living without hope for the future.

Father Marion took him to meet the Indians living along the Tongue River and in order to get close to the cabins, the young priest had to work his way around mean-looking dogs. They crouched low with ears back and growled as he hurried past. Sometimes the hurry changed into a lively sprint, with his long robe hiked up, and sharp fangs too close for comfort. At night the camp dogs ran in packs, stealing scraps of food. When someone died or friction upset the camp, the dogs felt the tension, grew restless, howled and fought among themselves. That was the non-Indian view. For centuries the Cheyenne people had depended on their dogs to pack belongings and warn them of danger. In times of famine, dogs became food and saved many lives. The Cheyennes loved their dogs.

Ranchers left their unwanted puppy litters outside Indian camps and the puppies wandered into the villages to be taken in and fed. On many occasions, ranchers later shot the dogs they had previously dumped on the Cheyennes. One rancher went into a rage when he heard dogs barking in a camp across the river on reservation land. He waited until the family had gone to church and then poisoned all their dogs and burnt down their house.

The nice frame house, only one month old, with new windows, curtains and furniture, had been built with money saved for years. The family lost everything they owned except the clothes on their backs and their team and wagon. That night they investigated and found the dogs had been poisoned with small sausages. The rancher's garbage contained 8 or 10 empty sausage cans.

The Cheyenne family quietly went back to living in their one-room log cabin. They didn't retaliate or call the sheriff because they were afraid that the next time, the rancher might poison one of their horses or even a child who might nibble on poisoned sausage. This was typical of the abuse they had endured since the 1880s when the tribe had first relocated on their own land.[37]

Father Marion explained to Fr. Emmett that despite their poverty, most Cheyenne parents dearly loved their children and took care of their elderly parents better than in non-Indian society. The village people possessed a goodness, a purity of soul not found among other races and they were exceptionally generous. Always polite, they helped one another and shared one another's sufferings. The more Father Emmett learned about Cheyenne history, the more he realized that their suffering was multigenerational. They had been starved, their religion banned and their cultural traditions forbidden.[38] It surprised him further that the Cheyennes had survived with an incredible sense of humor, perhaps their way of coping with the sickness and disappointments of every day life. Despite abject poverty, Father found Cheyenne humor hilarious. Their easy laughter and teasing had instantly broken the stereotype of the stoic Indian. He also noticed that when someone was injured or in pain, relatives tried to make the sick person laugh because they believed laughter healed.

In spite of himself, Father Emmett was beginning to like St Labre Mission, but when he remembered the so-called "vow of poverty" he had experienced in the palatial seminaries where he had studied for the priesthood, Father was ashamed that he had taken it all for granted. When he saw human beings living in real poverty, his youth passed from him and a new man emerged – a priest filled with compassion for the Cheyenne people of the Northern Plains. As time went on, he even learned to hunt (poach) and slept better than he ever had. The priests hunted for deer because they didn't have enough meat to serve the children.

One afternoon, a Cheyenne rushed into his office and begged Father Emmett to come to the Ashland camp. There was trouble. They jumped in the car and drove down to the Tongue River camp, less than a mile away. The man led Father to a decrepit outhouse, surrounded by barking dogs. Children sat naked in the mud and women yelled at the men with their fists in the air. Deer bones and brittle pieces of hide littered the ground around the tents and cabins.

When Father reached the outhouse, the stench from the two-seater was unbearable. He heard moans, hesitated, then opened the door. A woman, once pretty, her bloody dress shredded, slumped face down in the putrid hole. No telling how long she had been hiding in the out house. Worms crawled around in the feces and urine that covered her legs. Flies covered the inside of her nose and mouth.

Father Emmett stiffened and backed out. "Jesus in Heaven!" he said out loud. A wave of nausea passed over him and he desperately tried not to vomit. He turned the woman over and picked her up in his arms. Her face and body were covered with deep slashes and her eyes were swollen shut. She needed stitches; her throat, and face had been cut, her hair was matted in blood and all of her upper teeth had been knocked out.

A relative ran over to explain that the drunken husband had beaten his wife in a rage and here, giving excuses, staggered the husband, scum oozing from the corners of his mouth. "She ain't hurt," he protested. "Woman no damn good!" Still holding the woman in his arms, Father walked straight toward the man, who stood with a raised fist to hit her again.

"You have sinned against God and against this woman!" Father growled. "In the Bible, Jesus tells us that . . ." Father stopped suddenly and looked into the glazed eyes of the repulsive husband. "I realized," he told Father Marion later, "that nothing I could have said would have gotten through to him. You can't reason with a drunk."

Father pushed the man away and carried the woman to her tent and put her down on a dirty blanket, covered with rags and cardboard. He washed her face and neck in river water, prayed and waited until someone from the Mission came to drive her to the nearest hospital. His blood boiled as he drove back to the Mission to tell Father Marion what had happened. The older priest listened and then placed his hands on Father's shoulders. "Emmett, you must brace yourself. God will call on you to do things you don't even know you can do."

Father climbed up the hill above the Mission and asked God why He had sent him to Montana. Father knew that not all Cheyenne families lived in poverty and despair, but hopelessness permeated many of the villages. He was beginning to understand why priests did not last long at St. Labre, why many left physically and mentally broken men, and why some who stayed became jaded toward the very people they had come to serve. Praying for strength, Father realized that although God had not called him by name, He must have shown him this ghastly incident to strengthen his resolve to stay. Fr. Emmett wondered what else was in store for him.

Not long afterward, a middle-aged Cheyenne woman came to his office and begged Father to talk to her son. The young man had tuberculosis and wouldn't leave his home to enter a sanitarium. He was afraid that he would die there alone. Would Father talk him into going?

Father had no qualms whatever about helping the woman. He drove to the log cabin and got out of the car and walked up to the back porch. After knocking a couple of times, he stepped back when a pale, wheezing ghost of a man appeared at the door. His clothes hung from his emaciated body and he held his chest when he coughed. Father was standing about three feet from him when he opened the door.

"Emanuel," Father said. "Your mother is waiting for you in the car."

"I ain't goin'!" he shouted. "Leave me the hell alone!"

"Emanuel, it's time to go," Father insisted. "You'll get better in the hospi . . ."

In a split second, Father caught sight of the knife as it swept downward, ripping open his robe from chest to belt. Father jumped off the porch and ran for help while the young man stood holding the knife up in both hands as though contemplating suicide. As soon as Father realized that his bloody wound wasn't deep, he brought back several men who subdued Emanuel. They took him to a sanitarium, where he stayed for a year. As for Father Emmett, he physically survived the attack, but emotionally he couldn't forget it. He kept having recurring dreams of the knife blade plunging into his stomach. He looked down at his guts hanging out and woke up drenched in sweat.

After Emanuel came home, he went back to Mass at St. Labre as if nothing had happened. During Communion, Father placed the Eucharist bread on Emanuel's tongue and the young man became one with God. There was no need for either one of them to say a word about the incident. Father Emmett knew that malnutrition, poverty and disease had robbed Emanuel of his youth, his health and his reasoning. The assault had humbled Father. He realized he had to handle stressful situations with more compassion and caution.

Tribal members often asked Father to come to their homes and he especially enjoyed visiting the Charles Sitting Man Sr. family along the Tongue River. His son, Charlie Jr., usually acted as interpreter. On one such visit, Father asked the son about the drinking problems he had seen. Charlie told him that up until 1954, it had been illegal for Indians to drink alcohol on or off the reservation. That summer, the tribe learned that the government had given Indians more rights, among them the right to drink liquor off reservation (Eisenhower Administration Bill – H.C.R. 108 on June 9, 1953) This law opened the way for unscrupulous white men to open liquor stores just outside reservation boundaries. (The Jim Town Bar is located about five hundred yards from the northern boundary.) Since Indians could now drink legally off reservation, they went to the bar, bought a bottle of whiskey or wine and drank the whole bottle. They walked or crawled back to the reservation, not having broken any law.[39]

Others hid bottles in their coats and made their way home to make life miserable for their families. During the winter, many didn't make it back and were found dead in the ditches. Several white men had come and gone but all the Jim Town owners had made their fortunes on the misfortunes of the Cheyenne people.

Charlie told Father that Cheyenne women had started drinking as well and the result was child neglect. "It's a good thing you came now," Charlie told him. "Drinking cuts our villages in half like a log." [40]

Father Emmett asked to see his dad, Chief Sitting Man, and they went into the cabin. The elderly man stayed in bed most of the time, but he sat up on the edge when Father Emmett came in to give him Holy Communion. The house was quiet, save for the gurgling of boiling water in the coffee pot on the wood stove. Deer hides covered the pine floor. Father was given a seat at the table. Sitting Man lived well compared to many others on the reservation. Mrs. Sitting Man, dressed in a faded calico dress with a wide leather belt and moccasins, busied herself over the stove. Frequently, she glanced over at her husband's chest to watch his breathing.

Fr. Emmett pulled up a chair beside Sitting Man's bed and with his son interpreting (with his back turned), Father asked if the old man had any sins that he wanted to confess. If he did, he squeezed Father's fingers. The chief couldn't tell his sins in English and he couldn't tell them in Cheyenne either, because his wife and son were present, but the squeeze was good enough. Father considered that a squeeze was Sitting Man's confession. Then Father blessed him with the Prayer of Absolution. The chief solemnly bowed his head while Father and Charlie Jr. said the Lord's Prayer. Then the aged man lifted his head and touched his heart with his hand. Tears ran down into the deepest wrinkles and scars on his face. He rolled back down on the bed, his body relaxed and his breathing became less labored. The old warrior, still holding Father's hand, looked over at the priest, then he glanced up at the wall above his bed, at one of his most prized possessions – an American flag. On this last visit, a day before Charlie Sitting Man Sr. passed away, Father Emmett held his gnarled hand until the old chief fell into a lasting sleep.

CHAPTER 7

Underworld Connections?

T he Capuchins had been struggling for years to keep St. Labre Mission from closing. There simply wasn't enough money coming in to pay for building upkeep, heat, food, school supplies and teacher's wages, let alone the childrens' daily needs.

In the early days there was no money to pay a priest's meager salary out of church funds, let alone $80 for four Sisters; $45 for a cook; $60 for a teacher and prefect for boys; $45 for a fireman and janitor; and $50 for the farm foreman.[41] By 1955 Mission expenses had gone up, while more and more Cheyenne parents brought their children to school at St. Labre. Somehow, the Capuchins kept things afloat. Over the years, priests brought in lay volunteers to help. Fr. Emmett soon learned that many of the school improvements had been accomplished by a short, unassuming volunteer named Fintan Schaub. Fintan had barely survived a serious auto accident in Wisconsin and had promised God that if he were allowed to recover from paralysis, he would give his life to serve the poor. After his recovery, he dedicated his life to the Mission. At his request, the plain, little man, usually seen in bib overalls and an old hat, was never paid for his services and he played a prominent role at the Mission for over sixty years. From a dusty, dry place with few trees and no grass, Fintan created an oasis of beautiful lawns with orchards of fruit and shade trees and huge, bountiful gardens.

Fr. Emmett appreciated Fintan's good works, created for the children, most of whom had never seen a lush green lawn. Unfortunately, the lawn was the source of an incident that made Father Emmett furious with one of the Sisters. He had a touchy spot when it came to nuns, but

64

after he became a priest, he had learned to bite his lip on many occasions. One day, he overheard one of the Sisters screeching at the Cheyenne youngsters because they had walked across the grass. Descending upon her like a smoking freight train, Father told her in no uncertain terms that the lawns were planted FOR the children to walk on, lie down on and to enjoy. He said that if he ever caught her yelling at the children again, he would make a formal complaint to her superior. As it turned out, that is exactly what happened and she was transferred. Father Emmett refused to tolerate abuse, especially from a nun.[42] Yet his closest sibling, Sister Phyllis Hoffmann, remained his dearest friend and confident, mostly by correspondence.

Father hadn't been at St. Labre in the 1930s when the beloved Ursuline Sisters of Toledo left and were replaced by the School Sisters of Saint Francis. At that time, the Sisters were afraid of Indians and were worried about contracting the dreaded disease tuberculosis, which for over 50 years had plagued the Cheyennes. When Indians shook hands with the Sisters after Mass, the nuns ran to their convent to wash. Their fear of disease was not unfounded.[43]

The School Sisters had a difficult time getting used to Cheyenne ways and many hard feelings developed. The nuns had been shocked when they found children hiding rotten horse meat to eat in the evenings. The poor children had little to eat at home and they kept every scrap of food they found as a result of years of semi-starvation. One night, Sister Giswalda found a morsel of rotten meat tied up in a piece of flour sack in the girls' sleeping room. Sister scolded the young "culprit" and threw the food away. To her astonishment, the child waited until all were asleep, and then stole the food back and ate it.

Sister Giswalda finally left the Mission. Yet she somehow turned her life around after she went to live at St. Paul's Mission in Hays, Montana, among the Gros Ventre people. She was adopted into the tribe in 1951, and was said to have been "loved and entrusted with all that is traditionally sacred and treasured by the people who adopted her."[44]

It must be said that despite a few misfits, most of whom Fr. Emmett weeded out, much good came from the presence of the School Sisters of St. Francis. Poor children were fed, clothed and educated. Students with tuberculosis were screened, taken to hospitals, cured and returned to school, where their conditions were carefully monitored. When a parishioner died, or when a poor mother with children got sick, Sisters went to the home to prepare hot, nourishing meals. They washed clothes, cleaned cabins and comforted families, and when a parishioner died, they were sometimes called upon to prepare the body for burial. The elderly depended on the priests and Sisters in times of need.[45]

Over the years Cheyenne people told Fr. Emmett about many respected priests and Sisters who were fondly remembered: Capuchin Fathers Francis Busalt, Ludger Janowski, Benno Aichinger, T.O. Rocque, Marion Roessler, Joachim Strupp, Paul Reichling, Paschal Siler; and Sisters Etheline, Mildred, Cicily, Claver, Friedaburga, and Carla. These were men and women who had definite characteristics admired by the Cheyennes. They were polite, respectful, kind and most important of all, they knew how to laugh and have a good time. Sour, disapproving faces belonged to sour, disapproving people and the Cheyennes didn't want scowling religious around them. They had enough sadness and misery to deal with. Some remembered the early priests of their childhood and told others, "We were afraid of them."[46]

In comparison, Father Emmett's office was open to everyone all day. "I didn't have to make an appointment with him if I wanted to see him," Cheyenne elder Eddie Foote told a friend. "I just went in, sat down and told him what was on my mind." Father didn't plan a "typical day" because he never knew what was going to happen. He offered daily Mass for the children and they came to him for confession. They also came to him if they were mad at a teacher or wanted to run away from school, or they were too frightened to go home because a father or mother had been fighting. He listened to all the children's complaints and counseled and soothed hurt spirits. When parents came to him with worries about their children, he spent a great deal of time discussing ways to improve school and home situations.

Father was often called upon to visit the sick in hospitals in Miles City and Billings. Elderly Cheyenne wanted him to bring Communion to them in their homes when they were too ill to go to Mass. In addition, Father visited men and women in jail and counseled couples having marital troubles. He found that many intertribal (when the man and wife were from different tribes) marriages were troubled because of language barriers and because the wife missed family back on her reservation. The husband was afraid if he let her go home to visit, she would not return.

Interracial marriages had other problems. In these unions the husband

and wife loved each other but their white in-laws had either disowned them or made their lives miserable. When white grandparents, sisters or brothers constantly interfered, divorce often resulted. In these cases Father counseled the families to try and work out their problems, because he felt that in any divorce, children are the ones who suffer most.

Local sheriffs called Father when a suicide occurred or a crime involving an Indian. Non-Indian sheriffs and deputies were afraid to enter Indian homes and they had to get Father to go in for them. These were often sad situations and Father spent hours soothing grieving parents, bullheaded police officers or frightened children. He was called at all hours of the day and night, especially if a child needed to be rushed to the hospital. A domestic violence incident in the middle of the night sometimes only ended when Father came to pray with the couple.

Every evening, children in the dorms, kneeling beside their old iron beds, pushed together end on end, asked for Father Emmett to come and say nightly prayers with them. Some couldn't sleep unless Father blessed them with holy water, as his own father had done in his youth. In winter snowstorms, freezing rain or spring gumbo mud, Father could be seen trudging from dorm to dorm with his bottle of holy water.

Father Emmett especially enjoyed teaching Latin and Religion. When he first came to St. Labre, he was astounded when he asked his students a question. Not one child raised a hand to answer, and all eyes looked down. It didn't take him long to figure out that Indian children look down out of respect. They did not want to look like know-it-alls in class. Their culture had taught them to respect the feelings of others, especially elders, before their own. Having figured that out, Father found a way to get around it. He would ask a question and when nobody raised a hand to answer, he called upon a child saying, "Leland, I know you don't know the answer to my question, but tell me what you think anyway." The boy would then answer the question because Father had acknowledged in front of the others that the child wasn't a show-off or a person who wanted the other students to think he was smarter than the rest. Over the years, and in many Indian schools throughout the nation, non-Indian school teachers never learned this important lesson. They left reservation schools thinking Indians were slow and could not learn. This same lesson applied to college classes, job interviews, the military and in court rooms across the land.

The Cheyennes and their children never knew how difficult it was to keep St. Labre from closing. Father Marion had tried his best to raise money. Finally, he wrote to beg money from his old seminary classmates including Leo Dohn Sr., a brilliant, wealthy businessman in New York City. Dohn wrote back joking: "Your letter stinks!" Although not a professional fund raiser, Dohn had built up a mailing list of more than a million Catholic clients. His main and most profitable manufacturing business, Guild Arts and Crafts, molded plastic on nylon threads to create attractive rosary beads, a nice line of costume jewelry, interior decorations and statuettes of Jesus that Catholics placed on car dashboards and in their homes and offices. Mr. Dohn was himself a generous philanthropist and he sympathized with Father Marion's need for money to provide for the children of St. Labre.

Dohn offered Fr. Marion his client list and told him that he wouldn't charge him for it. If Father Marion could write a decent appeal letter telling about Cheyenne poverty, perhaps Dohn's clients would donate to St. Labre. Although Fr. Marion's heart was in the right place, he just couldn't write a good appeal letter. At the same time, he was ill with chronic asthma, had lost weight and could barely breathe, let alone take care of his regular business duties.

Leo Dohn Sr. had once studied to become a priest, but he had contracted tuberculosis in one of his legs and he was forced to leave the seminary. Dohn was a tough character. He acted something like the gruff actor, Edward G. Robinson, a man who walked around with a big Cuban cigar hanging out of his mouth, surrounded by curtains of smoke. But Dohn's deep Catholic faith belied his tough exterior.

Curiously, Dohn's right-hand assistant and closest friend, Italian-American Louie Congro, was a controversial individual with rumored Mafia connections. Some of Mr. Dohn's employees felt uncomfortable that Louie was always armed with a revolver, but his unquestioned loyalty to his boss prompted them to add: "Louie would take a bullet for the old man."

Years later, when Leo Dohn Jr. took over his father's lucrative business, he reflected: "I envied my father. He was out-going, a charismatic personality and he was sure of himself. He was also egotistical and an arch-conservative Catholic. He had a penthouse in Manhattan at Central Park West . . . and he lived an affluent lifestyle." But Leo's son didn't like or trust his father's confidant and bookkeeper, Louie Congro:

"Louie was an ex-bookie. He was a strong arm and did things on the shady side when it came to the IRS. He had friends inside the New York Police Department and he liked to give his buddies illegal police badges. When I took over my father's business, my father made one stipulation – I couldn't fire Louie Congro!"[47] The former bookie had his job for life, but the younger Dohn kept a wary eye on him because of his alleged underworld connections.

When poor health finally got the best of Father Marion, he resigned as Pastor and Superintendent of St. Labre. Father Emmett took over his position in 1955, just one year after he had arrived. The young priest knew nothing of bookkeeping or budgeting money, so he studied Father Marion's files and taught himself to balance the books.

After his first Christmas Mass at St. Labre, Father Emmett had gone to Muddy Creek to distribute Christmas presents to poor Cheyenne families. He wrote a letter to Leo Dohn describing the terribly impoverished conditions that he had seen. He told him about his vow to educate Cheyenne children and to provide for them in the best possible way. When Dohn received the letter, he was moved by Father's vow. He realized that Father Emmett was the one who should write appeal letters to donors. From then on, Fr. Emmett sent appeals to Mr. Dohn, who then had the appeal letters printed and sent to his Catholic clients. This was the beginning of one of the most successful direct mail campaigns in America.[48] Within a year, enough money came in to pay off all the Mission debts. The funds came in from all over the country, a dollar here or a dime there, and every penny was put to good use.

Father Emmett's fund raising success came from his ability to write his personal thoughts and raw feelings to donors in simple, everyday language. He also included interesting news about the Indian community. In the 1950s there were few direct mail appeals and little competition in Montana. When Father wrote true stories and included photographs he had taken showing reservation living conditions, people knew he was telling the truth and they were moved to donate. He wrote about Indian children being found in the snow, their illnesses and early deaths. He had to turn children away from the school because there weren't enough beds for them. Children were already sleeping in hallways. A letter to donors in 1957 read:

> Father Carl . . . brought little Jennie and Ann back to the
> mission because he could not bear to leave these two little ones

in their home, where they had been alone for days. Their father was away at work and their mother went in search of food. Partially starved, exhausted and ill, both girls managed to smile through the sadness and insecurity which filled their eyes. Soon they were cleaned up, fed and happily playing with the other children. And then it was discovered that Jennie's ear was draining badly. It was Saturday night and a 75 mile journey on slippery roads to the reservation hospital would probably prove futile, possibly fatal. The better solution was a phone call to Holy Rosary Hospital in Miles City and a rush trip. Immediate surgery was necessary, for the entire mastoid region had been destroyed by infection, which was approaching the brain. The surgeon allowed the child no longer than six months to live if this infection had not been checked at once . . . Jennie is alive today because of the care your generosity made possible.[49]

Funds raised for St. Labre went toward educating, sheltering and feeding Indian children, paying for food, heat, electricity, office furniture, beds, desks and chairs. The money paid for bus transportation, school supplies, school maintenance and plumbing repairs, boilers, roof repair, new buildings, teacher's wages and insurance.

Educating children and helping to organize industry to provide jobs were Father's answers to the poverty question. A man with a job was a man with self-esteem. Students with trade school or college educations were students with dreams for a better life.

Generous donors continued to respond to Father's appeal letters with suggestions and money. In 1956, 240 Cheyenne children attended classes at St. Labre. Donations provided: 2,800 two-pound loaves of home-baked bread, 3,200 pounds of beef, 3,500 pounds of pork, 30,000 quarts of milk, 2,200 pounds of butter, 6,000 large cans of vegetables and 32,000 pounds of potatoes, in addition to produce grown in the school gardens. Donors gave on average per year: 30 deer, 24 antelope, 6 elk and 3 buffalo, besides money for clothing, medical supplies, transportation and vehicles.[50]

After Fr. Emmett took over as director and pastor at the Mission, he worked 20 hours a day to keep the school running smoothly. But he still had a great deal to learn about life. One incident that opened his eyes was his first marriage ceremony, the wedding of Red Robe and Little Bird. The nuptials were scheduled on a Saturday in late December at precisely 10 a.m. On the wedding day, the temperature dropped and snow began to fall. At 10 a.m. the couple had not arrived. Despite the numbing wind, Father bundled up and drove the Mission Chevy down to the groom's log cabin and knocked on the door. He heard a man's voice inside say, "Come in!" so he opened the door and walked in. Not four feet away, the bride and groom were snuggled in bed together! The look on Father's face made Little Bird blurt out, "Father, we have to keep warm!"[51]

Father Emmett froze like a statue of Saint Francis. Innocent to the ways of the world, it must have been difficult to react as though nothing was out of the ordinary. He sat down on a chair next to the bed and discussed the weather. Miss Red Robe disappeared under the quilts, while Father rescheduled the wedding for the next week and then got up to leave. Driving back to the Mission, he had to chuckle at himself. He realized that the couple had probably been living together for years. It was a real eye opener. The following Saturday morning, Father Emmett married the couple at 10 o'clock sharp.

One aspect of Father's life – his obsession with time and punctuality – would never change. It didn't seem to bother the Cheyennes because they had grown to love him. As the years passed, he mellowed when it came to the Cheyenne people, but heaven help a white man or woman who was late for an appointment!

"You know how you feel safe around
your parents? That's how I felt about
Fr. Emmett. I trusted my soul with him."
Rubie Sooktis

CHAPTER
8

Irish Eyes

"That's a good lookin' guy!" Thelma Two Two whispered to her friends as Fr. Emmett walked past the women sitting on the grass near the friary. "Too bad he's a priest," she sighed. "That good lookin' is going to waste! Ayyy!"[52] When he heard the women giggle, Fr. Emmett stopped and turned for a moment, his neck, ears and face turned bright red and he hurried to the barn.

There never seemed enough time to finish all that Father set out to do. When he thought he might not get to a meeting exactly on time, one could recognize his trail by the nicks in the furniture. Despite his obsession with time, he usually saw only the bright side of life. His happy-go-lucky personality attracted children and they loved to see his awkwardness in the classroom, like getting his cincture (long rope belt) caught in his desk drawer. When he tried to stand up, the desk jerked him forward. Instead of quietly opening the drawer to extricate himself, he yanked on the belt, elevating the desk. When he saw that the kids got such a kick out of it, he kept on jerking the desk around the room. The children howled when he caught his long rosary on a door knob. The first time it happened, he tried to make them think he had done it on purpose, but they knew he was an awkward, fast-moving giant.

Father whipped around the mission, painting, fixing and tearing down with tremendous energy. He taught school, drove the bus, offered Mass, counseled, buried and baptized. He thoroughly enjoyed hard work and he expected everyone else to enjoy it with him. His sidekick, Frank Bollack, a layman he called "the genius electrician," had crippled, arthritic hands, but he was a patient teacher. He taught Father everything he knew about electrical wiring. One day, Father had to drive to Billings to pick up some wire, window glass and a few other things. Father and Frank jumped into the Chevy at 7:30 a.m. and drove off on the gravel road toward Billings. It was a good thing Frank had iron nerves because Father drove too fast, as usual. With a gleam in his eye and a wicked grin, Father turned his head and talked to Frank with one hand on the wheel and the other hand gesturing. "Ya know Frank," Father told him, "This car goes over 100 mph." Luckily, Frank knew better than to say anything and kept quiet.

After leaving the hardware store, they drove to Miles City to pick up Frank's daughters, Bonnie and Bobbi, who were arriving on the train. The teenagers climbed into the back seat with some of the supplies. It was getting late and Father wanted to make it home exactly on time for dinner. He and Frank were talking when Father made the remark, "Teenagers are sure wild drivers." At that moment they came up over a hill going about 70 mph. As they hit loose gravel, the Chevy began a rapid sideways slide and Father over-steered in the opposite direction. The girls screamed as the vehicle hit a rock and turned a high somersault head first into the air, landing upside down along the side of the road.

Father Emmett was afraid the engine might catch on fire, so he kicked the glass out of the window on his side and crawled out. Then he pulled Frank and the girls out through the same window, framed with sharp, jagged pieces of glass. In the roll-over, glass had shattered everywhere and the heavy iron bars had flown around like toothpicks in a high wind. Miraculously, besides bruises, nobody was seriously hurt. Frank then went around to the passenger side of the car and easily opened the upside down door. There hadn't been any need for Father to kick out the window. The young Capuchin had been at St. Labre for less than a year and he'd already burnt up all the winter fuel and wrecked the Mission car.

The warm-gold autumn months of 1955 passed and Fr. Emmett watched the leaves turn brown and die. From his office in the barn loft, he saw icicles form on the eaves and harden into tapered prisms, dangerous to those who walked under them. In December, arctic snows left the roads impassable, further isolating St. Labre from the outside world. The Mission car had been repaired and Father Emmett didn't mind the road conditions. In fact, he found driving on icy mountain curves thrilling.

One afternoon an emergency message came from the Ashland camp to pick up a pregnant woman already in labor. The woman lumbered into the back seat and they were off. The sun was going down over the hills and Father Emmett knew that it would be dark before long. They had to get to the clinic at Lame Deer, 21 miles away. He sailed over the icy, dirt road like a sloop in a high wind. Speeding around hairpin curves on ice didn't exactly help the woman take her mind off the radiating pain. Without warning, she screamed and Father hit his head on the roof of the car. A sharp look in the rear view mirror told him more than he ever wanted to know about childbirth. The woman was already in the delivery position. Later, telling the story to Frank, Father said that he gasped and started praying. "I can't do this Lord," he prayed, "Please don't make me . . ."

He braked hard and the Chevy spun to a stop on the edge of a curve. He got out and yanked open the back door. There he beheld what women since the dawn of time have gone through to give birth. The mother was in her last throws of labor. Blood smeared the back seat of the car that had just been repaired after the roll-over. The woman screamed, pushed and lost control of her bowels. Father staggered back. "Pull him out Father, pull him out!" the mother begged. Father didn't know if he could take it. "I was ready to puke!" he told Frank. The baby's head appeared and Father carefully slid him out, held the blue child up by his feet and gave him a whack on the bottom. The infant made no sound.

"Hit him again!" the woman commanded, and Father did as he was told.

After a little sputter and a weak gasp, the baby boy cried out. Slimy and cold, the infant shrieked and shuddered in the chill evening air. Fr. Emmett wiped him off with a serving napkin he found in the trunk of the car. The mother took care of the rest and they continued their journey to Lame Deer with Father Emmett hunched over the wheel with the window wide open. He knew he had witnessed the wonder of birth but it had also been a rebirth for him. He silently recommitted himself to his vow of celibacy.

Father later learned that this had been a relatively easy birth for an Indian mother, compared to the old days. A Cheyenne elder told about a woman who gave birth when the tribe was in hiding from "enemies:"

They took willow poles and put them over one another to
make a shelter. Then they put blankets over them, so they'd
have a place to sleep. In the middle of the night everyone got
spooked because one of the women was going to have a baby
. . . When the mother was near delivery, one of the old ladies
brought two dogs right into the doorway. She took a willow
stick and beat them until they howled. That's the way they had
to do it with enemies around in those days. When the baby was
born, the howling dogs covered up the sound of the baby's cry.
Then, the old lady let the dogs out . . .[53]

Many years later, when Father Emmett came to St. Labre, it was no
longer necessary for Cheyenne women to have babies in total silence,
afraid that an enemy might hear their crying babies and attack their
camp. Other invisible killers that were just as dangerous had crept up to
maim and kill their children, including malnutrition, polio, tuberculosis,
measles, typhoid, hepatitis, cholera, diptheria and influenza. Every
priest and Sister at St. Labre feared the sicknesses that white men
before them had introduced to the Northern Cheyennes.

The Cheyenne people were Father's best teachers. They put no time
frame on religion. They didn't say, "Well, this is the day and the hour I
will worship God." The more Father got to know the Cheyennes, the
more he realized they worshipped all the time, day and night. They
prayed for their neighbors and relatives, for a dead hawk on the road,
for a child every time he went out the door, for an unborn infant, for
victims of war, soldiers and prisoners. They thanked "Maheo," Creator
God, for giving them life. Over the years many priests and Sisters never
understood this precious and intensely personal sense of spirituality. To
them, a person had to pray at certain times and in certain places –
mainly in Church.

Father wasn't at all worried about Cheyenne spirituality. His appeal
letters continued to bring in funds and as soon as the old bills were
paid, Father began saving for his first major building plan, a new school
cafeteria and a convent for the Sisters. It would take five years to
complete and would cost over $250,000. Father wrote the donors
saying, "That sum staggers me." He never borrowed money and paid
bills with cash.[54]

There wasn't a building on the school grounds that would have passed a
health inspection but whenever Father talked of building, he heard

negative comments from other priests. "It can't be done," they'd say. Those words were sweet to his ears because there was nothing Father liked better than a challenge. He wanted the absolute best school for the Indian children, the best food the school could afford, and the best school supplies. Some of the priests thought that Indians could get along with second best, but Father didn't agree. There were times when Father Emmett didn't have enough money to pay a bill and he had to "kite" a check. He'd conveniently forget to sign a check. By the time the check came back, he had the money to pay the debt.

Father was admired, even idolized by the Cheyennes and by donors for his complete devotion to his calling. But his hard-driving ways to achieve his goals caused a few fellow Capuchins to criticize his tendency to push aside peers who said he was wasting his time trying to help Indians. His critics tried to make him seem autocratic, but he was a shy person with a simple faith, sincere motives and a fierce dedication to his work. This was obvious to all who knew him well, yet he sometimes lacked sensitivity when it came to priests and Sisters who weren't as motivated. He expected everyone to work as hard as he did. Despite his sometimes rude or indifferent manner with fellow Capuchins, he demonstrated the devotion of an inspiring priest and the faith of a great humanitarian.

 The Mission school was extremely isolated and it was rare when a Bishop or a Provincial came to visit. Over the years, every Bishop trusted Father Emmett completely after seeing his good works, excellent bookkeeping skills and how much the Cheyenne children loved him. When Father needed something done, he first wrote to his Provincial Superior for permission. Aware of Father Emmett's success in fund raising, the Provincial told him, "If it's okay with the Bishop, it's okay with me." Father Emmett then wrote to the Bishop who told him, "If it's okay with the Provincial, go ahead." Fr. Emmett interpreted this as "go ahead and do your thing." So he did. In this way, Father got things done and done right, with no interference.

While the Cheyennes were living in wretched poverty, the majority of Americans had discovered television. Grace Kelly was preparing to marry Prince Rainier of Monaco and the United States announced it would launch satellites costing millions of dollars. This at a time when out of 2,500 Northern Cheyenne, there were no college graduates, and the yearly family income was under $1,500. Ninety percent of Cheyenne families lived in one or two room shacks, with little or no lighting. Many log cabins had dirt floors and water came from the river or from contaminated wells. In later years, Tribal Chairman and visionary, John Woodenlegs, described the living conditions on his reservation in the 1950s: "We had nothing. We were right at the bottom . . . We had disease and sickness and my people were in the poorest health of anyone in Montana."[55] Father Emmett began a writing campaign to Senators and Congressmen to alert them to the poor living conditions on the reservation.

One summer in the late 1950s, a severe drought had turned the hills and valleys along the Tongue River into a desolate, cracked-earth landscape. Fr. Emmett watched the clouds of dust in his rear view mirror, slowly drifting across the road to settle on barren fields. As he drove up to a small log hut, he found elders Clara and Willis Red Eagle sitting outside on cottonwood blocks in front of an open fire. They were busy cutting strips of meat to dry. Near the fire lay a rotting beef carcass covered with dirt and flies. The couple told Father they were going to have beef to eat that night. Asking them how they had gotten the beef, Willis explained that a rancher had sent word to them that one of his cows had died a few days before and if they wanted it, they could come and drag it off. Father was just about to tell them how dangerous it was to eat rotten meat when Willis told him: "Maheo (God) blessed us with this food today." The old man's wrinkled smile and eyes, covered with cataracts, reflected sincere gratitude and joy.

Father studied the disheartening scene with dismay. Here was an elderly couple rejoicing to have been blessed with the carcass of a long dead cow that had rotted in the sun. They were using water they had carried a quarter mile from the river to wash off insect larvae from the putrid carcass. Because they had thanked Maheo for their good luck, Father knew better than to say anything. The pitifully poor people probably hadn't eaten meat for a long time and to them, a rotten cow was a feast.

Driving back to St. Labre, Father Emmett felt anger at the rancher for having gotten rid of a filthy carcass, knowing full well it might poison the old couple. He knew that he couldn't change the mentality of non-Indians who had taken away Cheyenne land. He couldn't change their hearts but he could do all in his power to educate Cheyenne youngsters. The only way to educate them was to provide the latest textbooks, teachers and supplies available, to provide the children with health education so that they could recognize contaminated well water and meat that was not safe to eat. He had to forge ahead no matter what stood in his way to find the money needed to raise the standard of living of every child who graduated from St. Labre.

When Father got back to the Mission he ran into "Bisco" Spotted Wolf, the man he had met after his first funeral service at the mission cemetery, when he heard a gunshot and had nearly fallen into the grave. When Father was made Superior at St. Labre, he asked Bisco to come to work for him at the Mission. He said he needed a man he could trust. Father handed Bisco the Mission keys: "If I ever find somebody better, I'll come and get the keys," he had said. That day never came.[56]

Father told Bisco about the Red Eagle family eating rotten meat, but the Cheyenne wasn't surprised. "You should have seen the food we had in the old days!" he told Father. "I remember standing in line with my mother on ration day. The government gave us flour, beans and rice from big barrels. I was just tall enough to look over the long table and watch them scoop out the food to put in sacks. Every time a scoop went into a barrel, mice jumped out of the scoop and ran up and down the table in front of me. When we got home we had to boil the food. The mouse parts and droppings came up to the surface and my mother spooned them out before we could eat."[57]

Besides his usual duties at St. Labre, Father worked in the print shop, hunted deer, skinned, cut and wrapped the wild game for the kitchen. He even delivered the mail. At 2 a.m. he fell into bed and worried most of the night that he wasn't doing enough. He needed a secretary to lighten his work load, but the Mission couldn't afford to hire anyone. The Marquette League for Catholic Indian Missions in New York City, came to his rescue less than a month after Father was appointed superior of St. Labre.

Thirty-one year-old Mary McGarvey, a vibrant young woman with shiny brown hair and striking blue eyes, an Irish American beauty from Bayonne, New Jersey, came highly recommended by her supervisor at the Block Drug Company, where she had been executive secretary to the manager for six years. Before that job, Mary had worked on the Battery in New York City, in a firm located on the third floor of a five-story building that had once been a commercial shipping warehouse. One hundred years before, wealthy merchants did a thriving business from the Battery to Roosevelt Street, facing the East River. Front and Water Streets were occupied by wholesale grocers and iron dealers or as warehouses for the storage of merchandise. Had the vivacious Mary lived back in those days, she would have been standing in the commercial house of a shipping merchant, where she could look out the office window at the countless ship bows jutting across South Street, over the bustle of sailors and clerks. Clipper ships and frigates crowded the piers and from the tops of the main masts fluttered the flags of every famous shipping line. It had once been an exciting harbor community, but in Mary's time, the romance of New York harbor had long since faded away.

World War II brought thousands of women into ammunition factories but Mary had gotten a job working for the U.S. Maritime Commission. She was the most efficient secretary her employer had ever seen and probably the prettiest. Mary's dark hair complimented her creamy complexion but she seemed unaware of her natural beauty. She had no need for makeup or tight-fitting clothes that accentuated the body that God had given her. Always well-dressed in plain, tailored suits, skirts and white blouses that her grandmother had made for her, Mary impressed people as a thoroughly professional and well-groomed young woman. But Mary's work was boring. In her journal she wrote that she longed, "to do something personally meaningful." She described herself as ". . . single by choice, living with my parents and sisters and still searching for a life of fulfillment."[58]

Mary's real happiness came from her Sunday visits to the New York Foundling Hospital, a temporary shelter for neglected and abandoned infants and toddlers, where she had volunteered for more than four years. A loving caregiver, she had long since resigned herself, as she wrote in her journal, " . . . to the fact that my destiny was to lead a single life but the related motherless role was a bitter pill to swallow."[59] Why she had given up on marriage so early in life is unclear but Mary possessed boundless energy and longed for something new that would give her more job satisfaction.

A friend put her in touch with the Marquette League and she was accepted for assignment to St. Labre Mission. Idealistic, as most volunteers were, she wrote that she "was determined to give my all to the most destitute."[60]

Mary signed a contract for a six-month stay at the Mission. She paid her own airplane fare plus a deposit for her return trip. On the evening of August 30, 1955, she boarded a "decrepit DC-6" at Idlewild Airport for the trip west. Mary's parents and grandmother went with her to the airport.[61] The McGarvey family was originally from Donegal, Ireland, a wild and mysterious northern county with high, misty blue mountains. Mary's grandparents emigrated to America where they had both found work. Her mother could neither read nor write and her father was in ill health, but with hard work they had made a living in their new country and saved enough to buy a row house in a working class neighborhood. Mary had always lived in Bayonne, New Jersey and had never flown in an airplane.

During the flight to Montana, she "began to have misgivings about the venture," imagining that it was a deathly cold place where the sun did not shine. "I might just as well have been on my way to some dark continent as fear of the unknown seized me," she wrote.[62] The sun was coming up just as her plane arrived in Billings at 5 a.m. Father Ludger met her at the airport in the Mission car that he had just recently learned to drive. The trip to Ashland took twice as long, while Father drove slowly over the bumpy dirt roads, he regaled her with stories about Montana.

They arrived at the Mission in time for lunch, and Sister Eustella Bush, the Mother Superior at St. Labre, took Mary to meet her new boss, Fr. Emmett Hoffmann. Now 29 years-old, Father's good looks and charismatic personality had not gone unnoticed among his parishioners. Mary wrote after meeting him that he was: "an extraordinary person."[63] It was clear that Fr. Emmett was equally taken by the trim, vivacious woman in the blue suit that matched her eyes. The color had risen in Mary's cheeks when they shook hands and Sister Eustella felt the strong, mutual attraction between them. She didn't like it. She would have to keep an eye on the pretty volunteer. As for Father Emmett, Sister had already given up trying to see what he was up to. How Father Marion had picked the reckless young priest to succeed him was beyond her comprehension.

Mary made a good impression with everyone she met. Her manners were impeccable, she spoke perfect English and she wrote well, although "Fr. E." as she called him, teased and mimicked her "New Joyzee" accent. They felt comfortable with each other from the moment they met, although both were intensely private individuals who kept their feelings to themselves. Usually warm in her interaction with others, Mary listened but didn't volunteer information about herself. People who knew her said she was "very outgoing" and a devout Catholic who attended Mass every morning with a missal and rosary in her hands. Jane Talbert (Wagner), Mary's close friend at St. Labre said of her: "She was beautiful, especially when she smiled. I liked her from the start but we never bared our souls to one another. We were both very lonely people."[64]

Sister Eustella kept a close watch over all the volunteers. She and Father Marion had worked well together and he had valued her opinion on school and religious matters. Now that Fr. Emmett, a much younger priest with new ideas and his own ways of getting things done, had taken control of the Mission, Sister Eustella may have felt that he was an inexperienced upstart. At first a cool disdain existed between them, but after Fr. Emmett became director and Fr. Marion left for extended periods of time for emphysema treatments, their relations deteriorated. Father Emmett told his father that Sister Eustella tried to "run me like she ran Fr. Marion and I'm not going to stand for it."[65] Fr. Emmett had grown up with a controlling mother and in many ways, Sister Eustella reminded him of his childhood.

Sister was especially critical of the volunteers sent by the Marquette League and it was clear she wanted to know where they were and what they were doing at all times. The criticism began when the volunteers played cards with the priests in the evenings and hunted with the priests during the day. Sister did not approve of this familiarity and made her complaints known. What really made her mad was that Fr. Emmett completely ignored her.

Meanwhile, Mary was of tremendous help to Father Emmett. She took over the bookkeeping, which allowed him more time for other responsibilities. She edited his letters for him and generally did an excellent job as his secretary. Before long, he grew to depend on her. Mary also went to work helping the nuns in the small boys' dormitory in the morning and evening and she supervised the small girls during the noon hour, as they washed and rinsed their luncheon dishes in the hall outside the classrooms. Lunch had to be served in the classrooms due to the limited space in the musty basement dining room. Mary also found crowded conditions in the dorms where the girl's beds had been pushed together to allow space for a few more. Every available space was taken. When she looked across the dorm room, it seemed like one enormous mattress. It was impossible for her to walk around each bed to cuddle and say good night to the girls before bed.

Mary only lasted two months in the dorm. She was too lenient with the children and the Sisters felt that discipline had to be maintained at all times. Mary disagreed, but said nothing. Privately, she felt that children, especially girls, needed more individual love and attention. Unfortunately, overcrowded conditions in the dorms contributed to epidemics of all kinds. When one child came down with the measles, they all did. Measles and mumps were always serious problems because Indian children did not have immunity against non-Indian diseases and they often experienced complications following childhood illnesses.

Mary loved to play with the children and she spent many happy afternoons on the school playground throwing volleyballs with the girls and cheering for the high school boy's basketball team. The girls wanted Mary to be a cheerleader but she wrote that although she was flattered by the request, she couldn't be a cheerleader because it would be "going too far."[66] When winter set in, the young secretary found, "the subzero weather exhilarating." Time went by swiftly because she loved the children and her work: "Being involved in satisfying work was a sure tonic for the (boredom) I had experienced at home," she wrote.[67]

Another reason for her happiness may have been her relationship with Fr. Emmett. One day he and another fellow took a couple of volunteers deer hunting. The efficient Mother Eustella must not have been minding her post that day. The men sat in the front seat and the women in the back. Someone offered Mary a candy "jawbreaker" and she plopped it into her mouth. As they bumped along the dirt road, she suddenly choked on the candy and couldn't breathe. Father Emmett slammed on the brakes, jumped out, yanked the door open and pulled Mary from the car. She had slumped over and her face was blue. The look of terror on her face made Father slap her hard on the back until the jawbreaker dislodged from her throat. The whole experience took only a minute, but it seemed like an hour to Mary. When she regained her composure, Fr. Emmett joked, "Boy, you'd do anything to get attention!" He always seemed to lighten a serious situation with a funny one-liner.

When Mary's six months at the Mission were up, she decided to stay longer. Working for Fr. Emmett was rewarding because she could see with her own eyes the good work being done to educate Cheyenne children. She had seen Father Emmett reach out to help many impoverished families. One day soon after she arrived at the Mission, Mary learned that Father had found a family with four children living in a dangerous log cabin. Two ceiling beams had fallen in and the adults in the family had to walk hunched over in order to keep from hitting their heads. The roof leaked everywhere and the children were constantly sick. Father got some volunteers together and they built the family a new log cabin with windows and a real luxury, a screen door. During the construction, Father could be seen with the other workers, wearing a baseball cap, white t-shirt and jeans with a mouthful of nails and a cigarette.

Mary was a little awestruck at how much Father got done in one day. Always in perpetual motion, he dropped in on classes and visited the children's dining room and the bakery, where the tall, wise Sister Friedeburga stood in the doorway as the children came in for meals. Sister could tell with one look if a child was sick or depressed. She then put a comforting arm around the boy or girl and took the youngster aside. A sick or distressed child opened up to the compassionate Sister. She seemed like a guardian angel to the little ones. Besides this intuitive knack that she had with children of all ages, Sister Friedaburga put her loving spirit into making delicious homemade bread and pastries. After Sunday Mass, her bread was blessed and offered to the Cheyenne parishioners, who never forgot this kindness. Half a century later, a Cheyenne said of her: After I ate her bread, I felt blessed all day."[68]

Father Emmett loved Sister Friedeburga's bread as well and she caught him on various occasions with his hand in the bread pan. He joked all the time so she tolerated his pranks. One of his long-time employees, Vivienne (Bollack) Wilbur, later characterized Fr. Emmett as "a shooting star."[69] He'd burst into the office, flash a smile, tell a joke, and cheer everyone up. Just as suddenly, he was gone. Special attention from Father Emmett, even for a moment, lifted spirits and made people feel good about themselves and what they were doing. He was a constant inspiration to everyone who worked at the Mission.

Mary found it easy to read Father's moods. He was either happy and fun-loving in the office, or sick (and wouldn't admit it) or worried and fidgety about bills. When he wasn't feeling well, she knew enough to clear out of his way because Father was known to become impatient and to lack consideration when he had a cold or a headache. Preoccupied with his many responsibilities, he sometimes ignored common courtesy, even with Mary. Bills, for example, always seemed to rile him, whether or not he had the money to pay them. When he sensed that he had hurt someone's feelings, he apologized.

At times, loneliness haunted Father, but he brushed it off. If the doldrums caught him unawares, he only had to look around him. He knew his loss of sleep and headaches were nothing in comparison to the suffering of the Cheyennes. The shock of going back and forth between cold, dirt-floored tents, seeing five semi-starved children hanging on to their tired and aged grandmother – to a well-lit and cozy friary with hot showers and nutritious food now made possible by donors – this culture clash was a constant recurring trauma that didn't help his chronic insomnia. At night he often thrashed in bed, thinking about complaining again to the Indian Bureau about reservation living conditions.

Father Emmett didn't tell anyone if he was sick (Mary could tell) but when someone else got sick, Father's compassion was much appreciated. The families he helped in times of medical need are legend. In a letter to Fr J. B. Tennally, from the Bureau of Catholic Missions Father wrote:

> The hospital bill mentioned was for an operation on Richard . . . the man was dying - he had TB of the bone and his whole leg was a mass of pus and rot. The odor was so strong one could hardly stand it. To save the poor man, we took him to Holy Rosary Hospital in Miles City where the leg was amputated. He is now a new man and we finally made arrangements to have him admitted to the TB sanitarium in Tacoma, Washington . . . I had to talk to Richard for quite awhile and finally I bargained – If he'd go, I would buy him two new shirts, new pants, a suitcase and a wool sweater.[70]

On long, cold winter days, Father fought hard to keep his vision. At times he asked himself why he was working so hard, why he had agreed to stay at an isolated Mission, a frozen Siberian tundra with temperatures 20 to 60 degrees below zero. The priests, Sisters, and lay volunteers were at St. Labre to teach Christianity to the Cheyennes and to provide a good education for Indian children, but there was a vast difference in vision between the Capuchin Friars and Fr. Emmett. He was there to improve the quality of life for the Cheyennes because, as he told others, "You can't teach religion or anything else to a child who is tired, cold and hungry."

Father was a pastor and a businessman but he left the proselytizing to others, a characteristic that irritated some fellow Capuchins. When they criticized him, he tried not be judgmental. Years later, Mary wrote in her memoir: "No job was too great or too lowly for him . . . there was never a job he would not tackle."[71]

In time, if a secretary is very efficient, she becomes her employer's right hand, and Mary was good. When Fr. Emmett became impatient, (everything had to be done yesterday) Mary worked her hardest to please him and to keep up with his enormous energy.[72] He was always searching the realm of possibilities and dreams, always looking for solutions to problems. Something usually broke down and had to be repaired and the added expense weighed him down with anxiety. Mary saw how quickly he became worried and frustrated over expenses and she kept quiet until it was time to step in and lend a hand. She was the only person who stood up to him and wouldn't take his impatient behavior when he was worried or not feeling well.

At first he didn't tell Mary anything of a personal nature, but when Father realized he could trust her, he told Mary of his dream to build a much larger, modern school for Cheyenne children. He wanted to encourage industry on the reservation and if possible, he hoped to set up businesses, factories and build decent homes for the parents of children attending the Mission school.

In turn, Mary confided in him. She was very lonely and feared she might never have a child. She worried about her father's terminal illness, throat cancer. She didn't know how much longer he would live. In the afternoons, Father Emmett and Mary took a few children up "Bunker Hill" where they could look down on the Mission, talk and admire the improvements.

Jo Miller, a widow with five children, was in charge of the mailing department that solicited funds from people all over the United States. Jo and her children lived in an apartment building for lay people called St. Francis Hall. The Miller family took a liking to Mary and she moved into a room at one end of their apartment, but she continued to eat at the convent. After Agnes O'Brien, her sister Jane Talbert and Jane's 5 year-old daughter Jeanne came to St. Labre from Mr. Dohn's New York office, the women all became friends. They were to supervise the campaign department including the opening of donor contributions. This left Father Emmett more time to spend on his numerous other duties. Mary felt more at home with easterners. After her clerical duties were finished in the morning, she enjoyed working in the campaign office. Jane Talbert never forgot the first time she spoke to Father Emmett:

"He was forbidding at first. I was afraid of priests, anyway. Three or four days later, I was standing in the road and Fr. Emmett came along in a pickup truck piled with mail bags. He stopped and asked me what I was doing standing there and I told him I was waiting for a ride. He motioned to the back of the truck and laughed: "'So get in with the rest of the old bags!'" We laughed and that was the end of my being afraid of him."[73]

With Mary around to help him, Father Emmett didn't have to rush around as much. It got so that he would tell her what he wanted to say in a letter and she would write it for him. Anyone who watched Mary type was astounded at her speed and accuracy. On the job, their communication was instant. If he needed something, she already knew it. She also enjoyed the pranks he pulled on people and joined in the fun with an infectious laugh. Sometimes Mary caught Father Emmett looking at her with more than appreciation, but she brushed it off as just her imagination.

The mission staff was especially lonely during the holiday season when the virtues of home were held most dear, where siblings and parents reaffirmed hopes and dreams and mothers outdid themselves with Thanksgiving turkeys and bubbly apple pies. But Thanksgiving at St. Labre turned cold and it snowed early in the autumn of 1955. Cold weather meant that everyone had to work harder. Machinery froze, cars wouldn't start, heat was expensive and the Sisters had to make sure that students dressed in warm clothes. This was a problem because many Cheyenne families could not afford winter clothing and boots for their children. For these emergencies, the Sisters set up what came to be known as "the old clothing room," where donors sent used clothing and stores donated new clothing that did not sell. Anyone could come to the clothing room and get something to wear, including the non-Indian ranch families living near the Mission. Over the years, thousands of children and adults benefited from the clothing room, and still do to the present day.

One snowy night at St. Francis Hall, someone accidentally let a dishcloth go down the drain in the leggy, old sink. Water came gushing up in the bathtub and before they knew it, Jane and Mary had an emergency on their hands. Fathers Emmett and Carl Pulvermacher came to see what was going on. Before they reached the building, Father Emmett put the wire plumbing snake inside the hem of his robe, so it billowed out like a hoop skirt. Then he filled his pocket with snow.

The men climbed the stairs and when the women opened the door, they collapsed with laughter at Father's ridiculous costume. Just when he had them laughing, he took a snowball out of his pocket and threw it at them, hitting Mary square in the face. That started a free-for-all that lasted long enough to keep everyone in a good mood during the plumbing repair. That night, Mary went to bed early and planned her retaliation.

The next morning, she was at her desk as usual after Mass. Father Emmett was out most of the time but he came in after lunch and was sitting at his desk looking over his mail. Deep in thought, he didn't hear Mary sneak in the door. Suddenly, he heard a sound and looked up, but it was too late. Mary had thrown the snowball. Whack! It hit him on the shoulder and some went down the neck of his robe. In an instant he was out of the chair. He lunged for the door and caught Mary as she turned to run. She was laughing so hard she couldn't escape. She twisted away from him, but not before he put a handful of snow on the nape of her neck. She yelped and tried to get away. "I gotcha now!" he laughed. They were standing in front of a window where Sisters and priests often passed by. A light snow was falling outside. Seeing that she couldn't get away, Mary gave a helpless glance upwards, his eyes met hers, the only warning before he kissed her.[74] Too surprised to resist, she experienced a disturbing warmth, an essence flowing over her, the strength of his arms around her. Everything in her being wanted to be horrified, wanted to recoil from him, but she couldn't. Her voice caught in her throat as she saw him clearly for the first time. This was the man she was to work for and impress, this was her companion, her best friend and this was the man that she loved.

He slowly released his grip and she slid her arms around his shoulders and their bodies came together in an intense, forbidden embrace. Then, as suddenly, he let her go and she stared at him in confusion, embarrassed. For the first time in her life, Mary felt an unfamiliar longing, the heat of a passion she had longed for. She stumbled out the door and Father fell back into his chair. "I wondered what had come over me," Father remembered. "I wanted to apologize but . . . it was all so spontaneous." In a few stolen moments, Mary had resisted him, but when the laughing stopped and she sensed his desire, she became soft and yielding in his arms. He had been so completely captivated by Mary's laughing eyes, her dark, soft hair and her mouth, that he had forgotten the Capuchin taboo about never getting close to a female, and "God forbid, never speaking in a familiar way to a woman."[75]

Mary went to Mass the next morning clutching her rosary beads and missal, no different than on other mornings, except that she hadn't gone to confession. Nor did she take Holy Communion. It would have been impossible to sit in the confessional and tell the man that she loved of the sin she had committed by kissing him. How could she kneel before him at the altar rail, look up into his eyes and place the Communion bread into the mouth that he had kissed? "This is my body and this is the cup of my blood which is offered for you," he would say. No, it would betray too much. She couldn't concentrate, she couldn't face him. And most certainly she could not accept the body of Christ from the priest whom she had desired. It was the first time that Mary McGarvey had missed Holy Communion since she was a child.

Yet, Father Emmett offered Mass as usual, or so it seemed. Inwardly, he knew that he was a different man. He, too, had not confessed that morning. What would he have told Father Ludger, his confessor? That he had held a lovely woman in his arms and smelled the sweetness of her hair? That he had prayed to God to give him strength and worst of all, that he felt no remorse, no regret, because deep down, he did not believe they had sinned?[76]

During Mass, Father was careful not to look in her direction, although he felt her eyes on his back as he consecrated the bread and lifted the wine chalice. Mary blamed herself for the reckless, forbidden kiss. She had committed a sin by desiring a priest. Had she deliberately enticed him? Did he love her? Would Our Lady forgive her or had she committed an unthinkable sin? Mary lingered in her pew after the parishioners filed out. Father Emmett waited by the door to shake hands and followed the people outside. Mary knew they could never go back to their former friendship. Now, life would take on a bitter sweetness. Kneeling, she prayed for her parents, for the orphans in the world, and finally she prayed for Fr. Emmett, that he would not blame her for enticing him. Then she went home with a terrible headache.

On Monday morning, Mary got to work before Fr. Emmett and was at her desk typing when she heard him at the door. He came in joking and laughing like always, expertly hiding what he really felt. He acted like nothing had changed but there was an unspoken emotion, an exciting tension in the office that hadn't been there before. Later that day, Father put his hand on Mary's shoulder and told her how sorry he was for what had happened. When he took his hand away, they stared at one another with an intense awareness.[77] They had to be careful. Mary knew that

Father loved the Cheyenne people. They couldn't let it happen. Later, Father went to confession but he didn't say anything about Mary. He didn't believe kissing was a sin, but he was in a quandary. Many times he asked God to help him to keep his vows and to be a good priest. There was no privacy, no time to be alone together and there were ears and eyes everywhere.

Many people looked up to Father Emmett. Mary knew that he was a man already staggered with heavy responsibilities but she also knew how glorious she had felt in his arms. It was clear that Fr. Emmett didn't live a life above reproach. He had the renegade streak in him, like some of the other men in his family, a freedom-loving rebelliousness that would not bow down to any man. But he was also the human being she admired and respected more than anyone else in the world, the man who would do anything in his power to help the Cheyennes. Their relationship was wrong in the eyes of the Church and Mary felt the guilt intensely. Her worst fear was that she could never have the only man in her life that she had ever loved. It was at this critical point that circumstance stepped in and changed Mary's life forever.

CHAPTER
9

Adopting Cooky

A Cheyenne tribal official called Father Emmett with news that a two year-old Cheyenne toddler, Clara Ann Crazy Mule, was returning from a tuberculosis sanitarium in Washington state. Would Father Emmett check to see if her biological father could take care of her? The nuns immediately offered to take the little girl and Father knew they would do an excellent job.

The Petter family, respected leaders of the local Mennonite community, also offered to take her.[78] Father tried to reach the child's father, Xavier Crazy Mule, but he was working on a ranch in another county so he decided to let Mary temporarily take care of the child. In his heart, Father knew he couldn't give Mary a child of his own, but he wanted her to realize her dream of becoming a mother, even for a little while.

Xavier Crazy Mule's other children boarded at the Mission. If Mary took her, the little girl could see her brother and sisters every day. For the time being, Fr. Emmett asked Mary if she could help raise a small Cheyenne child with many health problems. "Even before I heard her history," Mary later wrote in her memoir, "I was ready and willing. How often I had dreamed of having a little girl to mother but never expected it to come true."[79] It was settled. Mary had only two days to wait for the child's arrival.

Clara Ann Crazy Mule had endured cruel hardships in her young life. Her biological mother, Mary (Wooden Thigh) Crazy Mule, a tall, pretty, Cheyenne woman, was the daughter of Arthur Wooden Thigh, a respected employee at the Mission. According to those who had known the child's mother, Mary Crazy Mule was "a friendly woman, smiling, happy and laughing all the time. Nothing bothered her. She worked at the hospital in Lame Deer and liked to help people when they were sick."[80] Mary and Xavier Crazy Mule had several children, but nothing seemed to work out for them. After Mary was diagnosed with tuberculosis, she had to stop working. Weak and depressed, with a nagging cough, she tried to take care of her children as best she could.[81]

Mary was driving one day with her girls when she swerved on a gravel curve and hit the brake too hard. The car skidded and rolled several times down a steep embankment. The children were thrown from the car, as well as the mother, who sustained back and serious internal injuries. An Indian couple walking home found Mary but it was some time before six month-old Clara Ann was found. The baby, lodged in thick undergrowth, had nearly suffocated with her mouth filled with dirt. Her tiny body had catapulted down the steep ravine and both her legs had been broken. Mary and her children survived the accident, but the mother's internal injuries caused constant pain.

Baby Clara Ann spent months in the hospital at Crow Agency before her legs mended and she could go home. The child may have already contracted tuberculosis from her mother, who by this time had died from the devastating disease. Clara Ann had survived serious injuries, and the first separation from her mother while in the hospital. Death now separated them forever. The child was placed in a Tacoma, Washington TB sanitarium for ten months. She was finally released to an Indian Health Nurse who accompanied her home to Montana.

On March 5, 1956, the nurse dropped Clara Ann off at St. Labre, where Mary McGarvey was anxiously awaiting her arrival. "I shall never forget that meeting," Mary later wrote:

> As I approached the car, the most darling little girl emerged looking rather pathetic in an oversized plaid coat and a red velvet hat. Her eyes were dark and sad and I fell in love with her immediately. To my surprise, she came right to me although she did not utter a sound. We proceeded to Fr. Emmett's office where I removed her coat and hat. She seemed so tiny in a red corduroy overall. Her shiny black hair, cut in a Buster Brown bob, framed her bewildered round face.[82]

Mary took the child into the Church at St. Labre, where she and Clara

Ann knelt down and thanked God for bringing Mary the child she had always wanted.

Clara Ann's brother and two sisters barely recognized their little sister. Father Emmett sent word to Xavier that his daughter was at the Mission and early the next morning he came to see her. Since he worked away from home, he gave Mary permission to keep the child at the Mission near his other children. The confused toddler had arrived at St. Labre with a cardboard box containing clothes, pills (She called them "plills.") and cod liver oil.

Mary nicknamed Clara Ann, "Cooky" and the name stuck. The Sisters wanted Mary and Cooky to stay at the convent but Father Emmett had other plans for them. He moved them into another apartment, recently vacated by a former employee. Cooky begged to be held and begged to be rocked to sleep and she clung to Mary, afraid to let go. In her desperation to have a child, Mary may have misinterpreted the child's deep insecurities as evidence that the child had bonded with her. She lavished the girl with love and dressed her "like a little doll," in frilly clothes, a habit that was out of keeping with the child's tribal life, especially since Cooky's siblings couldn't dress in fancy clothes like their baby sister.[83] The unfortunate result was that Cooky stood out from other Cheyenne children at the school in the way she spoke and dressed – like a pampered "Indian princess." Cooky began calling Mary "Mama."

Cooky's health problems caused difficulties that would have been almost impossible for her father to have dealt with. She had severe, recurring nosebleeds, starting the first night of her arrival. Blood spewed from her nose and mouth in chunks and Mary couldn't stop the flow. "I have never seen such a hemorrhage in my life," Mary later wrote. "Fr. Emmett rushed her as fast as possible to Holy Rosary Hospital in Miles City. The child lost so much blood, she had to have a (blood) transfusion."[84]

A second Cheyenne child, "Doreen" had accompanied Cooky to St. Labre and two weeks after they arrived, Mary was asked to take her in as well. Now she had two young toddlers. That same week, one of the priests found yet another little girl nearly frozen to death in a pickup truck on a country road. "Dolly" suffered from malnutrition but she, too, joined the growing family within a couple of weeks. Mary had her hands full. ". . . it was quite a transition to have become Mama to three little girls in the short period of a month," she wrote, but she gladly accepted the children without realizing the enormous energy and time they would take.[85]

Father Emmett came to visit them as often as he could. He helped Mary with food and clothing, but she bought Cooky the best of everything and her savings account was soon exhausted. Mary's friend, Jane Talbert, remembered: "Fr. Emmett would do anything for Mary. What Mary wanted – Mary got. If she wanted to move to another apartment, we followed her. We'd get her apartment when she left. Father was a very lonely man before Mary came."[86]

Mary could now only work part-time as Father Emmett's secretary but he spent hours with her and the girls in the evenings, while Mary typed his letters. He started cooking their meals in the afternoon as Mary couldn't do everything at once. It got so that he would eat with them and then go over to the kitchen and eat a second meal with the friars. "The now limited office work had to be sandwiched in between, washing, ironing, housecleaning, and cooking, plus keeping a watchful eye on the girls at play," Mary remembered.[87] But something else was bothering her – Mary desperately wanted to adopt Cooky.

The winter of 1955-56 went by slowly; ice and snow enveloped the Mission in a frigid canopy with minimal movement advised. Indian children, used to the cold, went out to play and had great fun making paths through the deep snow. Mary, however, would not think of allowing her little charges outdoors in such weather. All winter long Mary and the children were cooped up together in the apartment while Cooky's nosebleeds continued to plague them. Father Emmett came over to nap in the afternoons on Mary's couch to get away from the noise at school. His relationship with Mary grew into a very special friendship, trust and love. After the girls were bathed and tucked into bed at night, they found time alone together.

Years later, Father Emmett told a friend: "We loved each other but we had an understanding that because of our religious backgrounds, training and beliefs, we could not become sexually involved. She was a scrupulously religious person. To do anything morally wrong would have been terrible for her. If either one of us felt romantic, the other was able to draw the line. But if she had not been as strict about her beliefs, I don't know what I would have done." Occasionally it was Mary who had to remind him: "Remember who you are." They were always discreet, or so they thought.[88]

Despite complaints from the Sisters and some of the priests, Father Emmett wanted all the children, including Cooky and her playmates at St. Labre, to learn as much as possible about their traditional Cheyenne culture. He had moccasins beaded for each girl in preparation for a pow wow. Father and Chiefs Charles Sooktis Sr., Charlie Sittingman Jr., Charles White Dirt Sr. and David Strange Owl Sr., had initiated interest in reviving Northern Cheyenne culture and dancing.[89] For many years the Cheyennes had simply concentrated on staying alive. They had no extra money to hold dances and giveaway ceremonies as they had in the past. Alcohol had quickly divided some families and the money that would have gone into the making of colorful dance costumes, often went to the bars instead.

Father Emmett planned to have the pow wow in a World War II Quonset building that was used as a gym. Donors provided prize money for the best dancers. Cheyennes from all over the reservation, as well as the Crow, Arapaho and Lakota (Sioux) attended the pow wow.

On the day of the event, Cooky and the girls were playing in their apartment when they heard the sound of bells. "(The girls) ran to the living room window to see what was making the noise. When they saw the Indian men dressed in colorful, feathered dance outfits, with bells and faces painted half black, or red and blue," Mary wrote, "they ran under the kitchen table like scared puppies."[90] She had to coax and reassure the girls that no harm would come to them. An hour later, all three girls, dressed in their colorful moccasins, were taken out on the dance floor by relatives to join in the dancing. They watched wide-eyed as elderly women danced slow-swaying traditional shawl dances, young male cousins jumped and whirled in fancy dance outfits and uncles displayed the dignity and manhood of the traditional movements of warriors long ago. Fr. Emmett knew that pow wows were important because the worries and humiliations of the day were forgotten when Cheyenne men became sophisticated and grand in their regalia and women elegant, demure and incredibly graceful. Passing each other on the dance floor to the beat of the drum made them one in spirit, one in tune with the memory of their ancestors, with their relatives and with their beloved children, who learned to dance beside them. It made them proud to be Indians. Listening to the advice of the elders, Father helped to revive Cheyenne cultural traditions by funding pow wows every year from then on.

94

That winter, Dolly came down with bronchial pneumonia and had to be hospitalized for a week. All three girls caught colds and ran high fevers. They were fussy and mischievous but they couldn't go outside, except for the short walks to Church for Mass. Jailed in a three-room apartment with three little girls for five months proved exhausting.

One evening in late winter, Father Emmett walked in and found Mary yelling at the girls. He remarked that she didn't have to scream at them. She demanded that he take out the garbage and he said he would take it out when he left. Furious, she yelled at him: "I'm tired! You bring me work and now I'm supposed to drop everything and get your work done! You have it easy! You can always just walk out of here!"[91]

Surprised at her angry outburst, Father Emmett tried to defend himself: "Mary, what can I do?" he said. "I'm only a priest!" She dissolved into tears and he tried to comfort her, but the resentment was out in the open and something had to be done about it. Jane Talbert noticed that Mary was on the verge of a nervous collapse. Her father's worsening health condition, her sudden responsibilities as a mother of three sickly children and her love for Fr. Emmett had left her feeling trapped and confused. Would she be allowed to adopt Cooky?[92]

Realizing that he had put too much of a load on Mary's shoulders, Father arranged for Dolly and Doreen to live in the convent with the Sisters and Mary and Cooky went home to New Jersey for a much-needed vacation. Mary found that her father's cancer had spread throughout his body. Everything had been done to make him comfortable and it was now only a matter of time.

Mary and Cooky stayed as long as possible and then flew home to settle into a more manageable routine. Father Emmett had planned a special birthday celebration for Cooky, with Doreen, Dolly and Cooky's siblings invited to celebrate with her. A month later, and one day before Thanksgiving, Mary's father died. She and Cooky left immediately for New Jersey and didn't return until after New Years. Accustomed to the dry, cold Montana climate, Cooky became seriously ill in New Jersey and Mary took her to the family doctor. He was aghast when he saw the sick child. "He was quite annoyed with me," Mary wrote, "and could not understand how I could possibly have taken on such a responsibility. He obviously would have advised against (taking the child) had I ever consulted him."[93]

Mary ignored her physician's warnings. Since Cooky's mother had died and her father was rarely able to visit, Mary knew that Xavier must be struggling to care for his other children as well. She also knew that strong family ties existed among the Cheyennes, but because of Cooky's precarious health and her need for constant medical care, she saw no reason to delay. She wanted to legally adopt Cooky in a Montana court of law. Lurking in the back of her mind was the fear that Xavier Crazy Mule would someday come to claim his daughter.

Father Emmett visited Xavier and explained Mary's desire to adopt Cooky. He told the widower how well Mary had cared for his child. They lived at the Mission where Cooky's sisters and brother saw her every day. The little girl loved Mary and under these circumstances, would it be possible for Mary to adopt Cooky? He could see his daughter anytime he wanted.

Xavier thought it over and finally gave his permission, although he had misgivings and wished it could have been otherwise. Nothing was said or noted until many years later, when Mary admitted that when Cooky's father visited his daughter, she immediately went to him and when he left, both father and daughter cried and the child held out her arms to him.[94]

Cooky's maternal grandfather, Arthur Wooden Thigh, a trusted Mission employee, lived alone with his adopted Cree son, Teddy, after his wife died. Arthur's land in the hills on Wooden Thigh Creek was one of the most beautiful forest allotments on the reservation. He had a sturdy log cabin, a barn and corrals. With the help of his son, he ran a small herd of cattle. Thick chokecherry bushes and wild plum trees grew in abundance along the creek with golden currant and yellow coneflowers. Every spring Arthur planted a garden with a horse and plow, and the harvest fed his family through the winter months. He carried water from the creek in heavy buckets to his garden and people wondered how "Grandpa" kept going like he did.

Father Emmett admired Arthur Wooden Thigh and he often took Mary and Cooky to see him. On these occasions, Cooky sat outside the cabin on her grandfather's lap in his favorite wicker chair. They visited and laughed and Arthur loved to tell stories. These were happy times because it was one of the only places that all four could relax together. Fr. Emmett always remembered to bring the old man his favorite Camel cigarettes, a bag of Bull Durham tobacco and oranges. Every Sunday without fail, Arthur rode his gray horse out of the hills and down to St. Labre Mission to attend Mass and to spend an hour with his little granddaughter. Cooky remembered that he smelled of strong tobacco:

> Grandpa talked Cheyenne and rolled cigarettes. He tried to make me laugh all the time – he'd say something and then he'd laugh and I'd laugh too. His face was covered with wrinkles and his hands were rough. We sat on the ground and leaned back against a building. The horse grazed and he lifted me up on the saddle and I could see the sweat on it's back. All of a sudden he'd start singing in Cheyenne. Our visits lasted an hour or so and it was always a happy time.[95]

Arthur spoke to Cooky in the language of their ancestors, who had fought and died for their homelands. He told her about the birds they saw in the trees and he mimicked the sounds they made. Many years later, Cooky realized how very much he had loved her. These were the earliest and happiest memories she had of her biological family.

Arthur Wooden Thigh was a faithful Catholic and had worked for the priests for thirty years. His patience and quiet strength made him a good father. In the evenings, he often told stories to his adopted son Teddy. One story in particular left a deep impression on the boy:

Back in the early days, one of the Sisters had died at the Mission and Arthur was asked to dig a temporary grave for her in the cemetery. Preparations were made to ship the body by train back to Wisconsin. Arthur dug the grave and stood beside the priest and Sisters as they placed a rosary in the Sister's folded hands, pulled her veil down over her face and nailed the casket shut. Arthur filled in the grave and later that summer the Mother Superior asked him if he would dig up the coffin because the truck was coming to pick it up for the trip east. Arthur did as he was requested to do and dug up the casket. Something about the way the coffin had turned slightly sideways in the grave didn't look right to Arthur. He removed the nails and carefully opened the casket lid to make sure it had not been robbed. What he saw left him with a haunting memory for the rest of his life. He dropped the coffin lid and backed away in horror, then ran stumbling down the hill to the convent.

Arthur burst into the Mother Superior's office but was unable to speak. The terrified look on his face and his mute response to her questions –

he could only gesture toward cemetery hill – told the Sister the unspeakable. All of the Sisters rushed up to the cemetery and opened the coffin. They sobbed and collapsed on the ground at the sight of the Sister's body, twisted in the lonely agony of death, her hands clutching her hair above her head and her mouth open in a silent scream. The wretched soul had torn the veil from her face when she woke up from the sleeping sickness and found that she had been buried alive. She had torn off her fingernails trying to dig out of the coffin. Years later, Arthur told the story to his son Teddy in order to teach him a lesson. "The Cheyenne people grieve for four days before they bury their dead," he told him, "because they believe the spirit of the deceased lingers behind. Our custom lets all the relatives know that the person is dead and his spirit can go in peace."[96]

Arthur's weekly visits to see Cooky may have worried Mary, but not for long. On the cold morning of November 30, 1961, Arthur Wooden Thigh, aged 81, died along the road. Although his horse was ill, he had wanted to see his granddaughter. He started off on foot and got almost 9 miles from his home in the hills before suffering a heart attack. The pain brought the beloved grandfather down, where neighbors found him frozen to death.

Fr. Emmett buried his old friend and wrote his obituary, saying that Arthur ". . . was the best dairy man the mission ever had. He was faithful to the smallest detail."[97] Cooky was too young to know that she had lost her grandfather, one of the finest men she would ever know.

Long before Arthur's death, Mary had wanted to adopt Cooky. She knew that, "Fr. Emmett was in favor of the adoption," but the child was sick most of the time.[98] When Cooky got chicken pox, it was the most severe case anyone had ever seen. She had survived tuberculosis but the severe, life-threatening hemorrhages meant that she would need constant medical supervision. Father thought she would be better off with Mary, who had proven herself ready to take on such a worrisome responsibility. He went to see Cooky's father and again explained the situation. Afterwards, he told Mary that Xavier "agreed without hesitation to the adoption." Nevertheless, when the time came to sign away his parental rights, Xavier Crazy Mule had second thoughts and hesitated before he signed the adoption papers.[99]

Mary went ahead with the adoption but when the date finally arrived, she "began to wonder if I was doing the right thing."[100] She waited anxiously in the courtroom for the judge's decision. Cooky, pretty in a pink dress with a pink bow in her hair and black, paten leather shoes, sat quietly beside her mother throughout the proceedings. Mary's "foremost worry" was that the Judge would disapprove of a single woman, a white woman, adopting an Indian child. She was surprised when the judge made his decision solely on the record and ignored her race and single status. Mary had taken care of Cooky for over two years, which already fulfilled the six-month probationary period. Cooky's mother was deceased and her father had signed the consent form. Mary waited anxiously until the Judge declared that Cooky, now renamed Carol Ann McGarvey, was her legally adopted daughter. Father Emmett had helped to make Mary's dream of having a child come true. He had, in a sense, given her a child they both loved. The adoption only brought them closer together.[101]

Mary now felt secure in her role as Cooky's mother and Father was always there to protect them, like the time Cooky was playing outside with her friends and a chorus of screams brought Father running from his office across the road. Cooky stood frozen in terror, staring at her feet. Father swept her up in his arms and away from a huge, coiled rattlesnake. This incident, as well as Cooky's precarious health problems, added to Mary's inclination to overprotect her Cheyenne daughter.[102]

Father, Mary and Cooky often went to Billings and it was not uncommon to see them shopping together. Cooky held on to Fr. Emmett's thumb on one side and her mother's hand on the other. "We were a family," Cooky recalled many years later. "I knew he was a priest, but I saw him as my own father. I'd look up at him and then I'd look up at her as we walked along. They were both happy and laughing together. Sometimes he took us to a high point in the hills and we'd have picnics of fried chicken, potato chips and soda."[103] Cooky felt completely happy and secure.

Jane Talbert recalled that "Mary was a doting mother with a capital D. She was a little hysterical over Cooky – almost smothering. Cooky fulfilled a need in her life because she had been so lonely. She wanted parenthood so much. She told me she had been engaged before she came to St. Labre, but there was a broken romance. We agreed that all of us who came to the Mission were refugees from unhappiness."[104]

The irony was that Mary, Cooky and Father Emmett were now happier than at any other time in their lives.

"Who the hell are you working for,
Father Hoffmann, or me?"
President J. F. Kennedy, 1961

CHAPTER
10

Nurse Viola

By 1958, Father Emmett had been at St. Labre Mission for four years. The Church policy was to reassign priests after a three-year term in one location. Father believed this rule destroyed the relationship between the Church and the Catholic Indian community. He was entirely without personal ambition to elevate himself within the Church hierarchy and one thing was certain – he didn't want to leave the Cheyennes. When the tribe found out that Father might be transferred, they passed Northern Cheyenne Tribal Resolution Number 128:

> Whereas, Rev. Emmett Hoffmann of the St. Labre Mission
> School has by his association, friendship and religious efforts
> won the admiration and respect of the members of the
> Northern Cheyenne Tribe; and whereas, said persons hereby
> express their desire to the Superiors of Father Emmett that he
> be continued at St. Labre Mission School in order that he can
> continue to carry out the work which he has so ably done . . .
> Signed, James D. king, Secretary and John Woodenlegs,
> President (Chief) of the Northern Cheyenne Tribe.[105]

Due to the tribal resolution, the Provincial Minister decided to allow Fr. Emmett to stay for another term. No one was more relieved than Mary McGarvey.

Cooky was still having nosebleeds at night. Viola Campeau, another Marquette League volunteer, came to stay with them so that Mary could get some sleep. An unassuming, practical woman, dressed in conservative plain clothes with short curly hair, Viola did not speak unless spoken to. Painfully shy, the trained nurse had a serious hearing problem. Viola arrived at St. Labre in the summer of 1957 from Minnesota, one of eleven children born to an American family of French Canadian descent. She was a loner, so quiet that her mother worried about her.

Viola had applied to enter a convent but after the entrance interview, she decided against it. A devout Catholic, she hoped for a life of service to others. After graduating from nursing school, she read an article about American Indian missionaries in the "Marquette Indian League Bulletin." She applied for a volunteer nursing position and spent a year in Arizona with the Navajo and then agreed to a six month stay at St. Labre Mission.

When Vi arrived at St. Labre, one of the priests dropped her off in front of a big tree with the comment, "Lady, you're home." Viola stood there for a long time feeling insecure. People walked by, but she didn't speak to anyone and nobody spoke to her. She was ready to leave when she met up with a woman. "How far is it to the nearest town?" she asked. The woman told her it was three miles and then added, "You have to catch the stage." Vi couldn't imagine herself riding in a stagecoach! Finally, a Sister came and took her to the convent. Later that day, when Vi first met Fr. Emmett, the young priest shook her hand, spoke to her for a second and then when he found out that she had worked with the Navajo for a year, he said: "Oh, then you know what Mission life is like!" He hurried off and Vi stood for an hour with her coat on, almost in tears and too shy to move. Finally, she was taken to her room, a small cubicle only big enough for a single bed.

That afternoon, Viola met Mother Superior Eustella Bush at exactly 4 o'clock and was told to "Keep your place." To Vi this meant that she should stay away from the priests, an odd thing to say to a new volunteer. After the first week Fr. Emmett asked her to teach the kindergarten class, but she told him that she'd never taught school before. "Don't worry," he chuckled, "I'll show you how!" He took her to a classroom, introduced her to the class, closed the door and left.[106]

Vi stood there dumbfounded with 12 little four and five year-old Cheyenne children looking up at her. One of them was Cooky McGarvey. "This was to become the most educational and rewarding of all my experiences at St. Labre," Viola later told friends. Most of the children couldn't speak English and they had never been away from home. Vi taught them the alphabet, numbers, rhymes and games. They had play time, singing, story reading, dancing and courtesy time. They went for walks to watch the ants build their homes and to look for pheasants and other birds, and to enjoy the out-of-doors. Soon Cheyenne parents came to see how their children were doing. "They took me into their hearts and homes in their silent, unspoken way," Viola remembered.

Dealing with the Sisters was something else again. One weekend, they didn't provide meals for Viola and she had no money to buy food. Volunteers were important at St. Labre and Fr. Emmett got mad at Sister Eustella for the way the nuns were treating Viola. They had been at odds for some time and this just made things worse. Father knew that when Father Marion had been Director of St. Labre, he had acquiesced to Sister Eustella's every wish. Now, things were different. He confronted her about the cruelty and when she objected, he lost his composure and used a few interesting words. He told her that Viola was doing a good job and that if she left the Mission because she had been treated badly by the School Sisters of St. Francis, he was leaving as well! For the time being, that put a stop to the abuse.

Viola felt she was a threat to the Sisters because the Cheyenne families had readily accepted her into their homes, but there was more to it. Sister Eustella suspected that Father Emmett was having a relationship with Mary McGarvey and now all the lay volunteers were suspect. How she found out remains a mystery, but it came from someone close to Fr. Emmett because Mary didn't share her personal life with anyone.

Vi later opened a small clinic at St. Labre, which then consisted of a chair, table, small cabinet, an old dental chair, plus odds and ends of antiquated medications such as mutton fat ointment, homemade, rolled bandages and two thermometers. No doctor came to St. Labre and the nearest Indian Health Clinic was at Lame Deer, twenty-one miles away. From 1957 until 1965, Viola averaged 60 patients a day, including school children and ranch families. The one telephone in town only worked from 8 a.m. until 4:30 p.m. and most serious injuries or sicknesses happened in the evening or in the early morning hours.[107]

Finally, Viola found a medical expert who cared, Dr. Ross Lemire, a Billings internist, who told her to call him day or night if she needed him.[108] "Before I met Dr. Lemire," Vi recalled, "It was only by the grace of God that I never lost a patient. I broke every medical and federal law in the whole country. The Cheyennes had polio, cholera, diphtheria, typhoid, tuberculosis, scarlet fever, you name it, they had it." Health officials reported that Rosebud County, where most of the Northern Cheyenne people lived, had the highest rate of tuberculosis in the United States except for one county in the southwest. Thirty years after a government investigation had found the Cheyenne suffering from "murderous neglect," little had changed.[109]

Besides teaching kindergarten, Nurse Viola was on call 24 hours a day. The Sisters disliked the fact that she could come and go as she pleased, but their complaints against her were to no avail. When Viola got fed up with the nuns, she told Fr. Emmett that she just couldn't take it anymore and was going to leave. He'd say, "Could you stay just one more semester?" Then she'd walk in the hills and come back to tell him, "Okay, I'll stay just one more semester." This went on every six months for five or six years and then both of them realized that Viola was not going to leave St. Labre.

Father appreciated Viola's good works. After going through many medical emergencies, he grew to trust Viola, but she and Father also disagreed about many things. During an argument, Father usually stood up for himself with a snide remark, but he had met his match in Viola. She wasn't afraid to argue with him, especially about the way she felt women were treated in the Church – like second class citizens. As in all friendships, awkward moments arose when both of them got angry and stopped speaking for a number of days. Vi was usually the one who threw up her hands and walked off, exasperated. But whatever problem or obstacle Viola experienced, prayer remained the center of her life; Mass, the Eucharist, the Scriptures, listening and speaking to God, and asking for His direction.

Every year at St. Labre, cholera broke out and hepatitis epidemics, measles and mumps and numerous other diseases made their fearful rounds. Mary was especially fearful for Cooky and kept her in the apartment until an epidemic abated, which sometimes lasted for weeks. It was a miracle that Father Emmett and the Sisters didn't catch illnesses more often than they did while caring for people like Jim and Bessie Twin, both devoted Catholics. The old couple lived about five or six miles from the Mission and people noticed them coming and going to town, Jim riding the white horse and Bessie walking behind. One day someone asked Jim, "Why doesn't Bessie ride?" Jim gave the man a strange look and replied, "She ain't got a horse."

Non-Indians never saw Bessie riding. They figured that Jim made his wife walk behind. The truth was that as soon as Jim and Bessie got off the beaten track, Bessie rode double with her husband. When they neared a town or a cabin, Bessie jumped down because she wanted to go one place and her husband wanted to go another. If she didn't walk, she'd have to go wherever her husband went and this she would not do!

In August of 1957, Father Emmett received an urgent message that Bessie was dying. The rain poured down as Father drove along the slick, muddy path. He found Bessie lying in her tent on a thin blanket, the only protection from the hard, cold ground. The spare tent contained no chairs, table, or bed. In the dim light of a kerosene lamp Father shuddered to see two dogs huddling close to the sick woman. When she moaned, they nestled closer. Father touched her burning forehead. He remembered seeing Bessie in early Mission photographs, a lovely young woman with shiny, thick braids.

Now Bessie's dogs snuggled close, while Jim knelt beside her. Father Emmett felt the nagging, helpless guilt come over him, the anger against the government for having broken every promise they had made with the Northern Cheyennes. They had never provided the tribe with enough food, with medical information, with decent homes. He couldn't do anything more for the woman except wipe her brow, give her a sip of water and pray with her. She prayed in Cheyenne while Father gave her the Last Rights. She relaxed then and after midnight, she slipped into a coma. As the morning sun began to rise over the eastern hills, the land of her courageous ancestors, Bessie Twin quietly passed away. Bessie was 65 years old at the time of her death, but for Indians the average age of death was 40. Every day for months, Jim Twin sat for hours beside Bessie's graveside, weeping and praying.

Meanwhile, Father was having a hard time finding teachers and staff who were willing to live and work in such a remote area of Montana. Ashland had no bank or drugstore and there wasn't much for children to do. People came to teach for a year and then left for jobs in Minnesota or Utah where the pay was better, the climate milder and the growing season longer. Since Father couldn't afford to hire teachers who had graduated from the best schools, he occasionally ended up with a misfit, but strange people were routed before they did any damage. The bottom line was that only the truly dedicated people, those who believed in helping the Cheyennes, stayed at St. Labre for years.

During the summer months, Mary and Cooky remained at St. Labre, while volunteers like Fintan Schaub and Viola left on vacation to visit relatives in Minnesota and Wisconsin. Over the years, Fintan became protective of Viola as though she were his own daughter. On at least one occasion, his ability to "sense" danger may have saved her life.[110]

The doorbell rang at the friary one morning and Fr. Emmett opened the door to a tall, thin man with big ears wearing a baseball cap. Jake Grundy was looking for a job. Father Emmett interviewed Mr. Grundy and found that he had excellent references. Father Marion, then living in Michigan, had worked with Grundy and had suggested he visit St. Labre. The Capuchins in Minnesota thought so highly of Grundy that he was affiliated with the Third Order of St. Francis. He was understandably proud of this honor and showed Fr. Emmett his card. As it turned out, Jake was a talented musician and singer, once a member of the popular swing group, the Fred Waring Band. He showed Father Emmett a photograph of himself with Waring's popular choral group.

Jake was hired as the boy's night dorm supervisor. The priests enjoyed hearing him sing and play the guitar when he visited the friary. Thanksgiving rolled around and like most of the employees, Jake went out of state to visit relatives in Cheyenne, Wyoming. When he returned, he showed Fr. Emmett a diamond ring his brother had given him. Jake was fun to have around but he was the nervous sort, jumpy and curious to know where people were going and where they'd been. The priests liked Jake but Bisco Spotted Wolf didn't trust him. "If you watch a guy," Bisco said, "You can tell if he's on the shady side. I knew from looking at Jake, that he was dangerous."

When Jake first came to the Mission he told Bisco that he had only 25 cents to his name. A couple of days later Bisco heard him jingling coins in his pocket. One weekend the high school boys stayed at the school so the coach could practice basketball with them. There was a pop machine in the old gym and Bisco was working in the building. When the boys went to supper, Bisco found the pop machine had been broken open and the money was gone. Jake immediately said that it must have been the boys who stole the money. Always observant, Bisco had been there the whole time and he knew the kids didn't do it. He suspected that Jake had stolen the money.

December snows covered the prairie Mission in an icy blanket, further secluding it from the rest of the world. The children had gone home and most of the staff left on Christmas break. Jake told everybody he was going to Salt Lake City, Viola left to spend Christmas with her brother and his wife in Minneapolis and Fintan was undecided. On Christmas Eve those who stayed went to Midnight Mass at the Mission and Bisco sat in his usual seat at the back of the church in the last row, right hand side. Behind him, a doorway led into the monastery. In the middle of Mass he glanced back over his shoulder and Jake was standing in the open door alone. "He saw me looking at him," Bisco recalled, "and I turned away. He was wearing a gray suit with a long overcoat that hung below his knees. I didn't want to take that second look. When we stood up, I looked back again. He was gone. I saw him the next day and he told me he had gone to Salt Lake City and come right back. He was driving a new green Ford. I knew something wasn't right."

Meanwhile, Fintan began to have a strange foreboding. One night, he had a terrible premonition that Jake was going to harm Viola! He packed a suitcase and caught the first train to Minneapolis. Vi was staying at her brother's home and was surprised when Fintan showed up at the door. He told Vi of his premonition. Sure enough, Jake had come to Minneapolis and had called Viola twice, making the excuse that he wanted to leave a suitcase with her. Fintan warned her, "Don't talk to him again." Viola had an uneasy Christmas knowing that Jake was lurking around.

Viola was still in Minneapolis when a young Indian girl at the Mission came to Father Emmett's office and stood in the doorway, too shy to come in. It was unusual for a girl to come alone to speak with a priest and Father thought she might be having problems in school. When the girl began to speak, she burst out crying. Jake Grundy had given her a ride home and had sexually molested her at knife point! Father immediately called the sheriff, but a thorough search of the Mission found that Jake had taken his belongings and fled.

Less than a month later, one of the Cheyenne boys in the dorm was looking at a forbidden "True Detective Magazine" with a flashlight under the covers one night when he saw something that made him take the magazine to Fr. Emmett, knowing he would get into trouble for having it in the first place. In an article entitled, "The Ten Most Wanted," was a photograph of Jake Grundy. He had brutally murdered his wife and escaped capture after police found blood stains on his clothing. Father Emmett notified authorities, Jake was apprehended and he was sent to prison for life. Viola felt that Fintan's premonition had saved her life. The staff and volunteers were a close knit team at St. Labre and the last thing Father ever wanted to do was to hire someone who might harm a Cheyenne child or an employee. Misfits, thieves and killers sometimes used Indian reservations as hide outs and Jake had been one of them.

Despite setbacks that Father blamed on himself, he could go to Mary and she told him that everything that didn't turn out right wasn't his fault. He had always been plagued by insecurities but with Mary there to talk to about problems, Father Emmett continued to "keep the miracle alive" at St. Labre. He worked on as if nothing else mattered in the world. His letters to donors, full of zeal and enthusiasm, caught on. In March of 1959, he wrote to donors:

> St. Labre Mission is 75 years old. These have been 75
> long and, at times, very difficult years of hard work and
> sacrifice . . . Six short years ago, our financial condition was
> so acute that it seemed only a miracle could save the Mission
> School . . . That miracle happened in the form of many friends
> like you. We now employ 70 Indians on the reservation, which
> helps them to support their families. When the history of the
> present period of St. Labre is written, these acts of your
> charity will be recorded . . . in gold where it truly counts,
> namely in the book of life, which is kept in Heaven.[111]

The 1950s were almost over. The United States had spent 67 billion dollars on the Korean War and Elvis Presley gyrated himself to fame, but Father Emmett was more interested in whether the Cheyennes had pure drinking water, were cared for during frequent epidemics of cholera and whether they had enough food to eat and clothes to keep them from freezing to death.

Donors responded with funding for the construction of a new student cafeteria with a seating capacity of 350, auxiliary faculty dining rooms, main kitchen, home economics department, school laundry and a new convent. The structure was completed in 1959, costing $436,650. The building was entirely paid for before construction ended. Father planned the work by studying the needs and worked with architects to provide the best possible usefulness and traffic flow. He raised the necessary funds through his direct mail appeals and during construction he supervised the construction with daily inspections of the materials and workmanship.[112]

Father also knew that the girl's dorm was overcrowded and some of the little girls had to sleep in a corridor leading down to a lower elevation (at a 20-degree angle). He launched a major campaign for a new dorm. In the meantime, he turned the cow barn into a trade school, a shed into a woodworking shop, the old Sister's dining room into a kindergarten and he converted two of the Sister's bedrooms and their old chapel into an infirmary so that sick children could be segregated until they were well. The Home Economics room became the Arts and Crafts Department and the Sisters' community room became a high school classroom and sewing room.

At the same time, Father was working on another idea – a factory. He wanted to start an industry on the reservation and he figured out how he could attract industry to combat the high unemployment rate. Leo Dohn Sr., Father Marion's old classmate, manufactured molded plastic items such as Catholic rosaries and religious statues at his New York factory, Guild Arts and Crafts. Father called to ask Leo if he had any assembly line work for Cheyenne workers. Dohn had been sending some rosary bead assembly work to the Cheyennes on a small scale and Father wanted him to think about expanding the business. Within six months, Mr. Dohn and Father had negotiated with the tribe to build a factory across the road from the Mission. That was the beginning. Next came the assembly of Indian dolls that were afterwards sent as premiums to donors. It didn't take Dohn long to realize that this type of work pleased the Cheyennes and they wanted more responsibility. Within a year, 150 Cheyennes were employed at the factory and a shuttle bus was set up to run between Ashland and Lame Deer. Most of the employees had never had jobs in their lives.

Cheyenne workers made address books and wall plaques, Indian novelty items and finally, a line of good costume jewelry. The donor response was overwhelming. Many satisfied Cheyennes took home pay checks to buy their families new clothes and furniture, cars and household appliances; washing machines, refrigerators, toasters and televisions. The factory work gave men self esteem and for women it meant a respite from housework and taking care of children all day long. Many learned new office skills; typing, filing, inventory, reception, job interviewing and filling out job applications.

Attractive tribal member Bula Bray and other young Indian women got the chance to model jewelry for the company brochures. The jewelry end of the business meant highly skilled training. The factory also meant half again as much work for Fr. Emmett but it was worth it when he saw the Cheyennes paying their bills with money they had earned, fixing up their homes and driving late model cars.

One day Mary handed Father a letter that shocked him to his shoes. Attorneys for the United States Postal Service were claiming that St. Labre owed $75,000 in back postage! Father figured out right away that the mail bags from St. Labre often sat outside the post office in Ashland for some time before they were finally mailed. Left outside in bad weather, the mail was weighed in sacks that were often rain soaked. Father had to do something and do it fast. The postal service filed a lawsuit and Father Emmett counter-sued. Leo Dohn suggested hiring a professional lobbyist to arrange an appointment for Father Emmett to visit the Postmaster General of the United States, J. Edward Day. Father Emmett was about to jump headfirst into playing politics.

Mary suggested that Father try to stay calm and professional, but he was understandably nervous when he arrived at the Postmaster General's office in Washington, D.C. Basically shy around people he didn't know, he tried to rehearse what he was going to say. Waiting for the official to show up was the first hurdle. Father's mind jumped around like hot popcorn as he waited for what seemed like hours in the Postmaster's outer office. He sat down. He stood up. He walked around. He looked out the window. He sat down. Finally, a secretary ushered him into a large room lined with dark wooden book cases. She gestured to a brown leather chair opposite a massive walnut desk emblazoned with the impressive emblem of the United States Postmaster General. Father sat down and desperately tried not to fidget.

Postmaster Day hurried in and apologized for having been late. They had just begun to discuss Father Emmett's problem when the phone rang. The Postmaster took the call, which annoyed Father Emmett, but not for long. It was soon apparent that the Postmaster General was speaking to the President of the United States, John F. Kennedy. "Oh yes, Mr. President," he kept saying. "Well, at the moment I'm tied up with Fr. Emmett Hoffmann from Montana. Can I call you back on this?" A growl heard clear across the room startled Father Emmett and he plainly heard President Kennedy say: "Who the hell are you working for, Father Hoffmann or me?" Father was so embarrassed; he wanted to crawl out the door on his hands and knees. That wasn't necessary, however, because the Postmaster General took care of everything. President Kennedy was in the middle of the Cuban Missile Crisis, but he was a Catholic. Within a month, the charges were dropped against St. Labre and Ashland was upgraded to a First Class Post Office.

The seminary had not prepared Father Emmett for life in an isolated rural community. He had to learn from scratch how to raise funds, coordinate building programs, deal with conflicting political forces, both tribal and government, learn about banking, investments and lawyers. The one life skill that he certainly never thought he would need and one the seminary instructors had warned him against – loving a woman – would nearly cost him his life's work.

CHAPTER
11

Scandal

The 1950s and 1960s were pivotal years in the history of the Northern Cheyenne tribe. Highway 212, the first paved road, was completed in 1956, and it ran directly through the heart of the reservation. Indian horses had to be shod and the women were thrilled that they didn't have to endure the dust and grime in open wagons when they traveled between Lame Deer and Ashland. The new road made life easier for everybody, especially the tourists on their way to the Little Bighorn Battle site, the truckers and the used car salesman who lined up along the reservation borders to sell old, beat-up cars to unsuspecting Indians.

Prior to automobile travel, Cheyennes rode many miles in wagons and on horseback to Mass at St. Labre. The dirt roads made trips to the Mission an ordeal. Everyone started out for Church fresh-scrubbed. Mothers saw to it that their children wore their best clothes and their hair was washed and braided. The two or three hour trip to Church in a high wind left the family with grit in their teeth, braids unbraided, babies crying and clothes dingy with dust. Despite these inconveniences, Indian families came far distances to enjoy the mystical ritual of Catholicism.

A poor Cheyenne family; father, wife and their little baby lived in an old log cabin a mile from the Mission. One night, the wife, Mary Lou, lit a kerosene lamp and it exploded in her face. Seventy-five percent of the skin on her body burnt away. The only place that wasn't burned was the patch on her stomach where she had been holding her little baby. A baby blanket saved the infant's life, although she too, was burned.

Screaming in agony, the sounds of which nobody ever forgot, the courageous mother walked to the Mission to get Viola. As quickly as possible, Vi rushed the mother and baby to the hospital at Lame Deer. Mary Lou suffered hellish pain but then she grew silent. "Vi," she whispered, "Please hold my hands. I'm so cold, so cold." The woman died the next day, but her child lived.[113]

With no hospital burn unit nearby, the woman didn't have a chance. Fr. Emmett had known her practically all of her life. As usual, he brooded about the death for weeks. He kept asking himself what might happen if someone had a heart attack, or God forbid, a student got run over by a car? What if Cooky hemorrhaged and nothing Mary or Viola could do would stop the bleeding? Father began thinking about buying a small airplane.

An airplane wouldn't have helped Jane Talbert, Mary's friend, when Jane answered a knock on her door one evening. She opened the door to a tall Indian pointing a rifle in her face. "Go to the office! I want money!" he growled. When she didn't move, he cocked his gun. "I was so frightened," Jane later recalled, "that I couldn't find my key to the office. I had my little girl Jeanne with me and I was sure he was going to kill us."[114]

The angry man held the gun on Jane while she rummaged wildly through her purse and her desk drawers. Finally, she came up with the key. They walked to the administration office and the man made Jane open two safes using light from a cigarette lighter. He grabbed $900 and ran off into the night. Jane rushed to the friary, told Father Emmett and the man was quickly apprehended. While the criminal had been fumbling through the safe next to Fr. Emmett's desk during the hold-up, he had missed the cardboard box sitting on the floor nearby. It contained $75,000 in cash donations that were to be deposited the next day in a Miles City bank. This frightening incident again made Father Emmett realize that if he had an airplane, he could fly the donations to Miles City every day and not have to worry about robbers.

Another close call caused nearly as much concern. Jane was sitting in her office during the Christmas holidays when Fr. Emmett came running in. "Get rid of the crew!" he ordered. "I just got a call from the FBI in Wyoming. They got a tip that we're going to be robbed!" Jane quickly told everyone to go home. "The following week was scary," Jane recalled. "We didn't know when the hold-up might happen."

FBI agents swarmed the school and one day, Father had to offer Mass while an armed FBI agent sat on the roof watching the roads and the people who entered the Church.[115] The week came and went but the robbery never happened. Nevertheless, Father Emmett slept with a rifle next to his bed every night and a gun near his desk in the office.

First Mary Lou died because she didn't get to a hospital in time, then armed FBI agents surrounded St. Labre. It was too much. Fr. Emmett began plans to shovel a runway at St. Labre. With a airplane, he wouldn't have to spend a full day driving 150 miles back and forth on ice-covered roads to get to the bank in Miles City with large cash deposits. And more importantly, if an emergency occurred, he could fly an accident victim to a hospital in time to save a life. But first, he had to get a pilot's license and a used airplane.

Father thought getting his pilot's license was "going to be a breeze." His flight instructor in Billings was impressed, but he told Father that he'd have to study hard for the written exam. "Piece of cake," Father quipped. Sure enough, he flunked the test and had to take it again. Then, he leveled a gravel runway next to the river at St. Labre and bought a used, four-seat Cessna 175.[116]

Not long afterward, a 10 year-old girl was badly burned in a house fire and brother Marion Kramer flew her and Viola to the Texas Shriner's hospital. The girl recovered. Later, Fr. Carl Pulvermacher was fixing the boiler at St. Xavier Mission on the Crow Reservation when it blew up, severely burning his hands and face. Brother Marion flew Fr. Carl to St. Mary's Burn Center in Milwaukee and he lived. The airplane had become a life-saving necessity at St. Labre.[117]

The runway also came in handy when donors like Ed Daly flew in to take a look at St. Labre. Daly, President of World Airways and a multi-millionaire, dressed in a cowboy hat and western wear. The generous benefactor flew in from California and liked it so much he came several more times. He told Father that St. Labre was his "quiet place" and he liked to fly his employees in for important meetings in a Convair 580, painted several shades of green, with a large picture of a leprechaun on the side. Father set up a tipi or two and Daly brought in men from all over the world. Rumor had it that he negotiated the purchase of a steamship line while staying at St. Labre.

Father enjoyed visiting with Daly, who had made his fortune during the

Korean and Viet Nam conflicts by chartering troops to and from Hawaii for rest and relaxation. Later, he flew one of the last planes out of Vietnam loaded with Vietnamese women and children. After Daly died in 1984, Father was shocked and grateful that the successful entrepreneur had left St. Labre half a million dollars in his will.[118]

An important part of Father's work was visiting prospective donors and this took him away from St. Labre more often as time went by. Mr. Harry John, a trustee of the Miller Brewing Company Trust and the Director of the De Rance Company in Milwaukee, was one of St. Labre's largest donors. His generosity over many years helped build a new school, a new chapel, and many other projects. Mr. John's donations made a sizable difference in the quality of education at St. Labre.

Talented television personality Carroll O'Connor, famed star of "All in the family," was a generous St. Labre donor, as well as Walt Disney, actress/singer Pearl Bailey and other celebrities. Father's personal contact with donors across the nation helped make these donations possible.

In return, Father remembered donors in his daily prayers and Masses and encouraged them to visit the Mission to see how their gifts were being used. When they came to St. Labre, he took them on tours around the school and many lasting friendships developed. He read all personal donor letters and with Mary's help, he answered every one. Exhaustion was the only problem about traveling so much to raise donor awareness to his cause, plus it kept him away from Mary, Cooky, and the children at St. Labre.

Three years again went by and when it appeared that Father might be transferred to another mission, the Northern Cheyenne Tribal Council, represented by Chairman, John Woodenlegs, circulated Resolution No. 98, which stated that the tribe: ". . . recognizes, approves, adopts and concurs in the petition being circulated for the stay of Father Emmett Hoffmann for another term as superintendent of St. Labre Mission, Ashland, . . . in order that he can continue to carry out the work which he has so ably done."[119] The resolution was sent to Father's Provincial, who agreed with the tribe and allowed Fr. Emmett to continue his life's work at St. Labre.

In the early 1960s, John Woodenlegs, Albert Tallbull and Harry

Littlebird officiated at a public ceremony making Father Emmett an Honorary Chief of the Northern Cheyenne Tribe, the first of only two white men in history to have been so honored. (The second was Episcopal priest and author, Father Peter Powell) During the moving ceremony, Tallbull put his hands on Fr. Emmett's shoulders and gave him the name "Soaring Eagle."

From the beginning, John Woodenlegs had supported Father Emmett's work and vice-versa. Under the tribal leader's administration, the Northern Cheyenne tribe saw more advancement than at any other period since their move to the reservation in 1884. Like Chiefs Dull Knife and Little Wolf, Chairman Woodenleg's success stemmed from the fact that he truly loved his people. He communicated effectively with federal and state government officials and with non-Indians in the community. Father Emmett and John Woodenlegs shared a mutual respect and admiration for each other. Part of the reason for Resolution No. 98 was Woodenleg's belief that Father Emmett was accomplishing a great deal for the Cheyennes and he knew that if Father was transferred, he would lose a valuable ally.

The tribal petition didn't help Father Emmett when a personal scandal rocked St. Labre. For years Mary McGarvey had been Fr. Emmett's secretary. Together they had dreamt of ideas to make St. Labre the best Indian School in the nation. Mary and Father Emmett took in neglected children, beginning with Cooky, Doreen and Dolly. This was the true beginning of what would someday be known as the "Cheyenne Home," eventually five group homes for at-risk Indian children. Father had planned to enlarge the school with new dorms, a new church and numerous other projects close to his heart. His relationship with Mary had saved him from the loneliness that had plagued him. She was always supportive and listened to his troubles. Although they were intimate in many ways, the bittersweet decision not to become lovers was Mary's.

Throughout the years, Father and Mary had assumed that people thought they were just friends. Some residents at St. Labre were jealous of Fr. Emmett, but he had ignored petty jealousies. But when he received a summons to fly to Detroit for a meeting with the Father Provincial, he knew something was wrong. The Provincial, Gerard Hesse, was a man Father Emmett respected. The Provincial's dark, dingy office was in the old St. Bonaventure Monastery, a red brick building not far from downtown Detroit.

When Fr. Emmett arrived, the Provincial squinted at him through thick, horn-rimmed glasses. Father Hesse told Emmett to sit down. In no uncertain terms, he told Father that he had been getting complaints about his "questionable relationship" with the Marquette volunteer, Mary McGarvey. Stunned, Father Emmett tried to explain that people at the Mission didn't believe that. Maybe the complaints had come from a jealous Sister or Mother Superior, maybe a family that didn't like him. The Provincial and Father Emmett sat across from each other smoking and before they finished their conversation, the large ashtray spilled over with cigarettes. What Father Hesse had to say, he said in a gentle, yet firm voice.

Father Emmett had built a reputation as a compassionate Catholic priest, an image of hope and goodness to the Cheyenne people. The woman in question might be a fine person, perhaps he was in love with her, but the time had come when Father Emmett had to make perhaps the hardest decision of his life. "Emmett, you have made a vow to dedicate your life to the Cheyenne," Father Hesse reminded him. "If you want to stay at St. Labre and continue to help the Cheyenne people, the woman must go. Otherwise, you will be transferred."

Father controlled his emotions in the Provincial's office but once outside, he cried. On the commercial plane trip back to Billings and on the long, two-hour drive to St. Labre, he tried to think of a way to tell Mary. Several times he was so overcome with emotion that he had to pull over to the side of the road. Father arrived at St. Labre with a broken heart. He knew that he was about to lose the woman and the child that he loved more than life itself. He walked into Mary's apartment with legs that felt as heavy as lead. Years later, he told a friend: "I will never forget how beautiful she looked that night."[120]

Mary saw Father's face and she knew that something terrible had happened. He started to cry and they fell into each other's arms. "I don't know how to tell you," he sobbed. Finally, he composed himself and told Mary that someone had complained about them to the Provincial. He didn't know who it was, he probably would never know, but it didn't matter. The Provincial had given him a choice. If Mary didn't leave St. Labre, he would be transferred.

They held each other and cried for hours. He asked her if he should leave the priesthood. They expressed their love for each other and he told her she would make a good wife. He could not imagine life without Mary and Cooky. But Mary had already made up her mind. "She told me that if she caused me to fall, she'd feel guilty all of her life. If they married, she feared that someday I'd blame her for leaving the priesthood. She couldn't have lived with that," Father told a friend. Mary kept worrying about her family. They knew how much she loved St. Labre. How was she going to explain her sudden departure from the Mission? "'What's going to happen to us now?'" she kept saying.[121]

Two days later, Mary packed up her few belongings and got Cooky ready to go. She put on the blue suit, the one she was wearing the day she had first met Father. It was his favorite. Then she went to her friend Jane Talbert to say goodbye. Mary didn't say why she was leaving but everyone already guessed what had happened. Bad news got around fast at the Mission and those who cared about Father Emmett didn't want Mary and Cooky to leave.

Father Emmett loaded their suitcases into the trunk of his car and Cooky's sister Marcella and her brother Floyd came to hug her goodbye. "Where ya going?" Marcella asked her sister. Quickly, Mary ushered Cooky into the car, the door shut and they drove out of the Mission grounds towards Billings. Mary stared straight ahead.

"We didn't say a word all the way to Billings," Father remembered. "Cooky fell asleep and every time I looked over at Mary, she was chewing her lip. Tears were rolling down her face. I tried to be brave but I could barely drive."

Autumn gold brushed the cottonwoods along the Tongue River. From the car window, Mary saw Indian women picking ripe plums and she heard the meadowlarks singing their last happy songs in the grassy fields. Usually, Mary and Father talked, sang songs and laughed at each other when they went to Billings, but now there was a sad, uncomfortable silence as they drove highway 212 for the last time. When Mary had first come to St. Labre, the dirt road to Billings had been full of ruts and potholes. Now paved, cars went faster and life was easier, but Mary probably didn't notice the road. She was grieving in silence, worrying about her future and what Fr. Emmett would do after she left. Having left St. Labre so quickly made her seem guilty of unspeakable acts, and she knew her departure would be the talk of the Mission. Was she running away, hiding her shame? Mary's dream had ended in silent heartbreak, but even if there was shame and no hope for a future in Montana near the man she adored, at least she had Cooky.

Father Emmett boarded the airplane with them in Billings and made sure they were buckled into their seats. Cooky didn't understand the move. To her, it was just another trip to see Grandma McGarvey. Father walked to the pilot's door at the front of the plane, then turned to look back at them one last time. Cooky waved and Mary's hand went up to her lips but she didn't wave. Their eyes locked for a minute. They had told each other that they were sacrificing their lives for God. It was His will. Then Father climbed down the stairs and walked back to the gate. He waited, crying, until the plane taxied to the runway and took off. He saw Cooky waving goodbye. "I never felt so alone," he said later.[122] On the way out of town, Father stopped and picked up a bottle of scotch.

Father Emmett never found out who had complained about Mary. Someone told him later that Sister Eustella had been smoldering over his relationship with Mary for some time. When she heard that Mary had left the Mission, she told another Sister: "Now he is damned to hell!"[123]

A week later, Father Emmett felt like he was already there. An old man had died in the Busby reservation community and Father was asked to conduct the funeral service. The Cheyennes had definite cultural beliefs about handling the dead. They didn't believe in embalming and were horrified that someone would touch their deceased relatives, let alone embalm them. The funeral was held at Christ the King Church and the night before the service, the family had the Rosary and then left the body of the deceased in the Church.

The next morning, Fr. Emmett arrived early to prepare. Apparently, the man had been dead several days before they found him because when Father opened the door, the smell of decomposing flesh made him gag. He tried to burn incense to kill the odor. The relatives, even the pallbearers, wouldn't come into the Church. The body secretions were seeping out of the clothes into the pine box. Father almost vomited, held his nose and offered a quick Mass. It was one of the most memorable services of his career. A year later he could still detect the odor. Every Sunday he smelled it. The incident was made all the more terrible because Father had known the man.

The 1960s marked the end of an era for Father Emmett and for the tribe. The last Northern Cheyenne warrior to have fought in the Battle of the little Bighorn died in 1957. William Yellow Robe, Is-sajahesha, had been thirteen years-old when Custer and the 7th Cavalry made their famous attack on the Indian camps along the Bighorn River. After the fight, Yellow Robe surrendered to General Nelson A. Miles at Ft. Keogh, Montana and became a U.S. Army Scout. When he died, newspapers reported that, "Hospital attendants bore witness to the fact that Yellow Robe's body was marked with numerous scars from the Sun Dance rituals of years gone by."[124] The old chief had converted to the Catholic faith in 1944 and rarely missed Mass on Sunday. Most of the priests attended the funeral and his entire tribe gathered to honor him. During his wake, people remembered how he always chewed Wrigley's Spearmint Gum and kept a good quantity in his shirt pocket for the kids, yet he died with all his teeth intact.[125]

In the 1960s, epidemics of typhoid fever struck the reservation camps and children began to die. Father Emmett and Viola moved quickly to bring the children to safety at the school. Medical personnel worked frantically to immunize them in order to keep the fever from spreading.[126] When an employee or parishioner needed surgery, Father flew the person to the hospital. In one of his appeals he wrote, "The good God who takes care of the lilies of the field and the birds of the air will not forsake the most needy of His children."

But Father's spirit would never be the same. After Mary and Cooky left St. Labre, he threw himself into his work as never before, pushing his feelings into a locked room somewhere in the back of his very active mind. At least that's what he thought he could do. After Mary left, his weight shot up to 235 pounds. He was overeating, smoking four to five packs of Camels a day and drinking at night. He told himself that having a drink was the only way he could get to sleep.

In 1962, a 10 month-old Cheyenne baby died from malnutrition, bronchial pneumonia and dehydration on the Northern Cheyenne Reservation. The resulting publicity sparked a reply from President John F. Kennedy: "Housing conditions on reservations are a national shame."[127] The media publicity stung tribal leaders who had been working for years to elevate the standard of living on the reservation. Tribal Chairman, John Woodenlegs, told reporters that many new projects were coming to the Indians of the west.

Father Emmett, John Woodenlegs and New York donor Leo Dohn had achieved something that would have been unthinkable just ten years before. The Cheyenne Tribe built the new Guild Arts and Craft Factory with 5,000 square feet of working space and it was a financial success from the start. The plant manager, John Seidl, told newspaper reporters, "There's no doubt in the world about (Cheyennes) being good workers. They're producing way beyond expectations." The owner of an agency store in Lame Deer noticed the impact of the factory on reservation economics: "The (factory) is raising the standard of living of the Indians," he said. "The Indians are clearing up old bills, and they are beginning to buy substantial items like appliances . . . things many of them never had before. Business has just generally improved."[128] John Woodenlegs was equally enthusiastic. "Our people are doing real well in the factory and I am very happy."[129]

The factory had its enemies, however, one man in particular who had never seen the reservation or met an Indian in his life. In the New York plant, Mr. Dohn had to fire an incompetent individual who swore to get even. The man called the IRS and made a false accusation against Mr. Dohn and against the new Guild Arts and Crafts factory on the Northern Cheyenne Reservation. One day several men came to St. Labre looking for Fr. Emmett. They said they were IRS investigators and they wanted to see all of the factory paperwork since its beginning on the reservation. "Take anything you want," Father told the well dressed men. "I'll show you where all the paperwork is stored." The attic in the old barn, built in the 1930s, served as the school records storehouse. Father took the men up the wooden stairs and switched on the light. Suddenly, hundreds of bats went berserk, flying all around the rafters and swooping low past the stunned visitors. "I guess you'll want to get to work," Father told the men." Then he left in a hurry. He hated bats.

Bat droppings covered the boxes, papers, and old filing cabinets in the attic. Mice had burrowed long tunnels into files, lovely nests for their babies. Once in awhile a mother skunk fought for turf and left her mark. The IRS men looked at each other in disbelief. They turned around, sprinted down the stairs and dropped their investigation.

"We should ask ourselves if we are being fair in asking the
Indian to stop being "himself" and to become like us. We are
actually asking him to go through a type of self-annihilation."

Father Emmett, 1965

CHAPTER
12

"The Candy Man"

N ine months after Mary and Cooky left St. Labre, Father Emmett
broke down and asked Mary to come back to Montana. It wasn't
an easy decision. He had begun work on a new dormitory, St. Rose of
Lima Hall, a gym and a recreation center with 4 bowling lanes. He was
already making plans for a new office building with mail rooms and a
bookkeeping department. Stress had taken its toll on him. Late at night
he tried to figure out bookkeeping problems. During the day he
supervised new building construction and ministered to reservation
communities. In addition, he directed all fund raising duties at St.
Labre. He was exhausted and he missed Mary's efficient skills and her
ideas, especially her gentle encouragement and her unconditional love.

Realizing that scandal would upset Mary if she moved back to St.
Labre, Father rented a modest home for Mary and Cooky in Billings.
He drove up on weekdays to see them and to bring Mary the work he
wanted her to do, which justified her being there. But this time, to
make matters more complicated, Mary's brother Hughie decided to
move to Ashland and work at the Mission. A tall, World War II Veteran,
Hughie was a severe alcoholic and a brute when he drank, but Mary
was too ashamed to confide that information to Father Emmett. During
the previous year in New Jersey, Cooky had watched in horror as
Hughie had beaten up her grandmother when she refused to give him
money to drink. Mary and Cooky were afraid of him but he lived in
Ashland and they rarely saw him.[130]

Meanwhile, the Civil Rights movement in Selma, Alabama began with
boycotts, sit-ins and protest marches. The crusade of non-violence

conducted under the leadership of Dr. Martin Luther King made a
sleeping nation wake up and take notice. Some non-profit organizations
that helped the poor were alarmed at the demonstrations, especially
when they feared their programs would experience a backlash of
opposition resulting from the movement.

But the Civil Rights Movement helped St. Labre. The southern Civil
Rights marches brought attention to the plight of the poor and
donations to St. Labre increased. Urban Indians watched African
Americans attempt to bring change through non-violent means, but
after Dr. King was assassinated, younger Indian men in the cities
thought the time had come for Red Power. The Red Power Movement
in the 1960s attracted Lakota activists and future American Indian
Movement (AIM) leaders. Native Americans, among them many Viet
Nam veterans, finally stood up and demanded better treatment from
non-Indians.[131]

During this time of national unrest, Jane Talbert remembered that when
Father was in a hurry, which was nearly all the time, he couldn't stand
to see anyone else slow down. "Get back to work and cut out the
bullshit Jane!" he growled in a joking voice. People noticed that he had
gained a lot of weight and wasn't taking care of himself. Jane knew that
he was drinking too much because at staff parties, he "went overboard."
At one party, Father was dancing with Jane (he loved to dance) when
suddenly he twirled her around and her wig fell off on the floor. Father
picked it up and put it on her head backwards laughing, "You look
better now!" Jane had to admit that he was always the life of the
party.[132] But his puffy eyes and face betrayed the exhaustion.

The winter of 1963 turned cold and icy with snow packed roads and
treacherous black ice waiting on the sheltered curves between Ashland
and Billings. With Mary in Billings, Father Emmett thought he could
spend an evening or two every week relaxing with her, but he soon
learned it wouldn't be that simple. His blood pressure was too high and
fatigue wore him down. Driving to and from Billings on dangerous
roads soon got tiresome. When he came to Billings, they went shopping
or out to eat, but Father noticed Mary was a little more demanding at
times. Cooky, nearly ten years-old, loved having the three of them
together again. Mary's friend Jane Talbert came to see her in Billings
but Mary and Cookie did not visit St. Labre.

Cooky was uncomfortable at St. Labre but it had nothing to do with the

Cheyennes or rumors of scandal. It had to do with brother Berthold Ascher, then 74 years-old. Brother Berthold had a severe heart attack and was taken to the hospital. To the children, the gaunt Capuchin brother with the pointed white goatee and bad teeth was known as "Brother Candy" or "the Candy Man," because he always had candy in his pocket for the children. The boys all liked brother Berthold and they followed him around like ducklings. When Mary and Cooky had first lived at the Mission, she and the other little girls followed him around as well. When Cooky was 5-years-old, she was allowed to accompany the Candy Man around the Mission at night while he turned off all the lights. One evening, Cooky found out that brother Berthold had more to give her than just candy:

> He sat down and pulled me onto his lap. "Do you want a piece of candy?" he asked me. "Yes!" I said. "Guess which pocket it's in?" he said. I stuck my hand down into his pocket to get it. I went for the candy and he kissed me. I could feel his scratchy beard. While I was eating the candy, he started touching my crotch and buttocks. I knew something was wrong so I jumped off his lap and ran. He had lured me with his "candy."[133]

Brother Berthold's behavior mimicked that of a pedophile, a man who craves sexual contact with young children. Viola, Fintan and everyone at the Mission seemed to love the old man and wouldn't have believed he was capable of child molestation. Father Emmett, however, once had an uneasy feeling about brother Berthold when he saw him pull up his great, brown mantle (cape) and encircle a child within it. Father watched and became concerned when the child did not emerge from the cape. Maybe it's a game, Father told himself. He walked toward the brother and the child ran off.[134]

Brother Berthold died after having been the "Candy Man" to hundreds of Indian children at St. Labre. At his funeral, one of the priests filled his pockets with candy. Before the services began, two boys rifled the pockets for the sweets. After gaining their trust, how many little Indian girls got more candy than they had bargained for? Cooky had been lucky that brother Berthold hadn't caught her. An isolated Indian school was the perfect location for a sexual predator. The people were poor, didn't speak English well and many of the families were headed by women. They were grateful when a brother or priest took notice of their children and taught them how much Jesus loved little children. The mothers had no qualms about brother Berthold taking such an active interest in their innocent little children.

Cooky never told her adopted mother about brother Berthold's sexual probings. She had instinctively felt uncomfortable and escaped his nasty grasp, but she didn't understand until many years later how close she had come to being sexually molested by the "Candy Man."[135]

Ashland residents who knew that Cooky and her mother lived in Billings were saying that Father Emmett was hiding Mary and rushing off to see her whenever he could get away. It was only a matter of time until Mary's brother, Hughie McGarvey, heard the rumors as well. He had been sober for some time, but after he heard the stories, Hughie drove to Billings and on the way, he stopped at a bar. Happy for her brother's recent sobriety, Mary had invited him to dinner. But when he didn't show up, she feared the worst.

Cooky noticed her mother's growing agitation and saw it quickly turn to fear once Uncle Hughie arrived drunk and belligerent. An argument started and Hughie turned mean: "You're nothing but a damned whore!" he yelled at Mary. She tried to get away from him but it was too late. "He hit and punched her so hard, she fell against the wall," Cooky remembered. "There were blood marks where she slid down." Cooky ran out the door to the neighbor's house for help. Once before she had locked herself in the bathroom when Uncle Hughie had beaten up her grandmother. This time she would do something! Cooky stood on the neighbor's porch begging, "Please, please come and help my mother!"[136] The neighbor quickly rushed over and threatened to call the police. Hughie staggered off into the night, still yelling, "You filthy slut!"

Father Emmett was away on a business trip and when he returned, Mary didn't tell him about the beating. He noticed that she seemed strange and distant and when he asked her about it, Mary told him she wanted to take Cooky back to New Jersey. Later, Father wrote a letter of recommendation for her saying: "(Mary's) daughter, Carol Ann, is now 10 years-old and it is because of the child that they returned to Miss McGarvey's home in Bayonne, New Jersey . . . The child's health, which has not been up to par, is a major factor for this move."[137] Hughie lost his job at St. Labre and followed Mary back to New Jersey. It is unlikely that Mary ever admitted to her mother that she had been beaten and Hughie may have held the secret over Mary's head from then on. Soon after their return to the east, Mary became seriously depressed and sick.

At St. Labre, Father Emmett tried not to think about what had happened to his relationship with Mary. He didn't understand her coldness toward him but he knew their relationship was over. The friendship would never end but the intense love they had felt for each other had changed. The irony of the situation was that Cooky was exposed to as much, if not more alcoholism and violence living with her adopted mother's family in New Jersey than she might ever have endured living with her biological family in Ashland. Despite the fact that Mary provided for Cooky's basic needs, the girl was raised in a fearful and dysfunctional atmosphere in non-Indian society.

The next three years flew by in a whirlwind of activity at St. Labre, but Fr. Emmett's letters to Mary and Cooky show that he wanted Mary to write more often. Perhaps because of her depression, Mary had stopped writing. In September 1963, Father wrote to Cooky: "I have been waiting for a letter from your mother, but I haven't had one for a long time. I do hope that everything is all right. I miss you and your mother very much, but I know that it is better for you to be back in New Jersey . . . don't forget to pray for me. I pray for you and your mother always. Love, Fr. Emmett."[138]

In June 1964, he wrote in an appeal: "As I write this letter, the quiet of St. Labre envelopes me. In fact, I must admit that I am a little lonely."[139] In September he wrote to Cooky and ended his letter with "Loads of love."[140] He still couldn't understand why Mary wasn't writing.

In 1965, Bishop William J. Condon, D.D. added the missionary work among the Crow Indians to the Capuchins. The Bishop announced his decision after dinner at his residence in Great Falls and Father Emmett was astounded. He went home distressed and wrote: "a new and heavy burden has been placed upon me . . ."[141] The Crow Reservation covered many thousands of miles of mountains and grassy hills, with a population of over four thousand people. Two schools, four churches and chapels and the combined missionary activity among the Crow was a huge fund raising endeavor. For eleven years Fr. Emmett's main focus had been on the Northern Cheyennes, a people far poorer than the land wealthy Crow. The Crow Mission churches were old and had to be rebuilt and this job was put into Fr. Emmett's hands.

The Crow had long associated with the white man and made friends easily among them. Great horsemen and formidable enemies with the Lakota and Cheyennes, the Crow eventually chose to ally themselves with the U. S. Government. For their work as scouts and as staunch government allies, they received a much larger reservation than the Cheyennes, who had taken a leading role in Custer's demise at the Battle of the Little Bighorn. The Cheyennes didn't like the fact that the Crow were "awarded" such a large reservation right next to the small Cheyenne Reservation. Whenever they got the chance, school children from both tribes pecked at each other like ducks on a bug. Putting Cheyenne and Crow youngsters together in classrooms and dorms was a daunting feat. The Capuchin Fathers and the School Sisters of St. Francis were determined to make it work and they did, but not without many bloody altercations.

Father Emmett had to expand his fund raising efforts twice as hard in order to pay for Xavier Mission and St. Charles Mission on the Crow Reservation. Because of this, he was sensitive to every social or political movement that might negatively affect his fund raising efforts. He looked upon the War On Poverty with some concern. Overnight, poverty programs on the reservation sprouted up and directors were hired at five times more money than the average Cheyenne was making. The jobs lasted a year or two and then evaporated. After making $25,000 a year, why would a man or woman be satisfied working at the Guild Arts and Crafts factory, although they were always paid above minimum wage? Several government programs lasted and proved beneficial; especially the Head Start Program, Job Corps, HUD and Native Action, while others came in with a rush and quickly melted away, leaving people frustrated and angry, with bills they couldn't pay.

Father's fears about the War On Poverty were not entirely unfounded but it didn't negatively affect St. Labre as he had feared. At the same time, he continued to have misgivings about government programs: "The War on Poverty sends the Indian on a mysterious search to find himself in a new cultural environment," he said. "We should ask ourselves if we are being fair in asking the Indian to stop being "himself" and to become like us. We are actually asking him to go through a type of self-annihilation . . ."[142]

By March of 1965, Fr. Emmett was so exhausted he could barely work, but he didn't tell anyone except Mary and his doctor. Mary had started writing to him again, telling him that she, too, had been sick. Father wrote a memorable letter to Mary and Cooky: "I love you very much. It is you and your mother who have given me the courage to keep on working, even when things are difficult."[143] In September he wrote to Mary:

> I wish I knew what is wrong with me. I get so tired that I can't move. I lost 30 pounds but I still look fat . . . Dr. Lemire wants me to take a good rest but that seems to be impossible. This afternoon I drove up in the hills to grandpa's place (Arthur Woodenthigh's log cabin) It really made me sad, and yet I had so many happy memories of us all being together. Everything is the way he left it. I could almost see him sitting there on his chair, holding Cooky on his lap. I sat around for an hour and sort of visited with him and with you again . . .[144]

The Federal Aviation Agency revoked Father Emmett's pilot's license when he failed his physical. His blood pressure was too high. He felt terrible about it and wrote to Mary:

> . . . Say a prayer for me Mary. I am worn out and tired. How much longer I will be able to go on I don't know. There are so many things I want to do for the Cheyenne before I pass away – maybe they won't all be possible. I know you have plenty of worries of your own and I shouldn't burden you with mine, but I don't have anyone else to talk to. It is good to tell you anyway.[145]

He didn't mention in writing what he meant by "you have plenty of worries of your own . . ." Father tried to keep up a show of vigor, but Leo Dohn Sr. wasn't fooled. Leo saw that if Father didn't get away from the worries at St. Labre, he might have a complete physical breakdown. After conferring with doctors, Mr. Dohn invited Father Emmett on an all-expense paid trip to Italy and then on to France, Germany and Portugal. Dr. Lemire agreed with Mr. Dohn and this time Father asked his superiors in Detroit for permission to go and the request was granted.

Father Emmett flew to New York and Leo took one look at him and said, "Your suit looks like hell. You're not going to the Vatican in that!"[146] Louie Congro and Mr. Dohn took Father Emmett to their expensive Italian tailor on 5th Avenue and after two fittings; a new black suit was finished in less than 3 days. It cost more money than all of the suits that Father had ever owned combined. But the tailor turned out to have a heart of gold. He told Mr. Dohn that his cousin worked at the Vatican and he would tell him when and where the Dohns were staying in Rome. Perhaps they could get together. Dohn winked at Fr. Emmett. They both thought the tailor was just being kind.

They sailed from New York to Naples on the cruise ship Michelangelo and Father was in a first-class room on the top deck. Half the time he didn't know what he was eating from the fancy array of food spread out on the tables in the dining room. They left the cruise ship in Naples and drove to Rome. Mr. Dohn was pleasantly surprised when the tailor's cousin called. He was none other than the influential Monsignor Donato de Bonis from the Vatican Bank. The Monsignor arranged for the Dohns to have a private audience with Pope Paul VI. That afternoon, Monsignor came to pick them up in his official Vatican car with Papal flags fluttering from the front fenders. At St. Peters Cathedral, Father Emmett sat in the Bishop's box with Montana's Bishop William Condon, about 20 feet from the Pope. "I was amazed by him," Father said later. "He seemed to glide across the floor." The Dohns went off to another room for a private audience with the Pope, but Father Emmett wasn't invited. He wrote to Mary that the Dohns: ". . . got to kiss the Pope's ring." From then on, Dohn sent a sizable yearly check to the Monsignor's orphanage in Rome.[147]

Leo had arranged for a car and a driver to take them to Assisi the next day, but he and his wife got sick from something they had eaten. Leo told Father Emmett to go on the tour by himself. Father was astounded when the driver arrived in a Limousine. He felt strange and uneasy about it so he sat next to the driver. Here he was a Capuchin beggar priest going to the tomb of St. Francis in a brand new Cadillac! One of the highlights of the day came when he stopped for lunch. A wedding reception in full swing saw a Limo chauffer open the car door for a young American priest. The groom at once invited Father Emmett to the wedding feast and Father was literally dragged into the restaurant with much toasting and singing.

Father enjoyed the tour but soon he was itching to get back to St. Labre. He sent Mary a bottle of perfume, a cameo broach and two rosaries blessed by the Pope. The group flew home to New York and from there Father returned to Montana. Instead of getting the rest he needed, he went straight to work in order to lose himself and his troubles. Hard work rested his mind but wore out his body. He had no idea that trouble was awaiting him.

In the midst of the War On Poverty, a newspaper reporter from the

Billings Gazette had interviewed Tribal Chairman, John Woodenlegs, about a Cheyenne baby who had died of malnutrition in Lame Deer. The reporter knew he had a story when Woodenlegs got defensive about poverty on the reservation, saying, and rightly so, that conditions had improved since he had been elected chairman of the tribe. Somehow, it came up in their conversation that Fr. Emmett Hoffmann was calling the Cheyennes the "Race of Sorrows" and Woodenlegs immediately countered with: "I don't want my people called the Race of Sorrows any longer. We are the Morning Star people."[148]

After antagonizing Chairman Woodenlegs, the reporter then called on Father Emmett. Stung by Woodenleg's statement, which the reporter was only too willing to repeat, Father told the reporter about the poverty he saw every day. He explained that General Nelson Miles had coined the phrase "Race of Sorrows" to characterize the Cheyennes in the 1880s and that although reservation conditions were improving, poverty still held them down. The reporter then printed what Father Emmett had said, in such a way that Woodenlegs was insulted and called for a Congressional investigation. Senator Mike Mansfield got involved and gave a speech that was published in the Congressional Record.[149]

The reporter had gotten his sensational story but the trouble he started greatly eroded the long friendship between John Woodenlegs and Father Emmett. The journalist evidently wanted to stir up a controversy that would sell newspapers. Father Emmett, now alarmed that publicity would decrease donor response, began a letter writing campaign to save St. Labre Indian School and the Guild Arts and Crafts factory. As he feared, the newspaper articles were blown out of proportion. The rift between the two powerful men widened. When donations slacked off, Father had to temporarily lay off workers at the Guild Arts and Crafts Factory.

Father Emmett wrote a blistering ten-page letter to Senator Mike Mansfield documenting the poverty he saw and countering accusations against him: "Frankly Senator, I was amazed that a respected leader of acknowledged integrity has been willing to accept untrue statements concerning St. Labre Indian School, without any attempt at personal verification . . ."[150] He also sent letters to state and national elected officials including Senator Stewart Udall, Lee Metcalf, the Secretary of the Interior, the Commissioner of Indian Affairs Robert Bennett, and Governor Tim Babcock.

At that point, Senator Mansfield realized his error in not checking the newspaper reporter's facts and he intervened to try to stop the antagonism between Chairman Woodenlegs and Father Emmett. The senator wrote to both parties and made his letter public in a press conference. He cautioned both Woodenlegs and Hoffmann by name and asked them to settle their differences. "It is my hope that all interests will work together."[151] He praised both men for all they had done for the Cheyenne people. Shortly thereafter, Father Emmett and Chairman Woodenlegs sat down together and discussed their differences peacefully, after which they issued a joint statement: "Differences can be negotiated and the matter is in the process of being solved. Further publicity . . . would serve no real useful purpose."[152] The battles were over but nobody had won the war. The misunderstanding sold a lot of newspapers.

When the BIA stated in the media that the Cheyennes lived in adequate housing, Father Emmett took photographs of the old log cabins and shacks they lived in. He sent the photographs and short interviews to the Bureau of Indian Affairs in Washington, DC. Sometime later in the 1960s, a per capita claim judgment went to each member of the tribe, with the stipulation that the money should be used for housing. Some people bought mobile homes but others paid contractors to build the homes they had always wanted.[153]

Father checked the quality of the home construction and realized that the reservation homes had been built with poor building materials. After tribal members moved into their new homes, they couldn't pay the electric and propane heating bills. Every winter they came in droves to the Mission for help. Cracks appeared in walls only a few months old and although modern plumbing was installed, no water flowed through the pipes because many sewer lines had been left unconnected. Wide gaps opened under windows and the people couldn't keep their houses warm or the floors clean without water. When a family couldn't pay their bills, especially during the winter, it wasn't too difficult to figure out what to do about it. Some moved back into their old log cabins or carried their wood burning stove to the new house, made a hole in the wall, stuck the pipe through the hole and kept warm in one room all winter.

Meanwhile, Father was working on plans with HUD to build 40, two and three-bedroom low-income houses for factory workers and their families, besides the 12 mobile homes he had already provided. He watched every phase of the construction to make sure the homes were well built. Nearly forty years later the homes are still a Godsend to the employees and the families with children attending St. Labre Indian School.[154]

In 1966, at the annual Northern Cheyenne Pow Wow, Leo Dohn Sr. was adopted into the tribe. He was presented with an eagle feather headdress and Pendleton blanket. Then Harry Littlebird and Charles Sitting Man Jr. danced beside him around the arbor. Hundreds of Cheyenne people shook Dohn's hand and many realized that without Mr. Dohn's brilliant fund raising skills, St. Labre might have ceased to exist. But Dohn credited Father Emmett with the success of St Labre. He often said: "If Father Emmett hadn't become a priest, he would have made a great President."[155]

"When a true genius appears in this world, you may know him
by this sign, that the dunces are in confederacy against him."

Johathan Swift

CHAPTER
13

Thoughts of Suicide

N eil Armstrong and his Apollo 11 crew landed on the moon on
July 20, 1969, in an area called, "the Sea of Tranquility."[156]
Millions of Americans were thrilled with the moon landing but there
was no sea of tranquility back on earth. The Vietnam War raged on,
domestic turmoil disrupted life in the United States and Richard Nixon
was elected the nation's 37th President.[157]

While the new political administration settled in, dreams were coming
true at St. Labre Indian School. Forty Indian families moved into new
homes at Cheyenne Village, located near St. Labre. The housing project
was sponsored by St. Labre under the HUD Rent Subsidy Program. It
enabled low-income families with children attending St. Labre or adults
working in the Guild Arts and Crafts factory to have a new home. One
week's salary went toward the rent. Some had been living in shacks
during the coldest winters and never thought they would ever have a
real home, let alone a new one.

Father accompanied one of the families when they moved into a three
bedroom house in what came to be known as "Cheyenne Village." The
mother, father and three children stood in front of the house and said a
blessing prayer. There wasn't a dry eye. Mother opened the front door
and peeked inside. She walked across the carpeting, turned back and
made everybody take off their shoes, even Father Emmett. Then she
saw the kitchen and stood in front of the new refrigerator and the stove,
running her fingers gingerly over the knobs. She turned on the water in
the sink and put her hand under warm, running water. She turned and
looked at Father with a big, smile. "Ese peve'!" (Really good!) she said.

The family moved in the only furniture they had; a table and two chairs, three trunks, suitcases and three mattresses with no bed frames.

Over the next couple of months, they bought furniture and a television set with the earnings from their jobs at the factory. Many people had talked about providing jobs for the Cheyennes but it had always been Father's philosophy to stop talking and start doing. Industry and jobs had improved the standard of living on the Northern Cheyenne Reservation. The building plan was such a success; Fr. Emmett began work on a second housing project for teachers and staff at St. Labre.

The late 1950s and early 60s was the era of Pope John XXIII, one of the most controversial popes in history, yet one of its most courageous. He surprised the world by calling a worldwide church council to update Roman Catholic religious life and doctrine. The Second Vatican Council or Vatican II, (1962-1965) has been called the most important event in the Catholic Church since the Protestant Reformation. Pope John died during the council and his successor, Pope Paul VI, continued the work. He and the council approved 16 documents that would change the Catholic Church forever.[158]

Nobody could have predicted the struggles that would take place at St. Labre after Vatican II. One of the difficulties concerned the wide schism between the older priests and the newer, younger priests. Father Emmett and Father Patrick Berther were Pre-Vatican priests, born before and during the 1920s. In examining the results of Vatican II, and the way priests responded to the new decrees, one religious scholar set older priests apart from the younger, saying that older clerics grew up, lived and worked "in . . . Catholic neighborhoods, schools, hospitals, newspapers and social groups . . . (They) grew up with Latin Masses, novenas, Benedictions, priests facing the altar (not the people) and Gregorian chant. They learned to pray, pay and obey."[159]

Priests born in the 1930s and 1940s and ordained in the 1960s, the Vatican II baby-boomers, or "progressives" experienced the "political tranquility of the Eisenhower years, followed by a sudden switch to the turmoil associated with the social movements of the 1960s." Under the auspices of Vatican II, the Catholic Church did a revolutionary, 180-degree turn. Such changes included the switch from Latin Masses to English Masses with the priest facing the people. Out came guitars and sometimes folk tunes replaced organs and a choir.[160]

Religious scholar James D. Davidson called the younger Vatican II
generation of priests ". . . a bit more schizophrenic than the others . . ."[161]
because much of what they had been taught in their younger years was
turned upside down by the time they were ordained. From 1966
to 1976, at least 20 younger, progressive priests and brothers were
assigned to St. Labre. Father Emmett, a pre-Vatican II priest, held the
reins at the Mission. The younger priests had prayed for change and
now that it came, they rejoiced and wanted more. In other parts of the
country, priests joined the Civil Rights Movement.

The struggle to modernize the Church included rules and regulations
that had been followed since the 1500s. The Northern Cheyenne and
Crow people were simply bystanders in this bewildering confusion of
changes within the Church. They had grown accustomed to and loved
the old, mystical rituals of the Church, as well as those of their native
religions.[162] They didn't understand why they were now told to do things
that had previously been called "sins." If they sinned, they would go to
hell. To sin was absolutely the worst thing they could do, according to
the Church. One of the sins they had been taught in school included
eating meat on Friday. Now they were told that it was up to them
whether or not they ate meat on Friday. Either way, they were now
assured, they would not go to hell. Over the years, "going to hell" was a
threat ingrained in them by the Sisters and the priests who had stressed
"damnation" as the final threat. Father Emmett had always thought that
the Friday meat taboo was foolish. Unless they could catch fish in the
frozen Tongue River in the middle of winter, how could they afford to
import fish and from where?

No longer would priests adhere to the doctrine that the Catholic Church
was the only true religion. The new Vatican II decrees stated: "The
church rejects nothing that is true and holy in (other) religions. She
regards with reverence those ways of action and of life, those precepts
and teachings, which though differing in many aspects from the ones
she holds and sets forth, nonetheless often reflect a ray of that truth
which enlightens all men." The new rules repudiated, ". . . any
discrimination or harassment . . . because of their race, color, condition
in life, or religions . . ."[163]

Freedom of individual conscience was one of the most important
affirmations of Vatican II and it gave the younger priests the most hope.
When the priests spoke English during Mass, the Cheyennes were
stunned. The children had already been told by the Sisters that changes

were coming, but the elders were taken off guard. They watched the priests in disbelief.

The Cheyennes knew when priests were unsure of themselves. A quiet scandal ensued among the elder tribal members who had loved the mysteries of the Latin Mass, including a priest holding up the shiny, gold Monstrance (large cross with the Eucharist at the center) in front of the procession. Bisco Spotted Wolf remembered: "I felt something special when they held it up. It glittered in the sun coming through the windows. When I saw that, it was like a blessing from "Maheo" (God). The elders especially loved the blessing of Sister Friedaburga's home-made bread and butter passed out to parishioners after Mass on Sundays. When it was announced and interpreted that this too, would stop, the Cheyennes shook their heads and asked each other: "Why have the priests changed their religion?" Some became cynical and stopped going to Church on a regular basis. Others merely shook their heads and watched the priests playing guitars and wearing modern vestments. After many years of close observation, they already knew that white people were strange. Why should priests be any different?

Father had been saving for a new church and friary for years and by 1969, he nearly had enough money to break ground.[164] But the people had grown fond of their old chapel at St. Labre, although it was always so crowded that many had to stand up during Mass. They loved the musty smell of the old hymnals, the wooden beams and the old-fashioned Crucifix. There was something familiar and lovely about the place where they had been baptized, confirmed and married.[165] But the old chapel sat less than 100 people, while the new church was designed to seat 300. More importantly, the old chapel needed a complete renovation and was on the verge of being condemned.

The new Church was large in comparison and the design was modern, yet it incorporated many Cheyenne religious themes. Completed in 1971, St. Labre Church remains today one of the most impressive Catholic churches in America. Inside, Christ is represented on the processional cross as a Cheyenne Dog Soldier. In historic times, the Dog Soldiers, a military society chosen as protectors of the their people, went into battle wearing the dog rope, a strip of buffalo hide looped over the right shoulder and left arm. A red painted picket-pin was tied to the end of the rope. In battle, the courageous Dog Soldier stuck his pin into the ground and pledged not to retreat until the women and children were safe. He was prepared to fight unto death to save his people. The ultimate Dog Soldier – Jesus Christ – had sacrificed Himself for His people.

The new Church, built in the form of a tipi or Medicine Lodge was made of local Montana dolomite, rich in earthen colors. The great wooden beam that ran through the ceiling skyward, rested in the smoke hole of the tipi. The shorter beam, visible from the outside of the church, formed the Cross. On either side of the Cross beam, glittering stained glass windows displayed the seasonal colors of the year. Many other Cheyenne symbols graced the church, including petroglyphs of the Stations of the Cross incised in rock by student artists. Father Emmett worked closely with architect Grant Crossman and artist Don Shephard to design and build the distinctive Church.[166]

The new Church was dedicated in the summer of 1971, with many guests in attendance, including the Bishop, the Leo Dohn family, and Mr. Dohn's controversial friend, Louie Congro. Everyone had a few drinks and Father had more than his share. He tended bar that night and later he took Louie Congro to a motel east of Lame Deer. On the way, a tribal policeman with his lights flashing pulled Father over to the side of the road. Officer Roger Old Mouse came up to the car and leaned down to Father's window. "Hi, Father Emmett! Say, I pulled you over because your wheels are wobbling kinda funny. You might have something wrong with your steering." He knew that Father had been drinking but he didn't want to embarrass him in front of his guest. Father Emmett thanked him – it sobered him up a bit – and he continued on to Lame Deer. He never got arrested for drinking and driving. He was lucky. The Cheyenne police officer was a former student at St. Labre.[167]

One day Father wasn't so lucky. He was speeding along when a policeman drove up behind him. The white officer got out of his car, walked over to Father Emmett's window, leaned in and asked sarcastically, "What do you think you're doing, flying an airplane? Where's your pilot's license?"

Father reached into his glove compartment and pulled out his old pilot's license. The astounded cop laughed so hard, he gave Father a warning ticket. Father Emmett's quick thinking got him out of trouble more than once.

Father was now the director of St. Labre Indian School Educational

Association, which included St. Xavier Mission and St. Charles
Mission. He supervised approximately 20 priests and brothers in the
area, while working with the construction team to build the Church.
He had also been elected to the Provincial Council of the Midwest
Capuchin Province of St. Joseph. This new post meant a great deal of
out-of-state travel. While he was gone, Father came under fire from the
progressive priests who thought they had better ways of raising money
and running the Mission. When he returned, they criticized his building
projects, despite the fact that his school and Church projects had been
hugely successful. They claimed that Fr. Emmett was "tight" with
funding. This complaint had been made over the years by many others
as well.[168] Father claimed he wasn't tight – he just wanted complete
accountability for all funds that were used.

They also criticized Father Emmett's drinking habits. They said he
became "boisterous and belligerent," and especially argumentative
when he was drinking. Friends outside the Church also noticed this
behavior, but none confronted him, not even the friend he was drinking
with one night when things got out of hand. Out of the blue, Father
looked down at the full glass of booze in his hand, got furious at
himself and threw the glass against a wall, shattering splinters
everywhere. In a letter to Cooky on September 29, 1966, Father told
her: "I am getting to be known as the alcoholic priest."[169]

Finally, in order "to show them" and to prove to himself that he was not
an alcoholic, Father stopped drinking for Lent, a one year vow. Most
alcoholics in recovery know that giving up alcohol for Lent is a sure
sign of an alcoholic. Nonetheless, despite the pressure he was under
from the province to perform his special tasks, plus supervising the
building construction, and the criticisms from his peers, he didn't drink
for the entire year. For everyone concerned, it was a very difficult year.
Father knew that alcohol was a real problem for him, but he denied it
was affecting his work or his relationships with others. He couldn't
accept or admit his weakness to others or to God. Yet deep down, he
was beginning to think it might destroy him.

When he finally realized that he had a serious problem, depression set
in. He had feelings of worthlessness, of not measuring up. He thought
nobody liked him and most of all, he feared dying drunk. Guilt over his
drinking made him stop believing in himself and his work. When he
woke up in the morning his hands shook and it wasn't until many years
later that he realized why he felt steadier after Mass – he had sipped

communion wine. In a Capuchin publication at the time, Father Emmett's writings should have aroused concern:

> The business of being a priest can be tough. Sometimes I get so down in the mouth that even suicide comes as a brief thought. That's how frustrated and lonely I get. I try to be a friend to my people – and half of the time I fail. But I keep trying – even when I know my best is not good enough.[170]

Suicide entered his mind at night when he couldn't sleep and was filled with terrible loneliness. Who cared if he was dead, anyway? Should he use a gun? He could hear his mother's hysterical response: "Stay away from guns Buddy!" No, it couldn't be a gun. If he decided to kill himself, it had to be in a car. He'd pick a mountain curve, let her go full throttle and happen to miss the curve. Some would say it was a suicide, but most would argue that he'd always driven too fast. It would look like an accident and they'd blame it on his drinking. But Mary would know the truth. The loneliness after she and Cooky left, had not only broken Mary's heart, it had also broken his. She had always boosted his spirits when he felt insecure. Now he'd lost her forever, lost the child he felt was his own. He was beyond love – he could only feel pain. Then he'd pray and doze and suddenly it was morning and there were people at his door asking for help, and the phone was ringing. Work saved him many a time.

Despite all of his good works, Father Emmett was haunted by his nagging fear of failure. Overwork caused many problems because he made himself available 24 hours a day. Donors called him at all hours of the night to discuss their problems. He had convinced himself that he had to be available to people who called because someone might be dying, or had been assaulted by a spouse and needed comfort and prayers in a crisis.[171]

Father's anger at the new breed of priests and his inner struggle to deal with his drinking problem caused loud outbursts that scared more than a few people. He believed the other priests and their radical ideas were trying to destroy his dream for the Cheyennes and as time went on, he was less able to control his anger.

During the Christmas season, Father Emmett relaxed a little because gift-giving was his special joy. He wrote to donors:

As I shuffled through the snow . . . I had to stop and gaze at
the gaily decorated dormitory and listen to the loud noise of
the children that echoed in the dark . . . A sensation went
through me, that I will never forget. To see and hear joy . . .
the children made a wild dash towards me and within seconds
I was surrounded. Each was holding my hand, my arm, or
clinging to my coat. They told me about the Christmas tree and
it made me happy to see them giggling when I passed out
gifts. Far too often their lives are filled with sadness and
despair . . . I felt a feeling of contentment and gratitude to our
donors.[172]

Nobody remembered Father's 25th anniversary as a priest except Mary
McGarvey. Father wrote to her: "I cannot really tell you how much it
meant to me that you remembered. I thought someone in the
community would remember. I had mentioned it in the friary a few
times in past weeks, but no one remembered the day."[173] As always,
Mary was there for him. He was careful what he wrote to her. Mary
kept all the letters that he wrote to Cooky, all the postcards and small
presents, but Mary usually destroyed his personal letters to her. She
didn't want her drunken brother to find them.

The Capuchins were in no mood to celebrate Fr. Emmett's 25th
anniversary. Every January the friars got together to discuss annual
budget plans. This included priests from several different areas on the
Crow and Northern Cheyenne Reservations. The meetings were like
serial showdowns at the OK Corral. Each priest had his own plans
including the hiring of new personnel, money for trips to town, retreats,
a new Church or rectory. New rectories were built but not before Fr.
Emmett had pared down the plans, sometimes until only the dry core
remained of the apple. They complained that he was spending more
money at St. Labre for the Cheyennes than at other reservation sites and
they were right. Father Emmett had begun his missionary work among
the Cheyennes and he was unabashedly prejudiced in their favor.[174]

Meanwhile, the rapid Vatican II changes meant that brothers, priests
and nuns could now more openly communicate with one another.
Before Vatican II, some convents did not allow a Sister to befriend
another Sister in the same order, let alone a lay person or priest. When
new rules unlocked doors that had been closed for centuries, keys
became lost and doors were left open too often. As a result, a minority
of Sisters, brothers and priests reverted back to the adolescent behavior

of which they had been robbed.

An example of this was a young brother at St. Labre who spent too much time with a woman lay volunteer. He talked about her to his fellow brothers. They noticed his obsession with the young woman and the priests confronted him. "You have to be careful," they told him, but their warnings were ignored. The two started seeing each other on weekends. When spring came they climbed the hill in back of the church at Kirby, an Indian community about 55 miles southwest of St. Labre. They reached the top, but their combined weight caused a landslide. When they finally landed at the bottom of the hill, the priest was bruised and the woman had broken her arm.

Gossip over this embarrassing incident didn't stop for months and the Cheyenne version was much more interesting. According to the Indians, the priest and the woman were making love on a sand ledge when the ledge gave way. They fell fifteen feet down the cliff and when they were found, the priest was semi-conscious and the woman was in a state of undress and she couldn't move! They had been found together, but according to other priests, the event wasn't half that exciting. The priest and volunteer, both hard-working people, left St. Labre and went out into the world to build a new life together. They had two beautiful children and their marriage has lasted to this day.

Sisters and priests had abandoned their adolescence when they entered convents and seminaries at the age of 13 or 14. Biological urges were repressed and many Sisters became non-entities – unhappy, hooded puppets whose hands, glued together in prayer, could not reach out to each other for friendship and comfort. When a new, good-looking priest landed at St. Labre, his arrival did not go unnoticed. To the lasting merriment of the high school children, one of the Sisters was so taken with a new priest that she hid in the bushes to watch him go by at the same time every day. Watching the lovesick nun became a favorite pastime.[175]

A Cheyenne bus driver recalled another, more serious story:

> One winter day I drove the basketball team to Rosebud. A
> Sister was with the cheerleaders and a priest was with the
> boys. After the beginning prayer, the priest went back into the
> boys' locker room. The cheerleaders went out on the floor to
> do their routine. One of the boys on the team ran back to the

locker room to go to the bathroom. He swung open the
bathroom door just 10 feet from where the priest and the Sister
were making love on a bench! The boy stumbled out of the
locker room and it's a wonder the team could play at all that
night.

After the game, all the players and cheerleaders knew about it.
The boy who had seen them in the locker room tried to get me
to do something about the wrongdoing. "Report them! They
are laying together!" he demanded.

"Report what? I never saw a thing!" I told him. I didn't dare
look in my rear view mirror going home. All the kids were
eyeballing each other and trying to get my attention. I knew if
I looked anybody in the eye, they'd all start laughing.[176]

Vatican II brought many lay women and Sisters into the Church to play
a more active role. Priests and brothers also aspired to do things that
would have been impossible before Vatican II. For example, after
Fr. Emmett could no longer fly the St. Labre airplane due to his high
blood pressure, other priests and brothers became pilots. When Fr.
Larry Abler first came to the Mission, he was shocked to find that he
had to learn to fly. He went up in the plane with Fr. Carl Pulvermacher,
whom he called, "The cowboy in the sky." Apparently, Father Carl was
usually conservative by nature, but not when he got into the cockpit of
a plane. Fr. Larry recalled: "He would put the plane into dives and pull
up suddenly. Then he'd say to me, "'I think I can fly this plane upside
down."' He kept threatening to do it. He scared the crap out of me."
One day, Father Emmett asked where the airplane was and he was told
that one of the brothers had taken a couple of nuns to Denver to see
"Jesus Christ Superstar." Father hit the ceiling and that was the end of
the airplane.[177]

The main reasons for having the plane in the first place had been to
save lives by flying serious medical emergencies to hospitals; to protect
the staff at St. Labre from robberies; (three times a week Father flew
the donation money to Miles City) and to save countless days of
dangerous travel on icy winter roads. The runway was rented to area
farmers for crop-dusting and donors flew in for special occasions.

The bank travel problem was solved soon after the airplane sold.
Fr. Emmett was one of the founders of the Ashland Cheyenne Western

Bank on Main Street. He was elected its first President of the board. By that time, hospitals were using helicopters to pick up medical emergencies. The runway at St. Labre could still be used for medical evacuations and for area crop dusters but the need for an airplane at St. Labre had come to an end.

The Catholic Church was changing and so was the country. According to some Cheyennes, President Nixon's administration was much better than Eisenhower's when it came to Indian policy. Nixon gave a message to Congress outlining his plans for "A New Era for the American Indians."[178] His message showed that his staff had researched the problems in great depth.

Nixon denounced paternalism as well and promised to fund programs. The Northern Cheyennes breathed a sigh of relief. Some tribes were ready to take over daunting fund raising duties and scientific analysis of donor response, but the Cheyennes had few college graduates. It was hard to attract Cheyenne graduates to an isolated reservation where the life expectancy was around 44 years and infant mortality at Lame Deer was three times the national average.[179] Father knew that unless they learned a lot more about direct mail fund raising, the tribe couldn't make a success of St. Labre. Separate groups within the tribe would try to take over power. He had seen this happen before. Without an interim period of several years when tribal members could be trained, Father felt the sudden move would set them up for failure. The younger priests, more avant-garde in their thinking, had decided that St. Labre should be given over to the Indians immediately. Without researching the move more thoroughly, the young priests moved ahead, sure of themselves and their "quick fix" liberation theology.

In the 1970s, Father was invited to attend peyote and sweatlodge ceremonies along the Tongue River not far from St. Labre. The memorable ceremony, which lasted all night, opened Father's eyes:

> We gathered around in the evening before we went into the tipi and there was a lot of visiting . . . Finally it was time to go in. The prayer leader sat in a special place at the back of the tipi . . . We began by making a cigarette with peyote in it, mixed with Bull Durham. We smoked and passed brewed peyote tea around. Everyone was given some to chew if you wanted it. They sang different peyote songs and they prayed. I got into the beat of the drum – it was like a heartbeat.[180]

During the ceremony Father prayed for the people he knew and for the projects he was involved in. The harder he prayed, the better he felt. He touched the Cheyenne spirit that night and almost seemed to understand the words of the Cheyenne songs. Sitting among the people he loved, peyote prayer songs made him one with them. He had heard that people who didn't have the right spiritual attitude sometimes vomited after taking peyote. He felt no such nausea.

The ceremony Father attended had elements of Christianity:

> In the ceremony they chanted the "Our Father" – that was really beautiful. I began to see that peyote was a Sacred Sacrament. I was invited to peyote ceremonies many times. It was an honor for me personally to be invited. I had to overcome the prejudice I had about peyote. I had heard the old priests call it "the devil drug." That just wasn't true. Those statements against peyote were made out of fear and ignorance.[181]

As Father prayed with the peyote, he realized that there were many different ways to reach God. It was a matter of prayer being good and positive in a person's life. It was a matter of faith.

When Father first came to St. Labre he couldn't imagine how peyote could help anyone. He knew the priests had been fighting against it for over fifty years and this had created many hard feelings. At one point in the 1930s the priests had made the Cheyennes sign an affidavit denouncing all religions except Catholicism. If the Indians didn't sign the edict, they could not receive Communion, their children could not be baptized and their relatives were forbidden from burying the dead in the Catholic cemetery.[182]

Father Emmett was probably the first director of St. Labre Mission to attend peyote ceremonies on the Northern Cheyenne Reservation. He didn't announce the fact to the other priests but he knew in his heart that he had come a long way towards better understanding the people he loved.

"Priests aren't poor!"
Fr. Emmett, 1975

CHAPTER
14

Heartbreak

F ather tried to remain calm in the middle of the furor. The young priests felt that Father ran rough shod over them and he thought their so-called priest's "vow of poverty" was hypocrisy at its highest level. The Church paid for everything the priests needed - their toothbrushes, their trips home to see families, their vacations, food, clothing, even underwear. "Priests aren't poor!" he told them. "You sit around pretending you are poor. Who are you kidding? We each have 12 years of higher education. You go to town to eat at a ritzy restaurant, have steak and then come back here. The Cheyennes know priests aren't poor. They're not stupid!"

Father Emmett, a missionary church, school and industry builder, never pretended to be an evangelist. The younger men didn't understand his goals and never would, so he proceeded without them. When he tried to tell them what life had been like on the reservation when he first came in 1954, they didn't believe him.

On his knees before God, Father had made his vow that he would educate Cheyenne children and improve the standard of living for their families and he was succeeding. He felt their future depended upon high school and college graduates and he wanted to see more industry on the reservation. There was still much to do. By the 1970s, reservation conditions were better for many, although poverty was still a terrible reality.

The younger friars didn't want to identify with the older priests.

Everything had to be done the modern way, separate from the accepted traditions of the old guard, namely Father Emmett. They always had to question any type of authority.

The other side of the coin was that younger friars felt that bureaucracy was taking over St. Labre. They believed that Father Emmett was so busy building and fund raising that business was becoming more important than Capuchin spiritual convictions and the conversion of the Cheyennes to Catholicism. Father Emmett questioned why they tried to "save" the Indian when they couldn't even save themselves. While older priests had courageously gone to the Missions and endured without complaint, the younger men couldn't take the pressure, the isolation. Easily distracted and lacking in spirit, they gave up and left, rather than stick it out for the long haul. There were no heroes in the bunch.

Father noticed that many of the young Capuchin priests were physically and emotionally weak individuals. Although he tried to brush this uncomfortable issue aside, underneath it all, he saw them as confused and sexually conflicted men who clung to their community because they felt safe nowhere else. He blamed the seminary for not weeding them out before ordination, but it dawned on him that many of the seminary novice masters were probably gay. Father had been taught to accept his brother priests but he couldn't help noticing that the young guard lacked vision, the guts, strength and endurance to get things done and worst of all – they had no long term convictions. All they wanted were the soft conveniences, things for their own comfort.

St. Labre's fund raising department had taken many pain-staking years to develop. Everything was in place and donor funds were flowing into St. Labre. The children had special programs, teachers and class field trips. The school was remarkably advanced compared to other educational institutions. Fr. Emmett feared that because of interference from young, inexperienced priests, St. Labre might lose funding sources.

Meanwhile, in New Jersey, Cooky McGarvey had blossomed into a lovely young woman, but her letters to Father Emmett revealed a teenager frustrated with her adopted mother. The more freedom Cooky wanted, the more Mary smothered her with religion. Mary had been sick for some time and this may have been the reason for her impatience. The two were at each other constantly. Cooky had been raised in the Church and had attended Catholic schools, but she backed away from the Catholic Church in her youth because of her mother's insistence that Cookie adhere to rigid religious rules. Cookie was questioning Church rules. She hadn't forgotten that a Capuchin brother had tried to molest her. She wanted to know more about her biological relatives and Mary felt betrayed.

Back East, Cooky had been treated like an Indian princess, but she had never felt that she fit in. She had no girl friends she could relate to. Cooky felt strange reaching out to a white person, although she had been raised white since she was a toddler. This is what set her apart from her classmates. Being raised white didn't make her white, it didn't change her soul. She couldn't racially or spiritually relate to them.[183]

In many respects, Cooky was no different than most teenagers who wanted to date and wear pretty clothes and makeup, but her mother saw her behavior as sinful and rebellious. Cooky started dating boys and Mary didn't like them. Both Mary and Cooky wrote to complain to Fr. Emmett and he tried to help each without taking sides. The Cheyenne girl had no knowledge as to the real reason why she and her mother had left St. Labre. In the back of her mind, something was wrong with who and where she was, and she felt it every day of her life. Cooky made a half-hearted attempt to get Fr. Emmett and her mother back together, but Father wrote: "Your letter was rather sad. I know Cooky, that you would like to come back to St. Labre. At times I wish very much that you were here with your Mother. It would be so nice to be back together. At the same time, I never know what the future holds for me. I could be called out of here at any time and we can't build your life and the life of your Mother around that. I am worried about your Mother still being ill."[184]

Besides his own determination to stop drinking and "white knuckle it" for a year, Father only got through the ordeal with help from his good friend, accountant Conrad Sump. Leo Dohn Sr. had hired Sump when his old Italian accountant in New York had passed away. "Connie" as he was called by everyone, went to work for Mr. Dohn in New York and then he took over the accounting department for Guild Arts and Crafts in Ashland as well. Connie came out to look over the factory's financial records in the 1960s, bringing with him his petite, attractive wife Ruth and their children, Linda and Conrad Jr. In later years, Connie added St. Labre Indian School as a client. Father's first impression of Connie turned out to be true. This was a man who thoroughly knew his business.[185]

Connie came along at just the right time to become a confidant and friend when Father needed him most. Sump's eastern accent made Fr. Emmett laugh, just as Mary's New Jersey accent had amused him ten years before. In addition to being Father's closest friend, Connie proved to be a genius at analyzing prospect mailings. He perfected a scientific test list before appeals were sent out, saving St. Labre thousands of dollars. This test would become the ignition switch to the direct mail vehicle.

Connie wanted to help the Cheyennes and he was willing to come to the isolated Mission ninety days a year. He encouraged Father to cultivate donors and to bond with them. In a way, Connie, too, was from the old guard – a man's man. That's why Father could tell him exactly what was on his mind without hurting his feelings. The accountant submitted detailed quarterly reports so that Father could see exactly where he could save money. Together they put together the annual budgets and accounted for every penny. Before long, Fr. Emmett knew they were an unbeatable team.

Connie admired Father and believed in his dream of what St. Labre could become, and they were both workaholics - work was recreation to them. Mr. Dohn's stock broker in New York, Paul Morigi, joined the St. Labre team in 1968.[186] With Paul's brilliant expertise, Connie's magic and Fr. Emmett's leadership, they successfully invested funds for St. Labre's endowments. For the next twenty-six years, they worked diligently for Northern Cheyenne children.

In addition to his annual audit, Connie completed the accounting and auditing of the Endowment Fund, the Tree of Life Scholarship Fund, the Emmett G. Hoffmann Scholarship Fund and the Annuity Fund. He maintained contact with the name brokers and analyzed the direct mail fund, which improved the efficiency of the development program. He also participated in five or six fund raising meetings held each year, reviewed all mailings and completed all the tax work necessary for the various agencies and prepared all of the regulatory and tax reports.

Connie also prepared the annual budget for St. Labre and presented an annual report to the St. Labre Board of Directors. He performed all of the accounting necessary for the pension plan and submitted to the actuary each year. Later, when St. Labre invested in other businesses, Connie advised school officials on negotiations with the Northern Cheyenne Pine Company (sawmill), the Cheyenne Village (housing project) and the Northern Cheyenne Business Development Fund (Business loans given to tribal members). Finally, he helped negotiate a stock deal with Guild Arts and Crafts International, which greatly profited St. Labre. In the years to come, Connie Sump would become a major factor in the transition of St. Labre Indian School from a struggling Mission school to a vibrant, financially solid, multifaceted social service organization with five, fully operational group homes for children at-risk.

It didn't take long for Connie to find out that Fr. Emmett didn't take criticism well. "He clams up when you disagree with him," he said. He got used to Father's messy desk and the way he always lost papers and had to look all over for them. He also got used to Father's irascible habit of fiddling with things on his desk or looking up at the ceiling when Connie was trying to explain something to him. "That's part of his personality. He gets bored," he said. Father Emmett's fellow Capuchins, however, considered him rude and insulting and it drove them crazy. "You'd be telling him about an important subject and he'd just look at his mail and tune you out," one priest remembered.[187]

The progressive priests disparagingly labeled Connie and Marlin Johnson, (St. Labre's insurance agent and Father's good friend) "the money men." After the work was done, Connie and Father sat in the friary, drank, laughed and forgot their troubles for awhile. Looking back, Connie described the rest and relaxation as "a release" from the stress of the times.

During squabbles in the friary, no priest stepped forward as mediator. On at least one occasion, a fist fight resulted in a black eye and broken furniture. The priests thought they covered these incidents up, but the Cheyennes knew about the confrontations. The constant stress finally got to Fr. Emmett and he ended up in the hospital with a pancreatic inflammation. His pancreas was beginning to digest itself. He knew what had caused it – his drinking. He went home from the hospital and slowed down for a week or two. But then he rationalized that he wouldn't drink scotch or brandy – he'd switch to wine!

While internal problems persisted at St. Labre, the Northern Cheyenne Native Action Program asked Father to donate classroom space at St. Labre, a program that would one day evolve into Dull Knife Memorial College. Fr. Emmett helped to provide classrooms for the study of welding, woodworking, diesel mechanics and heavy equipment operation. He also provided money for their meetings, activities and wages, in addition to the funds they received from the government. Many devoted Cheyenne people worked to see Dull Knife become a fully accredited Junior College and Father Emmett was proud to have been part of the effort.

Although Father thought he wasn't making excuses for his drinking, he told people at the time that he drank to make sure he could sleep. He told Connie: "I'm dying inside," but serving the Church and the people was of primary importance, whether or not he felt like dying. Father Emmett was just as hard on himself as he was on his fellow priests. For example, he saw that he had been paternalistic. This attitude of government and Church developed and encouraged Indian dependency and undermined self-esteem. The priests saw themselves as "Fathers" and the Cheyennes as "children." They imposed their way as the "right" way. Missionaries became enablers and co-dependents and when the Cheyenne lost their sense of self-sufficiency, they depended on government and Church for financing.

In later years, Father realized that the Church had encouraged paternalism. Indian artist Denver Horn told a story about Fr. Emmett's paternalism in the early days:

> One Sunday morning, Fr. Emmett had just gotten back from Billings minutes before Mass. I could tell he had been drinking the night before and he was a little hung over, but he got through it. After Mass I walked up to Father and showed him a painting that wasn't dry yet. "'I need money to go to Sheridan to visit my kids,'" I told him.[188]

Father knew the Sunday offering wasn't usually very much money and he was still holding the small offering bag as he left the Church. "Tell you what I'll do Denver," he said. "I like your painting but all I can give you is what is in this bag." Denver accepted the bag and he handed Father the painting. Afterward, Denver was ecstatic. He showed the $92.00 he had gotten from Fr. Emmett to his friends, saying, "This is the most I ever got for a painting!" Father Emmett thought he had given Denver about ten dollars.

Father's Emmett's health continued to decline. Photographs taken at the time show a young man with a furrowed brow, overweight and smoking. One night as he lay in bed, his entire body went rigid. He couldn't move at all. Slowly he moved one toe, but it took a long time before he could move the rest of his body. After this experience, which he wrote off as nerves, he went to the doctor and later wrote to Mary and Cooky: "After I saw the doctor I went away for 9 days. He told me just to get out of this place and relax before I dropped dead. Then I came back for meetings with seven FHA reps, plus contractors and subcontractors . . . It was pure torture. It was a terrible ordeal but Thank God we are getting the housing for the (Cheyenne) people."[189]

In the 1960s Larry Kostelecky took over as the first lay superintendent at St. Labre. Fr. Emmett wrote to donors about Larry's considerable contribution: "Because of his leadership and his interest in education, many new ideas have been implemented." Larry established a student teaching program in conjunction with Eastern Montana College and numerous other projects including a Career Opportunity Program that provided education and college training for many Indian adults. During his years at the Mission, Fr. Emmett praised the educator saying that "St. Labre has become a pace-setter for the state of Montana" because of Kostelecky's tenure at St. Labre.[190]

The talented new superintendent witnessed many changes after Vatican II, especially with the nuns. Larry was astonished in the changes that came over the Sisters. They came to his office: ". . . very upset over the fact that three of the Sisters were going to take off their veils. They wanted me to stop them. One of the elder nuns said, " 'Men will grope them. You can't let it happen! '" Larry reminded the nuns that he had no control over what the Sisters did or did not do. These matters should have been handled within their own religious community. Larry had always held Sisters and priests in high esteem on pedestals. Now he was beginning to see the truth – they were human beings after all. By the middle of the school year most of the Sisters had given up the veil. But that was not all. Over the course of the next two years, seven of the Sisters openly flirted with him. He was flabbergasted.[191]

One thing that never changed in the lives of the priests and nuns at St. Labre was their obsession with time. More than a few of the priests couldn't get used to so-called "Indian time," while it seemed to the Cheyennes that priests and Sisters were regulated more by time than religion. The religious centered their lives around bells and clocks. The Indians saw the priest look at his watch before he ate and he looked at the clock after he ate and before he prayed. Children attending boarding schools had to hurry to get up in the morning, hurry to dress, hurry to eat, hurry to class, hurry back to eat, hurry to clean up, hurry to more classes, hurry to church, hurry to prayers, hurry to play, hurry to work and hurry to bed. To the Cheyenne people, this seemed like an unnatural way to live.

In January 1974, Father got a bad cold. Drinking had compromised his immune system and the cold rapidly progressed to pneumonia. He stayed in bed a few days and then went back to work harder than before. In April, after recuperating from pneumonia, Father had severe chest pains and collapsed in front of his office door. Within minutes Viola had helped arrange his trip to Billings. He was in the hospital a few days and then returned to work. He didn't take the mild heart attack seriously because he joked to Cooky in a letter: "I'm restricting myself to one cigarette every 50 miles."[192]

Father Emmett's dad, Edward Hoffmann, had been bedridden in a Wisconsin nursing home, unable to walk or talk for some time. Months earlier, Father had visited his mother and dad briefly and Ed became frustrated and cried when he couldn't talk to his son. Father wrote to Mary and Cooky at the time: "Dad wants to die."[193] When the end finally came on June 17, 1974, Father Emmett was unable to make it to his father's bedside.

Cooky graduated from high school and entered nursing school, which pleased her mother and Father Emmett very much. He wrote to Cooky: "I was happy to hear that you and your mother are getting along better. I am sure being away from home helps. Now, you can appreciate each other more when you are together. I really worry about your mother and only pray that she will regain her health. I know being ill most of the time must be very depressing for her."[194]

Mary's mysterious illness kept coming up in letters but neither Father Emmett nor Mary told Cooky the truth about Mary's condition. In one of his many letters to Cooky, Father wrote: "Often I feel rather guilty because I was responsible or at least instrumental in your adoption. Three months later, he wrote: "I was surprised to hear that your mother has been existing on ginger ale." In this letter he told Cooky to "get the facts" from Mary's doctor.[195] Cooky wanted to come out and spend the summer at St. Labre but Father didn't think it was a good idea. Bedridden at home most of the time, Mary wrote letters of support and encouragement to Cooky, as well as a birthday poem:

You were much too small,
You don't recall
Our meeting
Seventeen years ago today.
We were strangers,
You and I,
A woman and child
With no special tie.
One bond brought us together,
A beautiful love,
That could only come
From God above.
As all kinds of love,
It has been tested,
But time cannot hurt,
The special union that evolved.
Whatever lies ahead,
And the price to be paid,
You will always be
Most precious and dear to me.[196]

Mary's poem could also have been written about her feelings for
Father Emmett. After Cooky finished her first year in nursing school,
Father wrote her a serious letter: "Now that you have completed your
first year, you must know that your mother has a terminal form of
leukemia."[197]

Cooky was devastated. "Nobody had told me!" she said. "I was beside
myself. I didn't know what to do, so I pretended that life was the same.
Everything was hush hush."[198] Cooky went back to school for her
second year, but quickly found that her mother was going downhill.
She dropped out of school and got a job as a nurse's aide at Bayonne
Hospital, close to home. Still, neither spoke of the wasting terminal
illness.

Mary endured constant blood tests and medication changes. Bills
started rolling in and Cooky struggled to pay them. One day Mary's
condition stabilized and she was happy, the next day she was so weak
she could barely move. When Mary began to lose weight, Cooky knew
the end was near, but they still didn't discuss it. Although Mary was
devoutly religious, Cooky was the opposite: "When I had continuous
nosebleeds as a child," she explained to a friend, "I watched her pray for

me on her knees, time after time. Nothing happened. I still suffered. After twenty times, you stop praying."[199]

Mary's brother Hughie continued to drink and harass them. One night Hughie came upstairs: "I awoke in my room," Cookie said. "He threatened me with a knife and his wife dragged him back downstairs."[200] Not one of the women pressed charges on Hughie, but eventually, he was hospitalized.

During all of the years Cooky had lived with her adopted mother upstairs in the McGarvey family home, she slept in a tiny room that had once been a bathroom. Cooky had no radio, no TV, no stereo. Instead of the blue sky and pine-covered hills of her Montana homeland, Cooky's view from her one small window was of Kahoots Mortuary, on a bustling working-class street where hundreds of people walked back and forth in the rain to work, to row houses, to the bus and to the train station. She often stood at the little window looking down on them, her heart aching for the Northern Plains in another place and time.

During her adopted mother's illness, Cooky got engaged. Mary didn't like the young man but she was resigned and said nothing. "I showed her my engagement ring but there was no happiness," Cooky remembered. "Mother laughed a lot, a nervous laugh. She trembled and I had to watch what I said to her because she would get upset over anything."[201]

Blocking her health problems from her mind, Mary tried to get Cooky to go back to nursing school. "She acted like she didn't know why I wanted to stay with her, that's why I don't think she knew she was dying,"[202] Cooky recalled. In truth, Mary knew about her illness because she had written about it to Father Emmett years before. They must have decided to keep it from Cooky until she graduated from high school. When Cooky hadn't gotten "the facts" from Mary's doctor, Father wrote to Cooky about her mother's condition, a striking example of Mary's lack of communication with her daughter.

Mary had lived longer than any other leukemia victim that her doctor had ever known. Finally, when Mary couldn't get out of bed, she experienced terrible pressure pains in her stomach, so bad that she had trouble breathing. Hospitalizations followed hospitalizations. "I was always at the hospital," Cooky recalls. "She was either having injections or having bone marrow tests. The doctor told me, "Keep her comfortable." That's all he told me. We'd get into the taxi and go to the hospital and they'd start the tests. In the late evening, I'd get up to go home and she'd say, "Be a good girl."[203]

On December 31, 1974, Cooky admitted her mother for yet another hospitalization and Mary had a blood transfusion. She weighed less than one hundred pounds. "She was quiet that night, calm but very weak," Cooky remembered. "I had a hard time hearing her because she had sores in her mouth and it was painful to talk. "I'm so tired," she whispered. "I'm going to sleep early." I made her some tea – she was so thirsty. Then I fed her lime green Jello. She had an IV in one arm, propped up on a pillow. She couldn't feed herself. She shook her head as if to say, "No more, please, no more."[204]

Cooky told her mother that she had been invited to a New Year's Eve party. "She was worried about how I was getting home and what time I was going home. "'The earlier you go, the earlier you'll come home,'" she whispered. I hugged and kissed her. "Happy New Years, mom," I said."[205]

Cooky went to the party, not realizing she would never see her adopted mother alive again. Early the next morning, she was sleeping when the phone rang. "Your mother is not doing well," a nurse told her. Cooky caught a cab and rushed to the hospital, but it was too late. Mary had lapsed into a coma and died on New Year's Day, 1975. The cause of death was cerebral hemorrhage. Mary was only 52 years old.

Frantically, Cooky called St. Labre to tell Fr. Emmett, but he had gone to spend New Year's weekend with Marlin Johnson's family at Big Sky, Montana. The doctor had suggested that Father take the week off and rest. Heavy storm warnings were posted and Father arrived just before a blizzard closed all the roads.

Father stood at the window watching the snow fall with a scotch in his hand. 'If I'm going to be snowed in,' he thought, 'I couldn't have picked a nicer place.' He loved the peaceful lake and the snow-capped Lone Mountain in the distance. The phone rang, a call for Father from his secretary at St. Labre. "Cooky just called for you. Mary McGarvey died this morning," she said. Father couldn't get his breath and had to sit down.

He always tried to look on the bright side of things but there was no bright side to Mary's death. He had not prepared himself for her loss. He telephoned Cooky. Distraught, she begged him to come to the funeral. She felt completely alone. He told her there was no way he could make it to the funeral. A blizzard had closed the roads and airline tickets had completely sold out for the holidays. He didn't have his suit or his collar with him.

Cooky wasn't having it. "I was surprised and angry that he didn't come," she said later.[206] She felt his ambivalence and she didn't understand. Maybe he didn't completely understand it himself. "It was the finality of it," he later recalled. "My years of loneliness and longing for Mary had suddenly ended. She had been my biggest supporter when nobody else was on my side. I had to face the grief by myself."[207]

Mary's passing brought a tragic closure to what had been a painful open wound in Father's heart. Cooky was the one who needed him now. She needed his strength and she needed to know that he still loved her and that nothing had changed between them. Unable to communicate the depth of his grief in front of others at Big Sky, Father was shocked into a painful silence.

Cooky thought he just didn't care – but he did care. He remembered Mary's face, her bright eyes, her softness and the way she felt in his arms. He remembered their stolen moments together, the snowball attack that had ended with unexpected passion, and the unforgettable evening when they realized their love affair had to end. He could still close his eyes and see the tears streaming down her face as they drove to the airport. He wondered if the remorse, depression and shame that Mary had felt when she left St. Labre had somehow made her ill. Consumed with guilt, he turned away from the window to the past and poured himself a double scotch.

As soon as the snow stopped, Father drove to Bozeman thinking he could get a flight to New York, but it was impossible. Holiday travel had booked all flights and skiers in the area and vacationing students were all trying to get home. He drove back to Big Sky and on the day of Mary's funeral he came down with a bad case of flu. Drinking heavily, he didn't want to feel the pain. He didn't want to feel anything. Mary was gone, his father was gone, his uncle, Father Herbert, had recently died, and his own physical breakdown with pneumonia had ended in a strange chest pains. The year 1974 had been a terrible nightmare. He usually left his personal problems on the back burner and now it was too late to tell Mary that he would always love her. She had given him her best, unselfish love and when she left the Mission, it was to let him get on with his life's work among the Northern Cheyennes. Because she loved him, she had let him go.

CHAPTER
15

"Don't call me Father Emmett!"

F ather pushed Mary's death to a corner of his mind where he could deny that it had affected him. Unconsciously, he may have feared a loss of control in front of Mary's relatives at the funeral, a clear indication of his love. On the day of her funeral, Father experienced tightness in his throat, shortness of breath, depression, as well as muscle aches and pains, lethargy and headache. In his book *Attachment and Loss*, Dr. John Bowlby wrote: "Adults who show prolonged absences of conscious grieving are commonly self-sufficient people, proud of their independence and self control . . ."[208] The problem with this response, however, was that Father's continued state of high tension, coupled with his overwork and perfectionism, left him with dangerously high blood pressure.

Throughout the month of January, 1975, Father couldn't shake off what he thought was the flu. He drank heavily at night, smoked and ate too much, as the stressful budget meetings went into a second week. Father wanted to build a new girl's group residence for the Cheyenne Home for neglected and abused children, but the Capuchins wanted to use the money elsewhere.

The importance of the Cheyenne Homes in Father's life cannot be underestimated. A special place in his heart belonged to neglected and abandoned children. Mary had been the first St. Labre caregiver to three little girls and he wanted to build this new group home in Mary's memory. By 1975, 56 children lived in the Cheyenne Homes, which consisted of a large Quonset building, plus 3 houses in Cheyenne Village, the housing development sponsored by St. Labre donors.

Children came to the homes from many tribes: Cheyenne, Lakota, Crow, Arapaho, Chippewa, Cree, Assiniboine, Gros Ventre and Northern Cheyenne. Living in the homes allowed youngsters the experience of a loving home environment while they attended St. Labre.[209] Eventually, the Cheyenne Homes affiliated with Father Flanagan's Boy's Town in Nebraska.[210] Without the Cheyenne Homes, many children would have been left to roam in search of a place to eat and sleep. Families that needed help to overcome divorce, poverty, alcoholism, prejudice, inadequate housing, poor education and insufficient employment opportunities were able to find comfort and aid from the Cheyenne Homes. As St. Labre became famous throughout Indian country, it was not unusual for troubled tribal families thousands of miles away from Montana to hear: "Take your child to Father Emmett at St. Labre."

January budget planning at St. Labre was always stressful, even under normal circumstances. Unable to sleep, Father tried to throw off his depression and illness with the busy work of planning the yearly budget. He didn't reach out to confide in anyone about his sorrow. Instead, he repressed his feelings with alcohol and awoke in the middle of the night having terrifying catatonic attacks of rigidity. He needed to achieve and he needed to be in control, but was he in control? His evasive stoicism and pride had deprived him of healthy escape valves. With Mary gone, he had lost the comfort of unconditional acceptance. Father had spent his life helping everyone else, but he couldn't help himself.

During the budget meetings, the Capuchin Fathers came in from the Crow and Northern Cheyenne reservations to meet with Connie and Fr. Emmett, just as the other department heads had done. During the meetings, Father lost the funding that he wanted and had to be satisfied with remodeling a 60 year-old dormitory for the older girls. After all the meetings were completed and the budget finalized, Connie and Father went back to the friary to unwind. Angry, Father drank more than usual, and then drove Connie to Billings. The next morning Connie flew home to New York and Father stopped off at Deaconess Hospital to visit a Cheyenne patient. A storm left roads icy and the drive home was nerve-wracking. Strangely, he didn't feel like smoking. During the hour and a half drive, he had time to feel the disappointment over losing the new Cheyenne Home that he wanted to name for Mary McGarvey.

When he got back, he walked into the friary kitchen to get something to eat. Suddenly, he felt nauseated. He wrote it off as stress and went to his room. He turned the door knob and a terrible chest pain hit him. Father Larry Abler somehow got to him, "Larry, I'm in trouble!" Father gasped. "It's my heart – pain down my arms and chest." He sprawled on the floor. The heaviness in his chest and arm immobilized his body and the pain felt like somebody was hacking him with a knife. Less than a month after Mary died, the denied, internalized grief over her death kicked Father in the teeth. He was having a massive heart attack.

Fr. Larry's face went white but he sprang into action. Of all the younger priests, Father Larry had remained a reliable friend. He usually sided with the younger men but he got along with Fr. Emmett as well. Fr. Larry found another friend, Father Gilbert Hemauer, and the two put Father Emmett into the back seat of the car.[211] He was in agonizing pain. Father Larry hit the gas and was speeding as fast as he could go when suddenly Fr. Emmett looked up over the back seat and demanded, "I may be dying, but you don't have to kill all of us going so fast on the icy road!" Even in mortal pain, he was back seat driving and trying to gain control.[212]

They took Father to the emergency room at St. Vincent Hospital and the doctor who examined him nearly went through the ceiling when Father told him he smoked 5 packs of cigarettes "on a good day." Father spent several days in intensive care and then he was moved to another floor. Viola visited him the day after his heart attack and later that day she wrote in her diary: "Went to Billings to see Father Emmett. There is something that is not right."[213]

Vi knew by his pale appearance and labored breathing that trouble lay ahead. Sure enough, Father had no sooner left ICU for the third floor, than he had a second heart attack. The awful pain hit him again while the staff on his floor were busy serving supper to patients. Frantically he rang the bell for help, but nobody came. Luckily, a man stepped out of the elevator next to Father's room and he yelled for help. Nurses rushed him back to ICU. As doctors and nurses worked to save his life, a strange and mystical feeling enveloped him. Later, Father told his sibling, Sister Phyllis Hoffmann:

> I felt a wonderful, peaceful feeling as life was slipping away.
> I knew that I was dying, and it felt nice. They were giving me
> shock treatments when I left my body. It was such a great
> feeling. I was floating above my body – completely at peace –

no more pain. All the grief, stress and worry in my life was gone. I looked down at what the doctors and nurses were doing to revive my body. I watched them. Then suddenly, I went back into my body again and opened my eyes. 'Damn!' I thought. 'Don't tell me I have to come back to life and go through this again!' I was shocked and disappointed that I was still alive.[214]

Father had lived through what is now known as a Near Death Experience (NDE). Dr. Raymond A. Moody Jr., an authority on the phenomena, wrote of Near Death Experiences: ". . . there are ordinary people who have been to the brink of death . . . but the traits of these episodes – no matter what they are called – all point to a similar experience . . . a sense of being dead, peace and painlessness even during a "painful" experience, bodily separation, . . . and feeling reluctance to return to the world of the living."[215]

The events Father remembered were all the classic characteristics of the Near Death Experience. After his NDE, friends and relatives noticed something different in Father Emmett's outlook on life. "There was a change in him after that experience. Life was more important to him," Sister Phyllis recalled. As with most NDE survivors, the event was filled with peace, serenity and love. He only shared the story with Sister Phyllis because she had always believed in him.

On February 10th Fr. Emmett came home to St. Labre and once again, Viola was in charge of his recuperation. She wondered if he would listen to her. Vi had not approved of Fr. Emmett's drinking and driving and she knew that smoking was dangerous. After working at her full-time job at school and looking after Fr. Emmett she wrote in her diary: "I drove Father E. to the doctor, would you believe? Thought he would have another heart attack."[216] She had made him lie down in the back seat. If Father Emmett hadn't been extremely ill, wild horses wouldn't have made him lie down in the back seat of a car driven by a woman! It wasn't manly. But a heart attack brings a man to his knees and Father was afraid to climb stairs, let alone get in and out of a car.

On March 11, 1975, he wrote to Cooky: "Each day I feel a little better. Right now it's a job to keep people from making me work." Someone suggested he keep his hands busy with needlepoint, but that didn't work. As he stared out the window, the old restlessness returned. He had cut back on his smoking and drinking but again, he was only fooling himself. Within a month he was back to his rigorous schedule.

He rested in the afternoon but worked late into the night to make up for lost time. None of Viola's warnings made any difference.

Father had been gone from St. Labre for three months and during that time, Fr. Larry had taken over Fr. Emmett's workload as director. Exasperated, Fr. Larry found out that Fr. Emmett was drinking again. "There's no reason why you can't go back to work," Larry told him. "I know you can do it. Just to prove that you can do it, I'm leaving Montana!"[217]

Father Emmett started crying. Before Mary's death, Father wasn't a man to burst into tears. But Mary's passing, two heart attacks and the Near Death Experience had changed him. His feelings poured out. During the summer months Father wrote to donors: "Seems there is something wrong, a feeling of loneliness; yes, even melancholy pervades."[218] He was finally grieving for the woman he loved.

Meanwhile, Connie Sump, who had a contact in the National Football League, helped arrange for a special donation. Ron Romans, head of the National Football League Properties Office, then working for Pete Rosell, arranged to fly Fr. Emmett and Connie to a Denver Broncos game and during half time, the NFL planned to present a scholarship to St. Labre. In return they asked if Father would act as Chaplain for the pre-game festivities. Since they were paying for everything, Father was happy to accept.[219]

A couple of weeks before the game Father flew to Denver to work out details. Ron Romans met him at the airport and they went out for the evening. After midnight, Mr. Romans took Father to a hotel for the night, and he went to bed after arranging a wake-up call for the next day. The call came in early and when Father answered the call, he was still hung over. Completely disoriented, he didn't know where he was. It scared him.

In October the NFL flew Father Emmett and Connie to Miami for the big game. Friday night, they had an elegant dinner on Pete Rosell's private yacht, an impressive ship with gleaming mahogany interior. They enjoyed a red gold sunset over the Florida Keys and later, the myriad of lights along the coast. The party cruised through calm waters outside of Miami and waiters were everywhere offering food and drinks.

On Saturday night before the big game, the NFL hosted a party with the press, advertisers and special friends with live entertainment, food and again, an open bar. The next morning, Father Emmett offered Mass for the staff, their families and guests. After a sumptuous breakfast, they boarded a bus to the stadium for pre-game celebrations. The bus was equipped with a bar and police buzzed them to and from the stadium, right through the heavy game traffic. Father had a great time. In fact, he and Connie had been drinking the whole weekend. He got up the next morning and said to Connie, "Oh God, why did I get drunk?"[220]

In November, Father wrote to Cooky and sent her money for nursing school: "The enclosed is not a loan but an educational grant," he wrote. "I have money budgeted for Cheyenne people going to school. I have a number of families I am supporting while the father and sometimes the mother goes to school. I also help other kids, recent graduates . . . Let me know honestly what you need. You should be able to continue your education in an ordinary fashion without any extra worries."[221]

In another letter to Cooky, one that illustrated that he was more open about his feelings, Fr. Emmett wrote: "Remember you are still my little girl and I want to help you and care for you. I guess no matter how old you get, you will always be my little girl with a special place in my heart. I guess that is what I mean when I say I love you, which I really do. I want you to succeed. Love, Father Emmett"[222] Physically, he couldn't be with Cooky, but his words comforted her. She had just broken off her engagement.

In the mid-70s, Viola Campeau celebrated 20 years of volunteer service as nurse at St. Labre. Day and night, with the help of a hearing guide dog called Charmin, she had given freely of her time, not only to the thousands of Indian children at the school, but to many non-Indians living around the reservation.[223] During her years among the Northern Cheyennes she had witnessed many changes. Catholic Churches on various reservations were now turning their boarding schools over to the Bureau of Indian Affairs and the younger Capuchins wanted to turn over St. Labre.

Father Emmett didn't approve of the rapid turnover to the BIA and he didn't want to be around when corrupt officials began siphoning off the funding that he had raised for Cheyenne children. He knew that tribal elders would have little say and that in the end, there wouldn't be anyone who could raise the funds to run St. Labre without interference from the Bureau of Indian Affairs and various factions. He went to

Fr. Larry's office and told him that he wanted to take a leave of absence.

Father Emmett got permission for a sabbatical year in New York City and the province gave him a loan, enough money for the trip and living expenses until he could find a job. During his leave of absence, he would have no vows – he would live like any other man. It was time to reflect on what he wanted out of life. After Mary's death, he desperately needed a new perspective – a rekindling of his spirit.

Leo Dohn Sr. did not attend Father Emmett's going away party. Their once close relationship had changed, and not for the better. Dohn disapproved of Fr. Emmett's drinking, although they had partied together as colleagues since 1955.[224] When Father first met Mr. Dohn, he was living in a spacious penthouse on Central Park West. After his wife Rose died of cancer, Leo lived in the penthouse alone and finally sold it. Later, he married Eleanor Kleczka, a professor at Fordham University and Father Emmett was honored to perform the marriage ceremony. The private, elegant wedding was followed by a reception attended by Louie Congro, who showed up with "mafia types" and many Italian priests.

Dohn lived in elegant homes, yet his home life belied his dingy office and his choice of cronies – some pretty rough characters. But Leo worked hard and possessed a wonderful gift of concentration. A colorful personality, yet a humble man, he truly enjoyed the fun-loving company of priests. To see him in Church, undistracted, dissolved in prayer and close to the Lord, left family and friends full of admiration for this generous humanitarian.

Dohn's office in New York was located in the Starret Leigh Building on the Hudson River. Huge elevators moved semi-trucks from floor to floor loading materials. The building covered a square block and was at least 13 stories high. The Guild Arts and Craft offices were drab with no carpeting on the floor. The worn, outdated furniture was at least practical. Mr. Dohn's small, dark office had little natural light. Since the floor was on a slight incline between the general offices and the assembly department, Dohn's chair rolled forward – straight to his heavy, well-aged, walnut desk. His squeaky chair accidentally matched his desk. The furniture needed refinishing, but Leo Dohn liked it just the way it was. While at work, Leo always wore the same tweed sport jacket with patches on the elbows and an old fedora. He smoked constantly and moved his hat from side to side as he visited, talked on the phone or worked at his desk.[225]

Over the years, when Father Emmett came to New York for business meetings, Dohn treated him to meals at the finest restaurants. His favorites included the Four Seasons and "Tony's Italian Kitchen." This was a safe place where he could relax with his business associates and Louie Congro. (Tony's was also a mafia favorite.) The waiters knew Dohn and catered to his wants. Father Emmett always had a great time in New York.

But times and relationships had changed. In the mid-1970s, oil producing nations raised the price of oil, causing businesses to fail and large scale unemployment around the world. The factory at Ashland could no longer make a profit. On December 14, 1976, the GAC Board of Directors in New York voted to liquidate their Montana operations, including the Ashland plant and the factory at Lodge Grass, on the Crow Reservation. The factories were closed after nearly twenty years in operation and Leo Dohn saw to it that workers got compensation and a bonus for every year they had worked for his company. Father's dream of providing a large scale industry and job opportunities on the reservation vanished. At that time, Guild Arts and Crafts was the longest running successful business in Northern Cheyenne Reservation history. A concerned elder remarked at the time: "The closing of the factory is going to make it tough . . . this factory was our only chance to hold down a job . . . now we will have nothing to do and less money to live on."[226]

Father saw the factory closing as a personal failure. His vow to educate Cheyenne children had succeeded, but to improve their standard of living for twenty years and then to see the poverty set in again, demoralized him. One day he walked over to the factory alone, unlocked the door and went in. He stayed for about 30 minutes, walking around, imagining the people were still there, happy and teasing him when he'd walk through greeting everyone. "Hey, Father, Did you come over to give us a raise?" The factory was cold and empty now, where once hundreds of Cheyenne people had brought home paychecks to feed and clothe their families. The memories gave him an eerie feeling. He turned off the lights and locked the door for the last time.

Closing the factory in 1976 had eroded Father Emmett's relationship with Mr. Dohn. When the doors closed, Leo Dohn Sr. and Father

Emmett didn't speak to each other for 7 years. Father was unable to discuss his personal problems with his mentor. In his heart, he knew it was the booze.

Father told Connie that he wanted a sabbatical because he could stop drinking if he got out of Montana for awhile. In other words, Father was looking for what recovering alcoholics call, a "the geographic cure."[227] Father wrote to Cooky to let her know that he was moving to New York. He promised they would see much more of each other. Cooky was surprised and thrilled that he was coming but she didn't understand the details behind his move.

After Mary's death, Cooky had graduated from nursing school and now she was living in a rooming house and working full-time at her profession. Cooky had always been a hard worker, never without a good job, but haunted about her former life in Montana and about her relatives that she rarely saw. She had adapted to life in the white world but something had always been missing, something spiritual that she could not touch, a meaningful part of her heart that felt empty. She could never explain this terrible void to anyone. Father Emmett was the link to her past, with who she truly was, and she was thrilled that he was coming to New York, she hoped, for good.

Before Fr. Emmett packed to leave St. Labre, he dreaded the thought of writing his farewell letter to donors:

> This is a difficult letter to write. My years at St. Labre have done something to me. I experienced Cheyenne suffering and their frustrations, so much a part of reservation life. Gradually all my worries about the needs of the children and their families began to take their toll. There were long days and often sleepless nights . . . I thought about the school children. What will be their future? Down through the years, everything that I have accomplished at St. Labre has been possible because you cared enough to help. You have really done me a great honor by letting me be the instrument of your caring and charity . . . I know my limitations . . . I love these people too much to stand in their way of progress.[228]

In June of 1977, Fr. Emmett left St. Labre and drove to Wisconsin. A year earlier, a southern black woman had given a sizable donation and property to St. Labre in her will. She had also given an old pink

Cadillac that she said was specifically: "For Fr. Emmett." The car was still in running condition. All it needed was a tune-up and tires. When Father drove out of St. Labre in a pink, Cadillac convertible, pulling a U-Haul, it must have been a strange sight, but he didn't care.

He stopped in Wisconsin to see his mother before going on to New York. But when he tried to explain his frustrations with the priesthood and how badly he needed a leave of absence, Regina Hoffmann didn't understand. "I just don't believe it!" she snapped. Father had hoped for a heart-to-heart talk with her, but that was not to be. He always had to be her perfect son, an ideal he could never reach.

From Wisconsin, Father pushed eastward. He couldn't wait to get to New York City, where his long-time friend and advisor, stock broker Paul Morigi, had given him a tip on a job at the United Nation's Plaza in Manhattan. Father interviewed and got the job ($25,000 a year), while Connie and Ruth Sump helped him look for an apartment. The apartments in Queens were dirty and infested with cockroaches. He inspected a tiny apartment with one bedroom and a kitchenette for $500 a month. The closer he got to the city, the more expensive the rent. Father couldn't believe that a small, efficiency unit with a rickety bed that folded out of the wall, cost over $1,000 a month, with no place to park his car. He ended up living much further away from the city in a high-rise called the Shore Towers. His 19th floor apartment had a distant view of the Manhattan skyline.

Father always woke up early before daylight for prayers, which always included prayers for Mission donors. He watched the morning light when it first struck the buildings of Midtown. Father could barely see Shea Stadium in the distance and he got up many mornings and couldn't even see the ground for the fog. Every morning he drove 8 miles, parked his car and rode the subway into Manhattan. He walked from the subway to his office building. It took a long time, but he needed the exercise. On weekends he sat on his couch and stared at the skyline, drink in hand. It took awhile before he felt comfortable enough to venture out on Sundays. One evening at dinner he told Connie and Ruth: "Please don't call me Father Emmett! Just call me Emmett."[229] Father was having serious thoughts about leaving the priesthood.

CHAPTER 16

"I am an alcoholic."

C ooky was disappointed when Emmett called saying that he had found an apartment outside the city. Anyway, he was in New York, closer to her than he'd been in years and that's all that mattered. On weekends she came to visit him and every time he got paid, they went out to eat at fancy restaurants. She felt important sitting next to him, just like she had as a child.

Meanwhile, Connie had been riding the fence between Mr. Dohn Sr., who was still his client, and Emmett. Connie knew that New York could destroy an individual and that Emmett had moved to the Big Apple for an exciting change, for the tremendous variety of experiences available to him. But at first, Emmett discovered little more than arrival and departure times of the trains he took to work. He was desk bound during the day in one of the plushest buildings in New York, a Manhattan worker, breathing the pollution that drifted over the city. Restaurants and bars were dark, overcrowded and feverish, – no circulating air and not enough light. Yet, Emmett enjoyed the endless spectacle and the tension, no matter how crowded and uncomfortable it got. Or so he thought.

When the hot summer months arrived, it was a different story. Summer nights brought aching loneliness. He soon found that nowhere is a person more alone than in the pulsating crowds of New York City. Downtown, in Times Square, he stepped over drunks on the sidewalks and inched around them in doorways and on benches, their feet sticking out from under old clothes and newspapers. He was horrified too see drunks piled like cockroaches one on top of the other in Times Square.

They clustered together – the lowest forms of degradation in one of the most exciting and colorful cities on earth.

But Emmett told himself that he wasn't in that heap of low-life bodies under the neon lights. He had a job, a nice apartment and he ate well. He told himself that he wasn't like those besotted wretches. He drank alone, at night, talking to Mary, to himself and to God. True, he wasn't in the gutter, but empty despair told him that moving to New York hadn't stopped him from drinking. The "geographic cure" didn't work because he brought his alcoholism with him. He couldn't run away from himself. Should he remain a priest when everything he had worked for seemed gone? Without Mary, without the familiar sounds of Cheyenne children at play, he thought about giving up everything. Besides, he had lost his mentor and friend, Leo Dohn, and he knew the demons of alcohol had ruined his health. Somehow, he held on to his vow to help the Cheyennes, but a vision now dimmed by booze.

During his former days as a priest, Emmett had offered Mass every day. He no longer did that. On Sunday, he attended Mass in different Catholic Churches but he never heard a decent sermon – every sermon was about money. He found it hard to be on the other side of the pulpit listening to trite messages, but it opened his eyes to what parishioners felt. He told himself that if he ever went back to the active ministry, things would be different. People were starving to hear something meaningful. Some of the Churches were magnificent buildings with huge crowds but parishioners had to move out of church fast before the next crowd came into the parking lot.

As much as he tried to hide it, word soon got out in his office building that Emmett was really "Father Emmett," a Catholic priest. Many embassies were located in the same building and it didn't take long before the people practically lined up to talk to him. They came to him saying, "Father, can I talk to you?" with pleading looks on their faces. It showed him that priests were needed – that he was needed.

New Yorkers came to work early in the morning, fought traffic for two hours, worked all day and by the time they got home it was 9 p.m. and they were exhausted. On Sunday they went to Mass and the priest would ask them why they weren't more involved in the church. Priests only kept office hours to see parishioners between 3 and 4 p.m. What chance did working people have to see a priest during those hours? It did him good to see the Church from the other side of the fence.

He learned to appreciate how hard it was for people to remain loyal to the Church. People needed heart-to-heart talks with a caring priest and they cornered Emmett in the elevator and in the street. He was experiencing his own inner turmoil, yet he saw their hunger to speak to a priest and he admired their deep faith when everything else was working against them. Underneath their sometimes rough exteriors, New Yorkers were a deeply caring and religious people.

Emmett worked as office manager for Wider Horizons, a business that promoted cultural diversity through world travel. They sponsored artistic groups from different countries like Jose Greco's flamenco dance group. In his new career, Emmett arranged cultural exchanges with U.S. high school students to live abroad for various lengths of time with foreign families.

Wider Horizons was the brainchild of a man who had innovative ideas but he wasn't a businessman. Emmett had made a one-year commitment to work for Wider Horizons, but the business was so messed up by the time he took the job, there wasn't much he could do. The owner whipped out his checkbook whenever he saw something he liked in Paris, Madrid or Copenhagen and he didn't keep a record of his expenses. Father cornered him about his spending but the man continued to spend with impunity.

Every morning Emmett left early in the morning and was at his desk by 7 a.m., a good time to get things done because he couldn't say no to the people from different countries who lined up in the hall to tell him their problems. After work, he'd also listen to their troubles and then stop off at the bars. On weekends he cleaned, did the laundry, ironed and washed the old pink Cadillac. Cooky came over from Newark on a regular basis.

Emmett got to know the city; lower Manhattan, Midtown, Harlem and the Bronx. At first he was afraid of the ghettos but he ended up walking around the streets of Harlem and met some nice people. Sometimes he went to a play or took Cooky to La Pensa, another of Leo Dohn's favorite Italian restaurants. Emmett didn't have to look at the menu. "You figure out what we want to eat tonight," he told a waiter he knew. They always had a marvelous meal. This special time together cemented Cooky's relationship with the father figure she had adored since childhood.[230]

Early one morning in August of 1977, Emmett noticed a man who bore a striking resemblance to Truman Capote, the author of *In Cold Blood,* staggering into the UN Plaza lobby. Emmett enjoyed watching the Tonight Show with Johnny Carson and he could have sworn he recognized this man from a guest appearance. He was right. The eccentric Truman Capote lived in a penthouse atop the building. It was said of Capote that, "he enacted most of the dramas in his life in public . . ."[231] This clearly seemed to be the case. Emmett didn't realize that Capote was fed up with life and was contemplating suicide. The author had recently been rejected by his gay lover and he was tragically consumed by anger and resentment, even revenge. One of Capote's biographers wrote that it was "perhaps the darkest depression he had ever known."[232] Capote always looked disheveled and was usually so drunk that he didn't know which elevator to take up to his penthouse. At first, Emmett felt sorry for him. He took him to the correct lobby, pushed the elevator button and waited to make sure the little man made it into the elevator.

Capote would often eat dinner at Quo Vadis or La Petite Marmite, then stop in at the infamous Studio 54 and end up at a bar across the street from the UN Plaza, where a noted fashion magazine editor said he acted like a "tiny terror."[233] Emmett usually found him early in the morning as Capote arrived from a wild night on the town. Hanging on to the wall to steady himself, Capote muttered to himself in babyish, nasal tones. He always wore a wrinkled beige suit and hat. After helping the man several times, Emmett started thinking that Capote was "really a weird guy. He gave me the creeps!"

Disco fever hit New York's night clubs at about the same time and it seemed that everyone wore bell bottom trousers and polyester suits – everyone except Emmett, who wore a pressed suit to work and a conservative tie. The movie "Star Wars" was a 1977 smash hit, but Emmett didn't see it, just as he hadn't seen the movie "Jaws" or the Statue of Liberty at close range. One of the places he found intriguing and thoroughly enjoyed was the exciting floor of the Stock Exchange. This was his kind of place. Once a month, he and Paul Morigi went to lunch and walked around Wall Street. This was his chance to spend time with a man he considered a genius in his field. For many years, Morigi had helped Emmett invest and expand St. Labre's portfolio in the stock market. The stockbroker was always a gentleman and Emmett greatly respected him.

A real eye-opener came when Emmett stood in the street near the UN Plaza and watched the demonstrations against the Shah of Iran. The Shah had ruled his country since 1941 but by 1977, his opponents were charging him with wide-spread corruption and the torture of political prisoners. Student demonstrators wanted the Shah, a long-time friend of the United States, overthrown, and the Ayatollah Khomeini to return from exile to lead an Islamic revolution. In New York, Emmett watched the demonstrations in the streets and was amazed to see that news reporters whipped the crowds into a frenzy with speeches and rigorous chanting. Then they filmed for the nightly news. The demonstrations he observed were staged. Within two years, 2 million people went to the streets in Iran to express support for the Ayatollah and hatred for the United States. The pro-western Shah fled into exile in 1979, and 63 Americans were taken hostage by students demanding the return of the Shah to face trial. Apparently, New York newsmen had played a dangerous role in inciting demonstrations that ultimately led to the hostage ordeal.

The Vietnam nightmare and the scandal over Watergate caused many Americans to lose faith in their government during the 1970s.[234] The general mood was of disillusionment and mistrust of world leaders, while at the same time, people began to appreciate the environment. The feminist movement gained new force, "The Godfather," starring Marlon Brando, portrayed America's organized crime syndicates, the first test-tube baby was born, John Paul II became the first Polish Pope and the first video game went on the market.

Back in Ashland, Montana, the Tongue River flooded its banks and the campus at St. Labre. Students took rowboats into the gym and played boat basketball, exasperating school administrators, who were scrambling to save textbooks and files. Viola wrote to Emmett about the flood and he expressed his condolences and his delight that he wasn't there to have to deal with the clean up. He was also glad that he had missed out on the Northern Cheyenne coal problem, a concern since the early 1970s, when the Bureau of Indian Affairs leased 56 % of the Northern Cheyenne Reservation to 5 large coal companies for prospecting purposes. A one billion dollar coal gasification plant was proposed by Consolidation Coal Company. They wanted to acquire mining rights to a billion tons of coal for 25 years.[235]

Tribal member Tom Gardner, Community Action Director, described the general Cheyenne debate over the mining of coal at that time:

We see prosperity from the coal, but we also see many thousands of white people – perhaps 30,000 miners and technicians and the people to serve them, when we are only a few thousand (tribal members). We see a population explosion, with bars, stores and discrimination against our people. My people are not competitive in the white man's sense and will be left out, swept aside. So it is not only coal we would lose and the damage to our lands, for a few million dollars – it is our way of life.[236]

Tribal members investigated the coal leases and found that permits which had been issued by the BIA involved gross violations of the law. The Secretary of the Interior issued a decision virtually stopping the coal companies from proceeding without further consent of the tribe. The final decision came just days before Peabody Coal Company, the nation's largest strip mining operator, was to begin a $7,000,000 mining investment on 16,000 acres of leased reservation land.[237]

Emmett had missed most of the coal developments and the flood clean up operations in Montana but in New York he found that he had to clean up a financial mess. By the end of the summer, Wider Horizons was in deep trouble and he finally told the owner that his business was beyond saving. Fed up with his job, the heat and the crowds, he yearned for the clean air and the wide open spaces of Big Sky Country. Emmett wasn't feeling well and sometimes he'd wake up in the night sweating in fear that he might die in New York and end up buried in one of the endless blocks of cemeteries he had seen on his weekend drives.

Viola went to New York for a short visit and Sister Phyllis arrived about the same time. One evening Vi noticed that Emmett was alarmingly short of breath. He had already told Sister Phyllis that he was returning to Montana and Sister decided that because of his health problems, she would help him drive back by way of Marathon, Wisconsin. While Sister Phyllis and Viola were in New York, Cooky joined them and he took them all to see some famous sites in the area.

Connie, Ruth and Emmett went out to dinner one night to a seafood place on the south shore. Both men got drunk. "I just have to get out of here!" Emmett told them. "I've experienced life on the other side. I've proved to myself that I can survive."[238] Connie was relieved. The pastoral work that Emmett was doing at the United Nations Plaza was satisfying but he couldn't follow through on many of the problems people came to him with, such as annulments and counseling. Life as a businessman didn't completely satisfy him either. He wanted to get back to active ministry combined with business. But he was sick, and he knew it. Sister Phyllis helped him pack and they drove to Wisconsin via Niagara Falls. They had a good time on the trip but Sister noticed that the closer they came to Marathon, the more agitated her brother became, possibly because of the meeting he was to have with their mother. He did have the forethought to buy a religious collar before going home.[239] His friends in New York and all of his family in Wisconsin were relieved when Emmett left the Big Apple.

Cooky, however, was heart-broken. "I was numb after he left. I didn't really get to say goodbye to him alone. When he came, he'd told me, "'I'm here for you now and I love you.'" She had been so lonely after her mother passed away and her engagement had ended. She had dreamt of a life with the only father she had known, but it was not to last. One night he took her out to dinner and told her he was leaving to return to the priesthood. "I was totally destroyed," she said.[240]

The day he left, Cooky went to work. Now in a haze, she went on her nursing rounds as usual, comforting others, giving loving care to critically ill people. That night as she got ready to leave the hospital, she broke down in sobs. The pain of losing the father she loved, once again took control, and she could barely make it back to her rooming house, which now seemed dark and empty. Her weekends came and went and she missed the exciting times with her charismatic dad.

Father Emmett called her often when he got back to Montana but Cooky was so depressed that their conversations usually consisted of his asking her: "Are you okay?' to which she replied, "I don't know." There were long silences. "Are you still there? he asked. She couldn't tell him how hurt she was that he had left her again. She didn't want him to return to the priesthood, but she couldn't tell him that either. It seemed so selfish. She was angry, hurt and very depressed for a long time. Years later she recalled: "That next year was hell."[241]

Father Emmett went back to Montana, but not as a Capuchin. He hadn't made up his mind about them yet. He worked as an interim Diocesan priest in the small town of Culbertson, in northeast Montana. It was a nice parish in a conservative ranching community, but the pace was too slow for him, especially after New York. His health had deteriorated, his weight skyrocketed and he could hardly walk across a room without gasping for breath. Finally, Father went to a heart specialist and the doctor told him what he already suspected. If Father wanted to live, he had to have bypass surgery.

Successful bypass surgery was performed in November of 1978, and Father Emmett was out of commission for six weeks. Viola helped take care of him after the surgery but she had misgivings. The day Father Emmett got out of the hospital, he ordered a drink with dinner. She protested, but he drank it anyway.

From Culbertson, Father was assigned to St. Bernard's parish in Billings, where he immediately saw that the Church had a seating capacity for only 200 people – not enough room. He hadn't been at St. Bernard's long before he started telling people they needed a new Church. He organized a building committee and started getting pledges. The goal was to raise $750,000 in two years. The parish needed half the money before they could borrow the balance from the diocese. As usual, critics said it couldn't be done. They were afraid they would never be able to repay the loan. Father Emmett had complete faith that it could and would be done. When the new Church was completed, it sat 1,000 people. Parishioners who had gone elsewhere to Church now returned and it didn't take long to pay off the loan.

Occasionally, Father Emmett heard negative comments from St. Bernard's parishioners about his drinking habits, but he ignored them. He was far too busy fund raising to worry about a few drinks. But everyone was beginning to notice his alcohol problem. Father was in complete denial about his occasional blackouts, his shaking hands and the attacks of rigidity. At Christmas 1980, he planned a big parish party. He delighted in Christmas, his favorite holiday, and he enjoyed decorating St. Bernard's. The party was a resounding success but a few eyebrows went up when the bartender for the night turned out to be a boozy Father Emmett.

Meanwhile, word of Father's drinking problem had reached the Provincial. Connie Sump got a call in January 1981 from Provincial Father Ron Smith. Apparently, he, Fr. Irvin Udulutsch and brother Paul Hanisko had decided to arrange an "intervention" in an attempt to convince Father Emmett to seek treatment for alcoholism. They feared that if he didn't stop drinking, it would kill him. The only problem with the intervention was their concern that Father might get angry when they confronted him. Nobody wanted to face Fr. Emmett when he was mad. Father Ron asked Connie Sump to take part in the intervention. With Connie present, Father Emmett would know they meant business. Connie was the only one who could handle him.[242]

The team planned to have the intervention in Billings where they could confront Fr. Emmett together. They wouldn't judge his behavior or accuse him. Instead, they needed to show grave concern about his drinking, using specific incidents to demonstrate how his risky behavior had been inappropriate. They were prepared for his denial. Connie was especially vulnerable since his long time friendship with Emmett was on the line. But he felt that unless Father realized the damage he'd done to friendships, his happiness, his self respect and job performance, he wouldn't commit to changing his life. Father Emmett alone was responsible for his success or failure at recovery and that meant immediate treatment at a good treatment center out of state. The team approach was the only way to show the powerful, stubborn priest that he was way out of line.

The Provincial called Fr. Emmett and told him that he and others were coming to Billings for a meeting. This was not unusual since priests came and went from Billings on a regular basis. The day came for the Provincial's arrival and Father Emmett greeted him. Later, Connie arrived and he spoke to the group for a few minutes. "Well, I better get outta here and let you guys go on with your meeting," Father Emmett told the visitors. He stood up to say goodbye.

"Emmett, sit down!" Father Ron told him. "We've come to Billings to talk to you!"[243]

Father Emmett immediately sensed they had come for an intervention. Before they could say anything, he piped up: "This is an intervention, isn't it? All right, I know I need help. I'm ready to go! " The team had expected hostility or at least a stubborn response, but Fr. Emmett was way ahead of them. They didn't get a chance to confront him about his self-destructive behavior, about how drinking had interfered in his relationship with others. They didn't get the chance to tell him that if he didn't go into treatment, they would have to reassess their friendship with him. None of that was necessary now because Fr. Emmett already knew that he was on the brink of losing everything he had worked for. He detested alcohol and wanted to get rid of the addiction that was strangling his life and work. Father was ready to surrender his problem to a higher power – to admit to God that he was powerless over alcohol.[244]

The next morning, Father boarded a plane for Lake Orion, Michigan, where he entered a three-month alcoholic treatment center for priests called Guest House. He had been there for a month when Connie came for a visit. Connie saw that Father Emmett was sober and ready to change his life, but it was going to take a lot of work.

Father completed 60 days of treatment and then went home on therapeutic leave for a week before returning for the final 30 days. During his stay at Guest House he had a thorough medical examination and began counseling sessions with a therapist he trusted. It was the first time in his life that he had opened up about his childhood. Now, he looked at his past behavior as an alcoholic.

Priests with alcohol problems were much harder to help than others, as they bore tremendous guilt for their actions. The program was designed to make them realize that although they would always be recovering alcoholics and need treatment, they could still be good priests. They had time to get back their self respect.

During counseling sessions, Father Emmett realized that his father had also been an alcoholic. Later, when he tried to tell his mother, she totally denied it. "Dad had blackouts like I did," he told her. But in his mother's eyes, a man could be a drunkard, but that didn't mean he was an alcoholic! Although Father explained about the treatment program and how much it had helped him to remain sober, Regina Hoffmann denied that her son was an alcoholic and she never changed her mind.[245]

Father Emmett left Guest House knowing that he could never take another drink as long as he lived. To remain strong in that commitment it would be necessary for him to attend 12-step meetings twice a week and to keep in touch with his sponsor, Connie Sump. He trusted Connie and they called each other every day and supported one another in their sobriety.

During Church services on the first Sunday Fr. Emmett returned to St. Bernard's, he stood up and astounded the congregation with a special, heartfelt announcement:

> Today, I have a confession to make. I am an alcoholic. I'm sure most of you knew that anyway. I want to tell you that I've been gone for months because I was in an alcoholic treatment program. I am now in recovery and I'm making a fresh start as

a sober man. I'm terribly sorry if I have offended anyone in the parish – I'm sure I did from time to time. I hope you will all forgive me.

I am a priest versed in theology, but something was missing from my life. I almost lost my spirituality. I came back here to find a loving God, to whom I could relate. Please keep me in your prayers.[246]

He sat down and the Church was so silent he could hear himself breathing. Suddenly, the whole sanctuary erupted in applause. It was the first time Father Emmett had gotten a standing ovation in church.

CHAPTER
17

Capuchin Power Struggles

C heyenne tribal visionary, John Woodenlegs, died at the age of 71 years in 1981. He had started out as a farm hand, then cowboy, road worker, coal miner and rancher. He served as president of the Northern Cheyenne Tribe from 1955-1968 and he was the first Native American to receive an honorary degree from the University of Montana. Woodenlegs was also President of the Northern Cheyenne branch of the Native American Church from 1946-1975.

Like Chief Dull Knife before him, the celebrated tribal chairman valued education: "The time is past when we have to keep living in some old, broken down way," he told his tribe. "Education . . . is the key to our future . . ."[247] Woodenlegs worked for many years towards the development of a tribal college and he lived to see his dream come true when Dull Knife Memorial College (now Chief Dull Knife College) became a reality. Many consider John Woodenlegs the greatest Northern Cheyenne leader of the 20th century. Often quoted, John told his people: "We have been mistreated in the past but we can forgive and forget because God forgives all people."[248]

Not long after Woodenleg's death, Father Emmett heard from Viola that morale at St. Labre during the 1982-83 school year was at an all-time low. Unrest and disagreements among staff and administrators had upset the entire school. The end results were student walkouts, fights among the staff and resignations.

Disrupted by complaints and school demonstrations, local newspapers picked up on it. "The atmosphere is not as happy as it once was," a student told a reporter. "School just isn't fun here anymore." In a local newspaper editorial, a parent wrote: ". . . the problems at our school are extremely out of control!"[249]

Before Father Emmett left for his sabbatical year in New York, he told friends, "If the BIA ever gives up on St. Labre, I'll be back." Word now reached him that Bureau of Indian Affairs officials and the tribe felt that problems were so severe at the school that something had to be done before donors stopped funding. That was all Fr. Emmett needed to hear. He jumped at the chance to return to St. Labre and once again took over the reins. His hard-driving way of achieving goals did not please everyone, but his dedication to his work was obvious to all who knew him well.

After the successful 5-day Centennial celebrations at St. Labre in July of 1984, Father resumed his fund raising efforts with gusto. His first letter to donors in 7 years came out in September: "I cannot rest until we have completed our work . . . I rededicate myself to helping every Indian family in this land of poverty and unemployment, to realize a part of the dream we all share . . . my hope comes from the love I saw in every donor's face during our Centennial celebration."[250]

Against all odds, Father had survived his bypass surgery. With God's help he had found sobriety and his original vow to dedicate his life to the Cheyennes had not faded away. The old spark of inspiration returned. On June 27, 1984, Billings Gazette reporter, Roger Clawson, wrote: "The history . . . of St. Labre is a roll call of legendary names . . . Mother Amadeus and the proud chiefs are dead but one man of the legend lives – Father Emmett Hoffmann." Clawson also noted: "When Montana's state governor faced a budget crisis in the early 1970s, Billings mayor, Willard Fraser suggested: "Put Father Emmett in charge for 60 days. He will have us back in the black."

After Father returned to St. Labre, he had so much to accomplish that he had no time to relax. Sobriety had not alleviated the nagging voice in his head that told him he wasn't doing a perfect job. He felt a sense of internal irritation with himself if he didn't perform up to his own high expectations. Now sober for three years, he faithfully attended sobriety meetings, where he shared his problems and sense of frustration with other alcoholics. He often told people: "The weak become the instruments of God to accomplish His great tasks." Before he attained sobriety, Father Emmett would never have referred to himself as "weak," but in the 12-step method of maintaining sobriety he tried his best to take life, "one day at a time."

One of the pitfalls of being a high-energy person was that at times Father unknowingly made other people feel nervous. They were afraid they couldn't perform as well as he wanted them to. This especially antagonized a small group of priests among the Capuchins in Montana. To them, Fr. Emmett appeared neglectful of his religious community. They felt that the true meaning of fraternity as Franciscans was to have a greater sense of unity and commitment to one another. Whenever they came to eat at the friary, it drove Father Emmett wild when he saw them sitting around for hours psychoanalyzing each other. He couldn't stand whining and complaining. "I'm not a person for meetings when nothing happens but navel-gazing," he told Connie. "They waste too much time with internal maintenance as it is."[251]

Father could never bring himself to communicate his uncomfortable feelings around priests he felt were not strictly heterosexual. He got along fine with most of the Capuchins but he couldn't deal with allegedly "unmanly" men, whether or not they were priests. In turn, they became defensive. Father didn't want to judge people unfairly so he ignored them – probably the only way at the time to deal with the reality of the situation.

From the old school, Father believed that men were men and women were women and that was that. If Father had told certain Capuchins exactly how he felt and how the Cheyenne people felt – that sexually conflicted priests should not be allowed to work with Indian children, he would have seemed homophobic. In those days, nobody in the church spoke of "gay" men and certainly the words "pedophile" or "ephebophile" were terms used only by psychiatrists. Father had heard that homosexual men were often promiscuous with young boys. St. Labre was a predator's paradise, a perfect set up for a priest looking to seduce a child. Indian reservations across the country had suffered in silence for many years with priestly child molesters in their midst.[252] In private meetings, the Cheyennes complained bitterly about priests whose sexual orientation worried them.

Catholic schools provided a better education for their children, but the question remained – should they trust their youngsters with priests?[253] Horror stories abounded. An Indian girl (not at St. Labre) impregnated by a priest was sent away to get rid of her baby. Instead, she brought the little girl back to her reservation. Countless Indian boys were molested in friaries. Short of outright violence or burglarizing friaries to scare priests away, tribal members could do nothing but seethe with disrespect for a Church that continued to let it happen.

Connie Sump, however, was not a priest and there was no question about his manliness. A strong personality, Connie seemed like a combination of several men; sometimes a wheeler-dealer with a cigar hanging out of his mouth, or a gruff longshoreman. He was also a brilliant CPA with a generous heart. Some people were immediately taken aback by his aggressive eastern manner of doing business, while others admired his forthrightness. But in the last analysis, Connie was the only white man who could get Father to slow down and have fun. He accepted Father's highly competitive nature, valued his friendship and was proud of his success. Connie's wholehearted support during Father Emmett's early years of sobriety strengthened their friendship, as both men reached the top in their respective fields of endeavor.

When Father Emmett came back to St. Labre, he began to make amends to family and friends, including Connie, one of the steps of a sober man in the 12-step sobriety program. He made sincere apologies to Leo Dohn and his son for his past actions while drinking. Leo had also been on the outs with his son for some time and Father took this opportunity to suggest a three-way reconciliation. Leo Sr. wasn't getting any younger. Perhaps it was time that all three men forgave each other. Soon afterward, Dohn and his son reunited and Father asked Leo Sr. to sit on the St. Labre Board of Directors. Leo accepted the invitation, ending 7 years of hard feelings between them. The Dohns were impressed to see Father sober and productive once again.[254]

Over the years Father considered Cheyenne friendships critical to his well-being. His Cheyenne colleague, Tony Foote, was a fine example of bi-cultural success. Born and raised on the Northern Cheyenne Reservation, Tony spent 14 years working for Guild Arts and Crafts. He started out as an assembly line worker. Determined to improve his career, he took evening bookkeeping classes at Miles City Community College and eventually worked himself up to the position of Office Supervisor at the factory. When the factory closed in 1977, Tony was hired as Comptroller at St. Labre.[255]

In his spare time, Tony led a Boy Scout group and was President of the

Employee Credit Union, offering savings accounts and small loans to employees. Fr. Emmett admired Tony's honesty, efficiency, diplomacy and unusual dry humor. Tony was careful what he did and never said much, but when he spoke, people listened. Lee Eckman, one of Tony's friends, said of him: "Tony had a keen sense of right and wrong. If he ran into a con artist, he had no use for him. He was unforgiving. If someone pulled a fast one on him, he never forgot."[256]

Cheyenne elder and longtime St. Labre employee, Eddie Foote, also held a special place in Father Emmett's heart. When Eddie's wife Regina had her hands and feet amputated due to diabetes complications, Eddie lovingly cared for her. He carried his wife to the bathroom, to and from the car, to visit relatives, to church, to the store and to pow wows. He dressed and fed her. Eddie's faithful devotion to his wife made him a role model for countless young boys at St. Labre and for all the younger men in his family.[257]

When it became necessary for Regina to travel to Billings three times a week for dialysis treatments, everyone in the family suffered because Eddie had to take off work. He didn't have enough gas money and Regina didn't want to leave her family. Father watched Eddie's escalating exhaustion, until finally, he stepped in. Father persuaded the Indian Health Service to install a dialysis machine so that Regina could spend more time with her family in the last months of her life.

Although Eddie's personal life was often difficult, he was a practical joker and he found his match in Robert Bement. Robert graduated from St. Labre and Western Montana School of Science, then took his first and last job, St. Labre's head printer. Sometimes Robert went golfing with Fr. Emmett, until Father found out that he was moving Father's golf ball off the green to replace it with that of a rival player. Father finally caught on and although he joked about it, he probably pulled a fast one on Robert later on.

One day Robert decided to play a joke on Eddie Foote. He put a plastic, half-filled pail of water over the door to the print shop. The plan was to drench Eddie when he walked in. But the day Robert implemented his scheme happened to be the day that Fr. Emmett was giving a television announcer a tour of the school. When they reached the print shop, Eddie, who was just about to go in, let Father go in first. The second he opened the door, the pail tipped and Father took a cold shower in front of his guest. Robert was hiding behind the press when Father found him. "You guys are always messing with me!" he laughed. Father could dish it out as well as take it.[258]

Due to Father's numerous contributions to the citizens of Montana, he received the 1985 Montana Jefferson Award for Outstanding Public Service Benefiting Local Communities. St. Labre employee Jennett Brey wrote the letter of recommendation for the award. She listed the buildings he had constructed and the programs he initiated and in closing she wrote: "Besides all this, he is a friend to one and all."[259]

Jennett Brey worked hard and at the same time, she took time to tease everybody. She made Fr. Emmett laugh, especially when she saw that he was under stress. A Chippewa Cree, Jennett's outgoing personality made her a favorite at the Mission. Every Sunday before Mass, Jennett and her daughter Patsy picked the best flowers from her "Friendship Garden" and decorated the church altar. Besides her devotion to St. Labre, "No sacrifice was too big when it came to her kids," remembers daughter, Patsy Brey, (a St. Labre employee for more than 40 years.)[260] "She was thankful for the Mission," added another daughter, Delores Little Coyote. "Mom worked in the clothing room and each Christmas she fixed a bundle of clothing, combs, toys and books for each student."[261] For thirty years Jennett saw to it that no child missed out on Christmas.

Indian women like Jennett were resourceful when times were hard, and they were almost always hard. Jennett had an interesting sideline that kept food on the table. Every morning in the dead of winter she went out to check her trap lines along the Tongue River. She rarely failed to bring home a beaver or a fox. She skinned and dried her pelts and sold them to a fur trader in order to feed her five children. Members of her family say that Jennett knew how to use a gun. One morning she found a bobcat attacking her dog. She raised her rifle and shot the bobcat right between the eyes.

Another aspect of Jennett's interesting personality was her fondness for poetry and literature, including her favorite works by William Shakespeare. Many non-Indians came to Jennett with their problems because she had a gift – she wasn't a licensed psychologist but she could heal a raw nerve and the wettest eye with her wit and her way of looking at life. Around Indian friends like Jennett, Father Emmett relaxed and laughed at himself. He joined in her teasing because he knew Indians weren't going to turn on him unless he really deserved it.

Besides his close friend, Bisco Spotted Wolf, whom he referred to as his "guiding light," Father regarded fellow Chief, "Jimmie" D. Little Coyote as his younger brother. When the new museum and administration building opened at St. Labre, Father asked Jimmie and his wife Juanita to develop the collections and design the exhibits. Over the years, Cheyenne friends had given Father many beaded gifts and he now donated his substantial collection, making the St. Labre Museum one of the best in Montana.

Jimmie, the son and grandson of Sacred Hat Keepers, was a Sundancer, a member of the Native American Church and the Northern Cheyenne Council of 44. His traditional Cheyenne name was Chief Appears In Sight. Little Coyote's many talents paid off and his friendly, diplomatic approach with St. Labre visitors made him a valuable employee.

One day a group of white people visited the museum. One of the ladies studied a buckskin dress displayed in a glass case and Jimmie told her it was a Cheyenne dress. "That is not a Cheyenne dress!" the woman insisted. "For heaven's sake, can't you tell it's not Cheyenne!" Jimmie, a full blood Cheyenne, smiled at the woman and led her to another exhibit. After the visitors left the museum, he went over and admired the beadwork and fringes on the buckskin dress in question. "That was my grandmother's dress," he chuckled.

At the end of his life, Jimmie spent weeks in bed at home or in the hospital, suffering from diabetes. During that time, more than 600 visitors came to see him in a steady, reverent stream. He told one visitor: "Fr. Emmett baptized me, he confirmed me, he signed my high school diploma, he hired me and he will probably bury me."

Before Jimmie passed away, the artist's face took on the handsome, chiseled look of his forefathers. His daughter Dewanda rarely left her father's side in a display of love so impressive that Fr. Emmett told a friend: "I will never forget her devotion. After Jimmie died, she became like an adopted daughter to me."[262] The hospital staff cried when Jimmie died. At the funeral, his 9 year-old grandson, Cordell James (CJ), became the youngest Northern Cheyenne Chief. With Bisco Spotted Wolf and Father Emmett by his side and with tears streaming down his face, CJ put on his grandfather's headdress as the coffin was lowered into the grave. Jimmie's gentle legacy lives on.

Throughout his years at St. Labre, Father Emmett had many Indian and non-Indian assistants. In May of 1985, he hired a new secretary, Mary Jo Burkholder, a young graduate of the University of Missouri. She was a non-Catholic who knew nothing about priests. Not long after Mary Jo came on board, Father Emmett was out of state when he suffered another heart attack. This time he was out of work for two months and as always, Viola nursed him back to health.

Although she had little knowledge of fund raising, Mary Jo earned Father's respect when she confidently filled his shoes during his recovery. She proved a good administrator by working with other school staff, including Father Emmett's co-director, Father Dennis Druggan, with whom she did not always agree. After a lengthy recovery period, Fr. Emmett returned to St. Labre with renewed enthusiasm.

Father Emmett asked donors to contribute to a college scholarship fund for high school graduates who maintained good grades at St. Labre. This had been one of his dreams, an example of Father's long term planning for Cheyenne and Crow students. It wasn't enough to educate and train a child through high school. He always thought ahead to what type of employment problems Indian graduates might have and the grade point averages they would need in order to obtain teaching, nursing, medical, law or business degrees. He also made sure that graduates received a personal letter of recommendation for jobs or grants – anything to help them after high school.

Father also planned ahead to help the children in the five modern St. Labre Cheyenne Homes. In addition to acting as surrogate parents to neglected children, Father wanted house parents in the group homes to teach the kids to cook and take care of personal hygiene, how to make good choices and how to apply and interview for jobs. Nothing made Father Emmett happier than to hear from a young person who had graduated from St. Labre and successfully started a career. Letters from graduates and donors were the perks that kept him going. He read every letter and responded to all of them.

Mary Jo worked on at St. Labre until 1991, when she began to hear that younger priests were backstabbing Fr. Emmett. She finally told Father that she wasn't going to sit idly by while fellow priests tried to undermine and destroy him.[263] This was news to Father Emmett. Lee Eckman, manager of the Northern Cheyenne Pine Company in Ashland, had also heard that some of the younger priests were ganging up on him. "Father Emmett had the ability to forgive people within his order that he shouldn't have forgiven," Lee recalled. When Eckman told Father about his concerns and asked him what he said to those who slandered him, Father Emmett told him: "I pray for the bastards!"[264]

True to form, Father tried to remain loyal to his fellow Capuchins by ignoring the intrigue swirling around him. "I can't get replacements for these men that easily," he explained to Mary Jo. "I have to work with what I've got."[265]

"Father wouldn't take my advice," Mary Jo said. "I felt helpless. He was very careful not to judge people and there was nothing I could do. His fatal flaw was that he had unfailing trust and loyalty in people and he gave them unlimited chances."[266] Since Father Emmett had embraced sobriety, he was making a monumental effort to work with his Capuchin brethren.

Before she resigned, Mary Jo and the other women in administration bought Father Emmett a white, 6 week-old, West Highland Terrier. "Fergie" as she came to be called, an adorable puppy that kept Father busy and entertained. He had to walk her outside during the day, good exercise after a heart attack. Fergie became popular with everyone as Father grew more and more attached to the intelligent puppy. Fergie's huge smile captivated the children and she was welcome wherever she went.

Without Mary Jo as a buffer, Father became more vulnerable to the negative undercurrent surrounding him. Outwardly, he didn't let it slow him down. Instead, he focused on positive accomplishments. He and Connie had long discussed a way to bring more industry and employment to the Northern Cheyenne Tribe. In 1987, they met with tribal leaders to investigate buying and renovating the local sawmill. St. Labre would renovate the old and dangerous equipment and the tribe would sign a ten-year lease on the mill, with the stipulation that tribal members were to have job priority. At the end of ten years, the tribe would have the option to buy the mill.

When a reporter from the Big Horn County News interviewed Fr. Emmett and Connie regarding the sawmill project, Father told him that the "(Cheyenne) people want to feel they can provide for their families. The sawmill will not only provide employment, but also hope for the future."[267] Connie agreed. "I've watched the mill open and close over the years," he said. "It came down to this: either we opened the mill and kept it open or we left it alone. The payroll was over a million dollars a year. That money would be circulated in communities on and off reservation. The sawmill would create badly needed employment."[268]

Father toured the facility and then brought up the idea of renovating the mill to the St. Labre Board of Directors. They agreed to the project. But later, when the new Provincial Minister, Father Kenneth Reinhart was elected to the board, he demanded to know who had authorized the purchase of a "sling sorter," a machine that eliminated the need for a man to lift unbearably heavy timber with his bare hands. "Why should the Cheyenne people work like slaves in a dangerous environment?" Father Emmett asked. It was almost as though the Provincial didn't consider them worthy of good treatment. "I refuse to throw scraps to Cheyenne workers like they're animals! For God's sake, treat them like human beings!" Father told him.[269]

When Father Emmett reported the latest renovation to the board, the new Provincial, in a disrespectful tone, asked: "How did you make the decision to buy it without coming to the board for approval?" Father Emmett was accustomed to earlier Provincials and Bishops who had trusted him to do the best job possible. When the Provincial, who apparently knew little about running a business, questioned his authority, it seemed like a slap in the face. Father Emmett and the donors had built up St. Labre, St. Xavier Mission and St. Charles Mission and there had never been a question of how the money was spent. Father's fund raising efforts over the years had amounted to millions compared to the sling-sorter" in question. The hard feelings that began with the Provincial's disrespectful approach at the board meeting, would have lasting and tragic effects on St. Labre, Father Emmett's career and the Northern Cheyenne Tribe.

At the same time, Connie looked for ways to attract more industry and employment. He met with Leo Dohn Jr. to bring up the possibility of moving a portion of Dohn's orthodontic supply business, Polysapphire, Inc., to St. Labre. Dohn had planned to build an assembly plant in Mexico but Connie and Father Emmett talked him out of it. In 1988, Polysapphire, Inc. opened for business at the Mission, providing 30 Indian employees with special training in delicate electro-welding skills.

When the 1980s came to a laboring close, the hard feelings and growing number of complaints on all sides had divided the Capuchin

Fathers in Montana. Many Cheyenne employees at St. Labre believed there was a plan afloat to remove Father Emmett from the school that he loved. A major breakdown had occurred but it was not the Indians who had lost touch with reality.

Not all Capuchin friars were involved in the power struggle against Father Emmett. Many of the older priests knew the Mission and school was his life's work and they wrote to tell him so.[270] Perhaps the Capuchins believed their Indian neighbors were unaware of the back-stabbing that divided the Mission. If so, they were mistaken. The most telling statement of Catholic Indian sentiment in the midst of the Mission controversy came from Tony Foote, Cheyenne Comptroller at St. Labre, when he said: "It's getting so that I have to watch every word I say. I'm always on guard. I try to stay out of it. One thing I've learned around here – if they'll turn on Fr. Emmett, you never know who they'll turn on next."[271]

White people living on the borders of the reservation were heard to criticize the intrigue of "tribal politics." It should have come as no surprise as to where Indians learned to operate like "political animals." Their view was to take the best the white man had to offer and to throw away the rest. With that in mind, the Cheyennes ignored what was happening at St. Labre. They had stood behind Fr. Emmett many times in the past and they felt he could handle a few young priests with new ideas. Anyway, since nothing else of interest was happening, watching the priests fight among themselves became a daily diversion.

Father Emmett assumed an air of bravado to hide his insecurities. He kept his problems to himself and smiled to mask worries. But what angered his detractors the most was their perception of something secretive behind Father's camouflage of mischief and good humor. He loved to arouse a laugh or a gasp, a trait they found irritating.

But Capuchin criticism of Father's Emmett's endeavors to provide employment for tribal members began to wear on him. In a 1988 letter to donors he wrote: "I try to remain calm . . . but worries have caused me to have heart attacks in the past . . . I cannot let this happen again. Should I give up and let someone younger assume these responsibilities and worries? Deep down I know the answer. "You can't walk away. St. Labre is your life's work."[272]

The following August, as he made his way home after visiting children in one of the dorms, he began to think about the Cheyenne families who would be living without heat during the coming winter. Suddenly, his chest tightened and he couldn't breathe very well. "Oh no! Not another one!" he thought. Within a short time Father was airborne in an emergency helicopter on his way to St. Vincent's Hospital in Billings.

Capuchins priests and brothers had been at St. Labre since 1926, yet few of them understood the people they had come to serve. If they hadn't been feuding among themselves, perhaps they might have learned that unlike the white man, the Cheyenne people are not human beings on a spiritual journey. Instead, they are born spiritual and are on a human journey. For many years, Father Emmett had been on that journey with the Cheyenne people and he was willing to sacrifice his life for them.

CHAPTER 18

FBI Agents

F ather Emmett spent weeks in recovery after the heart attack and while recuperating, the National Catholic Development Conference elected him their president for the second time. As President of NCDC, the largest association of religious fund raising organizations in the country, Father worked to help Catholic fund raisers across the nation.

In January 1991, Leo Dohn Sr. resigned from the St. Labre Board of Directors and was appointed Director Emeritus. At the age of 86, his health had failed and he could no longer travel. The Northern Cheyenne Tribe had adopted him in the 1960s, and his good works were well known to them. Perhaps it was God's wish that Leo Dohn was not on the Board when tragedy struck St. Labre Indian School in the early hours of May 14, 1991.

That morning, Father Emmett called Connie in New York: "You won't believe this! Fr. Dennis just fired me! He said he's taking over St. Labre!"

"What do you mean fired," Connie scoffed. "He can't fire you!"

Father Dennis Druggan, nearly 30 years younger than Fr. Emmett, hadn't concealed his ambition. After a disagreement over funding, he had demanded Father Emmett's resignation as co-director of St. Labre.[273]

Father Emmett had snapped back. "I'm not leaving St. Labre!"

A few hours later, with no prior warning, Bureau of Indian Affairs officials, FBI agents and representatives from three Indian tribes descended upon St. Labre in vans and a helicopter. The Mission looked like a war zone; flashing lights, armed vehicles and rifles in hand. Without explanation, Rosebud County Sheriff's deputies removed 14 children from the St. Labre Cheyenne Homes.

Father Emmett had no idea what was going on. It didn't make sense. What were the charges? When confronted with the crisis, Fr. Dennis didn't know what to do. Somebody had to take control of the situation and it fell to Father Emmett to speak to the authorities.

He found out that deputies had legal orders from a judge to remove the children. "It was a little like a Gestapo operation," Father Emmett told a newspaper reporter. "They didn't tell us why they took the children away . . . It was really sad when the children were leaving. The FBI agents were there with guns - it was a traumatic experience for the kids."[274]

As a helicopter buzzed overhead, the Acting Area Director of the Bureau of Indian Affairs told newspaper reporters: ". . . federal investigators learned of accusations of abuse . . ." He declined to be more specific and the secrecy escalated rumors across the reservation.[275]

The children removed from St. Labre Homes ranged in ages from 8 to 14. Annoyed, Father Emmett told a reporter for the Billings Gazette: "I've been expecting someone to call, but no one has . . . This thing seems to be a big secret – we don't know what's going on."[276] When he finally found out that the complaint concerned the alleged sexual abuse of young boys by a priest in authority at St. Labre, he was shocked.

Lawyers for St. Labre discovered that the complaint had come from a devout Mormon staff member who had just attended a sexual abuse workshop. The zealous man had come back to St. Labre looking for abuse. At that point, it didn't really matter where the complaint had come from – the damage was already done.[277]

By law, nobody could stand in the way of the alleged child abuse investigation. According to established church policy, Provincial Kenneth Reinhart recalled Father Dennis Druggan from Montana.[278]

As he was leaving, Fr. Dennis told Viola that he suspected that Father

Emmett had been responsible for the abuse complaint and for his embarrassing removal. When Vi told Fr. Emmett, he was astonished that Fr. Dennis would think he was involved.[279] I had nothing to do with it!" he said.

In the weeks to come, all of the children taken from St. Labre were questioned about the alleged abuse. Subsequently, no charges were filed by county, state or federal authorities. Father Dennis wanted to go back to work, but Father Emmett didn't think it was a good idea. At that point, Father Dennis had no choice but to move on with his life.[280]

Several aggressive young priests among the Capuchins still in Montana wanted Father Emmett to resign, but he didn't give up, despite two quadruple bypass surgeries. He held on to his vow to educate and care for Cheyenne children. That vow of loyalty had kept him going through all the peaks and valleys of his life.

Over the years, many thousands of devoted donors depended upon Father to budget funds in a wise and prudent manner. Father Emmett felt that the younger priests had no business sense and he didn't want them to control the donations. Donors had entrusted their hard-earned money to Father Emmett to use in the construction of churches, rectories and schools on two reservations, over 50 school buildings, homes and apartments, the renovation of a sawmill, three successful factories, and five group homes for at-risk children based on Father Flanagan's "Boys Town" model.

Meanwhile, the Northern Cheyenne people were never told the outcome of the sexual abuse investigation at St. Labre. This left many parents distrustful and angry.[281] In truth, Father Emmett and the rest of the staff were told not to discuss the case with anyone due to possible legal actions. State and federal regulations prevented the Indians from knowing what was going on.

At the next quarterly St. Labre Board of Director's meeting, all went well until Provincial Ken Reinhart pulled Father Emmett aside in the hall during a break. With a straight face, he said: "Emmett, you have been accused of child molestation. I'm going to bring it up to the board." Father Emmett stared at the Provincial in disbelief.[282]

"What the hell are you talking about?" he said.

Poor posture made the Provincial appear shorter than he actually was. His small, darting eyes gave Reinhart, known as "Lance," a strange look.

The Provincial told Father Emmett that an unidentified woman had accused him of sexually molesting her when she was a five year-old girl back in the 1950s. The Provincial also said that a young friar had also accused Fr. Emmett of trying to have sexual contact with him.

Father Emmett told Connie what happened next:

> Suddenly, I saw the connection. It was like a light bulb going on in my brain. Ken Reinhart wanted to destroy me. I looked into his beady eyes and I said to myself, you lying SOB, if you thought I was guilty of such crimes, why didn't you report it to the police? That would have been the lawful thing to do.

Connie thought the Provincial was acting like a vengeful adolescent, making Father Emmett pay because he felt Father had deliberately driven Father Dennis from St. Labre.

After the break, the Provincial seemed cool and calm when he told the board members about the alleged sexual abuse complaints against Fr. Emmett. Father sat in shocked silence and looked at first one and then another board member.

Then Father Emmett broke the awkward silence. "I didn't abuse anyone and I'll do whatever is necessary to defend my name!" Later, he told Connie: "I looked around the room at my friends – the ones who knew me well – Paul Morigi, Dr. Ross Lemire – they'd have felt betrayed if I'd done something like that!"

The board members sat in their chairs aghast. Seeing he was losing the floor, Provincial Reinhart continued: "Well, we'll investigate this matter and report to the board at a later time." Disgusted, Father told Connie that night:

> The Bishop was there, many people I had known for years. I sat all afternoon across from the Provincial. He had this nasty, smug look on his face – like he was thinking, "I'm finally getting rid of you Emmett!" I just looked back at him, but I was so angry. The accusations were ridiculous, but he was

determined to take me out. It was a clear violation of justice and a cheap shot.[283]

Father Emmett barely heard what went on during the afternoon session. At last, the meeting ended and Dr. Lamire came up to Father to show his support. The doctor knew that Father was as mad as a bull. "You have done wonders for St. Labre," he told Father. "I've watched you break your health for this school. You've done a fine job. . ."[284]

Father could barely acknowledge the compliment – he felt so betrayed by his brother Capuchins. 'How am I going to fight this evil? Where do I go from here?' he asked himself. Writer Rosemary Ruether summed up Father's position when she wrote: "To defend the rights of the poor is to make oneself the marked target of those in power . . ."[285]

Despite Father's distinguished record of achievement and many awards for outstanding community service and leadership, a cloud of humiliation and grief passed over him. He knew that the allegation the Provincial had made against him was false, but the obvious hatred his superior felt toward him was real and powerful. He considered the abuse accusation a form of "moral violence" against him – as serious as murder would have been to him. Fr. Emmett didn't want his name and reputation linked to it, but how could he stop the rumors? He couldn't go across the reservation from door to door proclaiming his innocence to the Cheyennes – complaining that certain priests had ganged up on him. No, if he publicly denounced the conspiracy, donors might wonder what on earth was happening at St. Labre. The risk was too high.

The Provincial had been especially insulting. Father Emmett felt that if the Provincial got control of St. Labre, there was no telling what kind of unstable, deeply flawed priest he might send to the Mission to take his place. Based on the quality of the sexually confused men coming out of the seminaries, he couldn't tell which ones were homosexuals and which ones were pedophiles, or if neither applied.

Father Emmett detested the Church policy of covering up sexual abuse by priests. Whatever they did to get rid of him, Fr. Emmett had no intention of fading away. Through the worst kind of personal humiliation, Father Emmett hung on. He would try to maintain his composure, but how was that possible now?

Trying to remain focused on his work, and not swallowed up with vindication and anger – that was the challenge. Father began to take stock of what he had. Friends suggested that he get a lawyer but he wouldn't do it. He was innocent of the charges. Why should he retain a lawyer when the money spent would come from funds that were supposed to feed and educate Cheyenne and Crow children? No, he would not spend a penny of donor money on a lawyer. He kept busy, but work no longer had any joy in it. The lines had been drawn. Under incredible stress and to his credit, Father maintained his sobriety and his loyalty to the Capuchin Order.

Weeks passed without a word. Finally a letter came from the Provincial saying that Father Emmett was to undergo psychological testing in Chicago. "Good!" Father told Connie. "Let's get this over with!" Father knew that unless criminal charges were filed, he was under no obligation to undergo tests, but he wanted to prove his innocence and there was only one way to do it. On July 21, 1991, he flew to Chicago.

When he arrived for his 9 a.m. appointment at the Chicago Medical Center, Father had no idea what to expect. A short, balding technician led him to a room that resembled a small theater with a large screen in front and a slide projector set up against the back wall. The tech didn't waste any time. "Drop your pants," he told Father Emmett. Father unbuckled his belt, unzipped his pants and let them fall to his ankles. The tech pointed toward Fr. Emmett's crotch. Father slid his boxer shorts down and clinched his fists. Whatever came next, if this guy tried to touch him, he'd blast him in the face.

The tech instructed Father to sit down in a recliner in front of the screen. Then he handed the priest a rubber ring and instructed him to slip the ring over his penis. The ring was connected by wires to a Plethysmograph in the next room, a machine designed to show deviant sexual arousal in men who craved sexual contact with children.

"Nobody can imagine how foolish and humiliating it was to sit there wired up to a machine! The tech looked like he was getting a sick charge out of the whole thing," Father remembered. The machine tested penal size while pornographic pictures of children flashed onto the screen. Audio recordings of heavy breathing accompanied some of the lurid photographs, while others showed children in unwilling positions experiencing pain. An unseen narrator said: "You are hurting him, but his cries excite you." The machine clicked several times a minute as it measured penal circumference in millimeters.

The tech put on a recording of a child begging, pleading with a rapist not to molest him. "Mother of God! So this is what they get off on!" Father mumbled. "Oh Jesus, it's disgusting!" He experienced the true meaning of powerlessness and called upon the Blessed Mother for help. Some of the photographs were of young girls just coming into puberty with breast development and pubic hair. The tech kept changing back and forth between boys and girls.

It seemed like an eternity before the test ended. Father got dressed and went back to the tech's office. This time the repulsive little man took out pornographic cards and laid them out on his desk with the nonchalance of a Saturday night poker player. He learned forward slightly in his chair, winked at Father and asked in a whispery voice, "Now, which ones turn you on, little boys or little girls?" A slight look of enjoyment crossed the tech's face, like a mentally disturbed boy pulling off the wing of a Monarch butterfly. Revolted by his slimy implication, Father grit his teeth, "Neither," he said. The tech's face fell. He was clearly disappointed. "At that moment I wanted to strangle him." Father later recalled.

An hour later Father went to the top floor of a university medical building. It turned out to be a mental ward. The heavy doors clanged shut and Father thought it looked like the film set of a horror movie. A man in a white coat carrying a set of keys took Father Emmett through a series of locked doors and down a long corridor with small windows. If Jack Nicholson had jumped out with a butcher knife, bared his teeth and arched his eyebrows, it wouldn't have surprised him. Nothing could have been worse than what he'd already been through.

Father met with the psychiatrist for an hour and he could tell by the doctor's apologetic demeanor that he had passed the tests. The doctor knew he was not a pedophile. Their meeting over, he then led Father through the inner sanctum and out to the elevator, they shook hands and the psychiatrist went back to his work.[286]

Besides an occasional faraway clanging of a door, Father Emmett stood in complete silence. The red elevator light above the door came on, a bell rang, the door opened and he stepped inside the empty elevator. He pushed the button for the ground floor and waited for the slight jar as the elevator began to descend. As he passed floor after floor he saw the shimmering stained glass windows of St. Mary's Church in his hometown of Marathon. He saw himself offering First Mass and Holy

Communion to his family – his dad, mom and sisters – kneeling at the altar rail. Lifting the Eucharist, he told them: "Behold the Lamb of God who takes away the sins of the world. Happy are those who are called to His supper . . ." Facing the parishioners and moving to the row of kneelers, Father said quietly, "The Body of Christ." Edward Hoffmann raised his head and Father Emmett placed the Communion bread into his dad's cupped, callused hands. Ed made the sign of the cross and whispered, "Amen."

The elevator stopped with a jolt on the ground floor and Father quickly made his way outside into the sunlight. He knew that he was innocent of the false charges – that was all he really cared about. The Cheyennes knew nothing about the unjust accusation and thank God, Mary McGarvey and his parents were not alive to hear of it.

Months later, during a break in a chapter meeting, the Provincial took Fr. Emmett aside. "Here." He reached into his pocket and took out the test report. "Well . . . the evaluation was good," The Provincial added offhandedly, "There's no reason to suspect you as a child molester." Father Emmett read the report for a minute and then the Provincial quickly took it and put it back into his pocket.

Father's face and neck turned red and he glared down at him. "The damage is already done! Don't you see? I feel degraded, especially after the penal test!" The Provincial's eyes sparkled and Father realized that he had told the man exactly what he wanted to hear – it appeared to have given the Provincial satisfaction. "I had been trying hard to see some good in the man," Father told Connie afterward. "But instead, I saw only evil."

The accusations against Father Emmett evaporated. Later he read in a Milwaukee newspaper that while Provincial Reinhart had been vigorously trying to destroy him, Reinhart had been stalling on many urgent complaints of sexual abuse against at least five Capuchin priests in Milwaukee. The allegations were serious. Eight young men who had been seminarians in Wisconsin had brought charges. A headline in the Milwaukee Journal, December 20, 1992, read: "8 men tell of sex abuse by friars: ". . . several (alleged victims) are seeing psycho-therapists, two fear repercussions . . . and three say the sexual episodes were factors in their attempting suicide."[287]

In the same article, a 32 year-old victim recalled being molested:

". . . (the priest) gave a back massage that led to sexual contact . . . the priest forced his penis into (my) mouth. I remember being paralyzed and unable to move," he said. ". . . (I) then bit the priest's penis . . ." Yet another student reported that he was "raped anally at the Capuchin pre-novitiate house in Detroit." The rape victim said he attempted suicide a short time later.[288]

After extensive rumors, and according to newspaper articles and complaints, it seemed to the victims that Reinhart was trying to hush the matter up, but the citizens of Wisconsin would not let it go away. Furious over the delay, the victims went to the press claiming: "The Capuchins have not taken appropriate disciplinary action." Finally, other former seminarians also claimed Capuchin priests had sexually molested them and Reinhart agreed to pay them thousands of dollars for psychiatric help. But in return, the young men had to sign a contract agreeing: "to keep confidential all the facts and circumstances giving rise to this agreement."[289]

After signing the agreement, victim Peter Isely and seven other young men came forward with the information. Victim Michael Rocklin described more than 50 sexual encounters with a teacher and principal at a Wisconsin seminary in the 1970s and 1980s. The offensive scandal reached the front page of every newspaper in Wisconsin and United Press International covered it across the nation.[290]

While Provincial Reinhart's name was being splashed in newspapers across the United States, he had been vigorously pursuing his allegations of abuse against Fr. Emmett. It seemed strange that at the same time, Reinhart was dragging his feet on serious sexual abuse charges right in his own back yard. The young friar who supposedly had made the abuse allegation against Fr. Emmett had serious mental problems and had left the order, but the Provincial hadn't bothered to tell Fr. Emmett.

After weighing all the scandalous reports and his own horrific experience, Father Emmett felt ashamed and disappointed in the Capuchin Order. It seemed to him that someone should be cleaning house. In his journal, Father wrote:

> Things have changed since I was in the seminary. The whole orientation has changed. Unless you're gay, you can't make it. I am concerned about this just from my own observation. We

get a bunch of young candidates that come into the seminary and most of them will drop out after three or four months. The ones who stay are gay.

Gays were ordained because of the great shortage of priests. These men take a vow of chastity but many start sexually acting out. Their superiors don't have the guts to question their behavior. The seminary formation has fallen apart. Any priest who molests a child or a teenager should be treated like any other criminal. I'm not condemning chaste gay men, but as far as I'm concerned, priests with sexual identity problems should never be assigned to Indian reservations.[291]

After Father Emmett's name was cleared of abuse accusations, he found out that Joseph Cardinal Bernardin of Chicago had also survived a false accusation of sexual abuse. In his book, *The Gift of Peace*, Cardinal Bernardin wrote of the accusation against him: "I tried to get beyond … and return to my work, but this lurid charge against my deepest ideals and commitments kept consuming my attention. Indeed, I could think of little else . . . As never before, I felt the presence of evil . . ."[292]

During his ordeal, Cardinal Bernardin had meditated on the first of the sorrowful mysteries, Christ's agony in the Garden, and he told the Lord: "This is the first time that I have really understood the pain and agony you felt that night." Cardinal Bernardin's accuser finally admitted that he had lied about the accusation and he asked the Cardinal's forgiveness.[293]

Father Emmett had some of the same feelings as Cardinal Bernardin during his ordeal. He now knew that his last years at St. Labre would be difficult. He also knew that if he retired, the small group of Capuchins he considered "conflicted" would celebrate his demise.

Father Emmett consistently denied that he was bitter, but he told others: "It's hard not to feel bitter!" As a priest he had been taught to accept all of his Capuchin brothers, but that was now impossible. The main objective was to survive with dignity and keep working. Every time he walked across campus and the Indian children ran to his side, he knew that nothing in the world was as important as their well-being. At all costs he would protect them.

Once Fr. Reinhart found out that Father Emmett wasn't budging from his position at St. Labre, he went after him again. In February 1993, the Provincial, still embroiled in the Wisconsin sexual lawsuits, wrote a scathing letter to Fr. Emmett, implying that Father had privately obtained stock in the Cheyenne Western Bank. Indeed, Father had founded the Ashland bank and was elected its first board president. The bank policy stipulated that the president of the board had to own stock in the bank, so Father had purchased shares. Now the Provincial demanded that his stocks were to be handed over to the Capuchin Province immediately, as well as any will or life insurance he might have. Father Emmett was open about his life insurance policy: "When my heart attacks started destroying my health, I took out a million dollar life insurance policy . . . with St. Labre as the beneficiary – then I didn't die."

As a parting shot, the Provincial veiled a threat of media coverage about the old accusation against Fr. Emmett. In still another letter he told Father that he had received another accusation against him. He also said that he would now be forced to inform Fr. Emmett's superiors at St. Labre (new Board members) of the accusation. Offhandedly, Reinhart added that the information he had received was not sufficient to take any action, but he would tell people anyway.

Father Emmett immediately sent a copy of the letter and his reply to Montana Bishop Anthony M. Milone D.D., saying:

> I feel that it is necessary for you to know what is happening. It's the second time he has come up with accusations to put me in a bad light. My concern is not for what he does to me, but what will happen to St. Labre. It is my opinion that he has effectively taken over St. Labre. He publicly professed that he wanted me out before his term of office ends in June . . .[294]

Father told Connie: "Reinhart's actions constitute a "personal vendetta" against me. I put the blame on several of the friars who will have to answer for themselves in the eyes of God."[295] By informing the Bishop, Fr. Emmett believed he had gotten the Provincial and his cohorts off his back.

However, one month later, in May, 1993, Father received yet another threatening letter from Reinhart, this time saying that the board had employed outside, (competitive) stockbrokers to complete a study of St. Labre's financial standing, including all outside corporations.

He admitted that he had been the one to recommend this action to the board. Since Connie Sump's accounting firm had masterfully represented St. Labre for nearly thirty years, Father couldn't understand why the Provincial was insisting on what seemed like an investigation, disguised as a financial report. Naively, Father had always believed that good people are rewarded for efficient and diligent work. He learned the hard way that people with unhealthy motives can be found in religious orders as well as in the general population.

Coincidentally, this last threatening letter from Reinhart arrived just as Father Emmett was preparing to dedicate the Soaring Eagle Center, a magnificent, multi-complex recreational facility, the only one of its kind for children and adults in the surrounding area. Constructed of slabs of Montana marble and brick, the facility included an auditorium with stage, an Olympic-sized swimming pool, basketball court, weight room, indoor running track, saunas and racquetball courts. For years Father had planned to provide Cheyenne and Crow youngsters with a sports center as an alternative to drugs and alcohol on the reservations, especially during the winter months.

With Lakota Olympic Gold Medalist, Billy Mills as special guest, the dedication celebration honored Father Emmett for his nearly 40 years of service among the Northern Cheyenne. To Father, what the Indian people thought was what really mattered.

During the ceremony Father told the audience: "Today there are more than 400 women and men employed by St. Labre, Polysapphire, Inc., and the Northern Cheyenne Pine Company with its spin-off industries, such as logging and trucking. I know of no other reservation in the country that can compare to this reality of private industry working with the Indian people . . . Thank you my friends. You have made my life meaningful and worthwhile."[296]

This honor wasn't the only one Father received in 1993. Ironically, at a time when he found little comfort from fellow Capuchins, Father accepted the Outstanding Fund-Raising Executive Award from the Montana Chapter of the National Society of Fund Raising Executives. Again he credited others, including Mr. Leo Dohn Sr., for helping him over the years. Unfortunately, Mr. Dohn could not be there for the awards ceremony. He had passed away on June 25, 1993, at the age of 88 years. "The old man" as his staff lovingly called him, had a long history of health problems. Dohn's generous contributions had benefited thousands of Cheyenne, Lakota, Arapaho and Crow children, as well as an equal number of African American and European children.

Hoping to replace Connie's accounting firm and Paul Morigi as stockbroker, Reinhart's competitive brokerage company made a negative report on Connie Sump and Morigi's handling of St. Labre's investments. The report stated that St. Labre had lost a great deal of money in the stock market over the years, a small sum compared to the 600 million dollars that Connie, Father and Paul had raised for the school. Furthermore, Reinhart indicated that St. Labre intended to sue Connie and Paul for damages.

For nearly 40 years, every field trip, every book, every bowl of hot soup, every band aid, Bible, teacher's salary, table, chair and school bus, virtually every item, building and bill paid at St. Labre had come from funds generated through the generosity, wisdom and expertise of Father Emmett, Leo Dohn Sr., Conrad Sump, Paul Morigi and thousands of donors from across the country.

On November 11, 1993, the St. Labre Board of Directors held a special meeting at a Catholic School in Billings. Father Emmett sat with the board but he had no idea what was going to transpire at the meeting. Connie and Paul Morigi were sequestered in a small room and told to wait their turns to meet with the board. The men sat for hours. By the time Connie's turn came, it was already 2 o'clock in the afternoon. Finally, he was ushered into a large room where people sat at the front and along the sides. He was told to sit at the farthest end of the room at a small table. A lawyer on the board took the microphone and for over an hour she grilled Connie about St. Labre's investments over the years. Later, he said, "I felt like I was in a McCarthy Senate hearing."[297]

During the meeting Father Emmett sat at the front with the board. Connie could tell from his position at the far end of the room that "Emmett was going crazy the whole time." Paul Morigi then underwent the same interrogation. Father was so upset about how rude his friends were treated, he said, "It was the maddest I ever got." Because the Provincial and his lawyers couldn't destroy him, they had gone after the people closest to him, the men he admired most in the world. If they had planned to murder Fr. Emmett, they couldn't have hurt him more. He had to sit by and watch them throw a false net of suspicion around the two people who had worked the hardest for Cheyenne and Crow children. It was more than Father could take.

Afterward, he tried to eat dinner with Connie and Paul but during the meal, Father felt sick to his stomach. He hadn't eaten lunch and his body ached. He returned to his hotel room and threw up, then went to bed early, burning with fever. Around 11 p.m. Father called Connie. "I'm having another heart attack!" he gasped. "Get me to the hospital!"[298] Connie jumped out of bed and rushed Father to an emergency room. The next day, Roger Clawson, journalist with the Billings Gazette, tracked Fr. Emmett down. From his hospital bed, Father Emmett told him: "I don't know what's going to become of me . . ."[299]

On November 12th Father Emmett was listed in satisfactory condition, but doctors wanted to operate. Father didn't have a choice. Without surgery, doctors advised him that he might live a little longer but with a greatly diminished quality of life. If he lived through the surgery, he might be able to work again. The question was - could he survive another major operation? On November 22, 1993, hours before his second bypass, Father wrote to St. Labre donors: "Time seems to be running out for me . . . I don't know how long I can continue."[300]

Furious with the board's alleged actions against Sump and Morigi and the disrespect shown to Father Emmett, more than three dozen staff members walked off their jobs in protest at St. Labre Indian School. Johnny Russell, a Chief of the Northern Cheyenne Council of 44, was interviewed on a local television station. "Why are they doing this to Father Emmett?" he asked. "He is just like one of us."[301] Another chief, Leonard Elk Shoulder, agreed. "He is always supportive of the children and elders."[302] During the protest march, a woman held up a sign that read, "Please come home Fr. Emmett. We need you!" Another read, "Come back to us Fr. Emmett!"

But Father Emmett was too ill to come back. At that point he thought he might come back in a coffin. He couldn't seem to bounce back from surgery. Walking exhausted him. It was during this recovery period that Viola and Father had a talk about their future. Father was not optimistic about his last years. Since he and Vi had been platonic friends for nearly 40 years and since Vi had cared for other Capuchins when they were in ill health, (she had been affiliated with the Capuchin Order since 1970) why not help one another in their old age? Both agreed that it made sense. The arrangement was a great source of relief for Father. His fear, like that of many others, was that he might end up in a nursing home. After his heart surgery years before, he had relied on Viola's nursing skills. Physically he was now in bad shape and he didn't think he would make it this time.

Father wanted to go to California, a warm climate where he could recuperate and clear his head, but he knew he couldn't take care of himself. He asked Viola if she would consider coming along to look after him. Luckily, she agreed to go. Father told a friend: "Viola is a solid citizen - a good person without evil desires." With many years of experience, Vi knew that heart attack survivors who become depressed have a significantly higher risk of dying within six months. After every one of Father's heart attacks, Viola had worked hard to keep Father's spirits up.

Fr. Emmett and Vi didn't always get along, however. When stressed, the one thing Father could never completely control was his impatience. Because of Viola's profound deafness, it was often necessary for Father to repeat himself, or she sometimes misinterpreted what he said and hard feelings developed. Both had infirmities and they were getting older.

On November 17, 1994, Father Emmett made a decision that would change his life forever. By that time, Fr. Kenneth Reinhart was no longer a Provincial. Fed up with the hostility and harassment perpetrated against him by certain members of his order, Father Emmett wrote to his new Provincial, Rev. Anthony Scannell:

> It is not easy to put into words the reason I am asking for
> a dispensation of my religious vows. I cannot in good
> conscience, continue to live as a Capuchin friar . . . a new
> brand of Capuchins (has) emerged and a "violence . . . not a
> physical violence but rather a spiritual or moral violence . . .
> against me (has prevailed). They . . . decided "Emmett" had
> to go. This was publicly vocalized. Violence was no longer
> something outside in the streets but had entered our
> community. For my own serenity and spiritual growth I could
> no longer act as if all was well . . . After forty-nine years of
> religious life . . . it was not an easy decision. For my own
> peace of mind, spiritual growth and serenity, I humbly ask to
> be dispensed from my Capuchin vows. I will live out my life
> as a priest in the Diocese of Great Falls – Billings.[303]

The Capuchins as a whole were not to blame, but several conflicted priests had spiritually murdered and cannibalized one of their own.

> . . .Whoever hates his brother is a murderer,
> and you know that a murderer does not have
> eternal life in him. 1 John 3:15[304]

CHAPTER
19

"I know I'm a renegade..."

I n September 1994, Father Emmett underwent a Doppler Ultrasonic test at the Eisenhower Medical Center in California. The report showed that only 20% of his heart was functioning normally. He immediately questioned the data. How was that possible? Finally, after a week of denial, Father had to accept the findings.

Concerned donors with similar problems had written to him about Chelation Therapy, an intravenous infusion of a solution containing minerals, vitamins and a special man-made amino acid that had the effect of removing toxic heavy metals such as lead, mercury and arsenic from the blood. Among other things, the treatment was used to reverse the affects of hardening of the arteries "by unplugging and improving the condition of blocked and hardened arteries." Scientific literature reported that it also benefited people with diabetes.[305]

Father Emmett read that Chelation Therapy had been used since 1941. Victims of lead toxicity in World War II provided ample opportunity to test humans and the exciting results laid the groundwork for Chelation Therapy. The treatment improved circulation, one of the leading causes of heart problems and many other diseases. Administered by licensed physicians, Chelation still wasn't sanctioned by the Federal Drug Administration. Some believed it hadn't been sanctioned because a therapy that led to a cure for diabetes and heart problems might put some drug manufacturers out of business. FDA regulations stop health insurance companies from covering the treatments. Never one to try alternative therapy, Father listened to his donors on this one. They wrote to tell him that Chelation had given them new leases on life.

Under a doctor's supervision, Father began the treatments. Within a month, his shortness of breath improved enough that he could walk 3 to 4 miles a day. It seemed like a miracle – just another miracle performed by the benefactors of St. Labre. Donors had given him advice over the years and their concern about Father's health paid off. Donors were not generally rich – they were caring people with love in their hearts for Indian children and for the priest they compared to Father Edward Flanagan of Boys Town and to Dr. Albert Schweitzer, who had spent his life helping impoverished people in the Congo. Some even wrote comparing him to Dr. Tom Doolittle, who ignored danger in Southeast Asia to bring medical help to the poor.

Bishop Anthony Milone accepted Father Emmett into the Diocese of Great Falls/Billings in December, 1994, just a few days before Father's retirement from St. Labre. On December 27th Father Emmett wrote to His Holiness Pope John Paul II, outlining the reasons for his request to leave the Capuchin order. Knowing that it was just required paperwork, he didn't expect the Pope to read it, but he wanted the information placed in the record. None of the Capuchins mentioned Father's decision, except to say that they marveled at how he could make such a decision after 49 years in the order. He told them he had no regrets, but he felt sure they didn't know the full story of what had happened to him. He could have ranted about the priests who had tried to destroy so many lives, but he knew it wouldn't have done any good. Instead he told them: "I know I'm a renegade in many ways but I have always been faithful to my Church."[306]

Father had been robbed of great personal satisfaction in retirement, but he was still winning awards. He won another Outstanding Fundraising Executive Award from NCDC. Later, the Boys and Girls Club of the Northern Cheyenne Nation honored him for his many years of dedication to Indian children. In his home office at St. Labre, his staff presented him with an Appreciation Award for Outstanding Achievements: "You have inspired in us complete loyalty and dedication . . . Thank you for being a kind, caring and understanding person. We know you care. You are not just a boss and this is not just another job. We can see it on the faces of our children . . . (Our children say) "'Oh, Mom, there's Father Emmett. Can I go see him?'" . . . They know who you are . . ."[307]

When the Cheyennes thanked him, it meant everything. While awards were nice to have, Father still had a hard time feeling good about his work. The nagging reminder that Connie Sump and Paul Morigi were still suffering, gnawed at any real happiness he felt. He canceled his retirement party when he left the school because it didn't seem right to celebrate when others close to him were hurt and discouraged.

Finally, he was asked to move out of his office in the administration building to make room for a new staff member. This brought an instant outcry from the staff. Vivienne Wilbur, daughter of the late Frank Bollack, and then a 55-year employee at St. Labre, (She worked 64 years total.) wrote a note to the acting director: "How do you justify Friday's terrible, heart-breaking eviction of Father from his office . . . To many of us this appears to have the elements of a very cruel personal vendetta on someone's part. How long before his house at St. Labre is taken from him?"[308]

Tribal member Bula Brey, a 38-year employee, agreed. "When Father Emmett was here he was like the captain of a big ship. Everybody knew their jobs. We all pulled together. Now that he's gone, the new director has started throwing things overboard. The ship is rocking back and forth. Fr. Emmett knew that the captain can't row the oars, pilot the ship and do every job himself. Father always trusted the Cheyennes to do our best and we lived up to that trust."[309]

Meanwhile, Connie was having serious problems. Retirement negotiations with his accounting firm broke down after the St. Labre Board of Directors made their complaint of alleged wrongdoing. Father Emmett wrote to Father Gil Hemauer on February 22nd, 1995, saying: "Isn't it strange that one day Connie receives a letter from Bishop Malone thanking him for his friendship and help and the following day his partners tell him he cannot draw his retirement because of possible litigation. There is something seriously wrong in what is happening. Does the Board of Directors realize what they are doing to people's lives?"[310]

After working hard for the Mission for nearly thirty years, Connie was disappointed and completely disillusioned with St. Labre. This tore at Father's heart. Connie had risked his life traveling from New York to Montana 6 to 12 times a year, when others wouldn't come to the Mission at all until spring weather made flying and road travel less treacherous. This meant approximately 250 trips and thousands of hours of travel time by plane and by car, over ice-packed roads on the Crow and the Northern Cheyenne Reservations. Connie had plowed through ice, sleet and snow many a time when Father needed him. He was always a big personal contributor to St. Labre, and the time and energy he expended on behalf of the children cannot be measured. Now, with false accusations against him, he became disappointed and depressed.

Connie felt that his thirty years of physical and mental effort had been in vain. The threatened lawsuit against him and his probable counter suit caused untold heartache. It was only a matter of time until his health began to break down. One night he woke up in a sweat with strong pains in his chest. Two days later he suffered a heart attack. During his recuperation, St. Labre filed a formal complaint against Connie and Paul Morigi, stating that while they were working for St. Labre, the school had lost money in the stock market.[311]

Paul Morigi had been a successful stockbroker since 1945. He later said that the St. Labre complaint against him "changed his whole life." He had prided himself in honesty and hard work, helping Father Emmett since the 1960s. Paul was completely discouraged by the allegation of wrongdoing. For over 50 years he had built a thriving business. Peace of mind means everything to a reputable, highly successful businessman. Unscrupulous people walked away from accusations of misconduct without a backward glance, but men of "The Greatest Generation" rated honesty in business above all else.[312]

Realizing they would lose the law suit before it ever went to court, the St. Labre Board wanted to "settle," which meant that instead of going through a long, costly court battle, they wanted Connie and Paul to "settle" with St. Labre by paying a large amount of money. Connie said he'd rather "walk through fire" before he'd give the Board one hard-earned penny.[313] It was a matter of principle. Connie's lawyer sent a letter to the Board on November 10, 1995, saying: "St. Labre was not just another client to Conrad Sump. It was his life's work. During his tenure, St. Labre's endowment grew from approximately $500,000 in 1964 to more than $42 million by 1994 . . ."[314]

After all the depositions, an independent mediator accepted by all parties, made a thorough evaluation as to whether or not St. Labre had evidence for a lawsuit against Sump and Morigi. Meanwhile, the veiled threats and rumors continued, with St. Labre Cheyenne comptroller, Tony Foote, Father Emmett's protégé, caught in the middle of a difficult situation.

"The board must be crazy!" was Tony's first response. Connie and Fr. Emmett had been Tony's mentors and friends nearly all of his life. He was disgusted when he felt that he was being nudged into the board position against Father Emmett and Connie. Tony was unforgiving when it came to anyone he felt was hurting St. Labre and this situation fell into that category. When pushed to side with the board, Tony got the direct impression that his job was on the line.[315]

Interviewed about the allegations against Sump and Morigi, Tony said: "If spies for the Provincial see my car parked out in front of Father Emmett's house or vice versa, I might lose everything I've worked for." Tony thought he knew where to place the blame: "Reinhart started this whole thing," he said. Tony knew that stress aggravated his diabetes. Thinking that he was now witnessing an attempt at "character assassination," he tried to stay out of the furor.[316]

When a Capuchin priest was interviewed about the pending lawsuit, he told the interviewer, "If Father Emmett died, St. Labre would be better off." This astonishing comment, made by an ordained priest sent to teach God's love to the Cheyennes, demonstrated the level of hypocrisy and hatred within the Capuchin Order in Montana.[317]

On May 9, 1996, legal mediator John Mudd sent his evaluation of the complaints to law firms on both sides of the table. The final report read:

> An evaluation of the potential claims, the legal principles and the available evidence lead to a strong conclusion that for all the questions here, the evidence does not support a claim that the defendants defrauded or otherwise misled the School in making the investments in question.[318]

The case was dropped and members of the board who were on the investigative committee either resigned or their term of office expired. The St. Labre Board of Director's complaint proved to be without merit. Conrad Sump and Paul Morigi were fully exonerated.

At the end of a long, expensive and needless controversy, in which reputable men's lives, health and futures were jeopardized, Fr. Emmett felt the "wrongdoing" had occurred because Father Reinhart wanted to hurt him by destroying the lives of his old friends. Reinhart had gotten his revenge but the bills for attorneys representing St. Labre and the fees for the mediator were rumored to have totaled nearly $1 million dollars. The true amount may never be known. The loss of funds made the children of St. Labre the ultimate victims.

When the controversy ended and Father Emmett retired, he could finally go fishing, travel and visit relatives. Chelation treatments continued to help his circulation problem and gave him an energy perk. In May, 1996, he wrote in his journal: "Justice came before my religious vocation of 49 years. God works things out in His way and His time."

Father Emmett felt that he had to be doing something productive, but he wasn't sure how productive it was to stand for hours with a fishing pole in his hand. On May 19, 1996, he noted: "Today while fishing, I picked up 108 aluminum cans around the lake." He had many bags of cans that he had found while walking Fergie or fishing. When he made a run to Billings, he took the bags, sold them and used the money to buy a tank of gas. It was sad in a way, that he had to justify taking time off to go fishing or to walk his dog.

Father Emmett soon got "Booored," as he put it, in retirement. He felt he wasn't doing enough to help others so he got a consulting job with Fenske Media Corporation. "It's fun to be creative again," he told friends at the Mission. School children still dropped by to see him and he kept busy gardening and writing in his journal. In April 19, 1996 he wrote: "The best way to describe today is to compare it to a race horse that comes out of the shoot first, leads for a little while and begins to fade and ends up dead last." But Father was making good money for the first time in his life, plus he had received a lucrative CEO retirement package from St. Labre. The first thing he did was to buy himself a shiny, black pickup truck.

Now, instead of worrying about St. Labre, he wrote in his journal:

> "I was up at 5:15 a.m. It is my best time of the day. I enjoy seeing the early morning sun and the earth coming to life. It's very peaceful." He felt especially good because he now had time to experience a renewed closeness with Cooky. She had graduated from Nursing School and married Italian American, Joseph Kunkel, with Father Emmett officiating. Cooky and Joe had three children, Joe Jr., Justin and the lovely Cara George, named after her "Poppie" Father Emmett George Hoffmann.

Cooky and her family still lived in New Jersey. In April, 1994, Father wrote in his journal: "Cooky called . . . Many things between us have been left unsaid all these years. We haven't really talked about our feelings. We had a great visit – the most we ever talked on the phone – a real bonding. Without actually saying the words, we said we loved each other very much. Now we can talk about it." The next morning he woke up and wrote: "It was one of the best night's sleep I've had in years."

"The way things are now, I don't think those old
chiefs and warriors could stand it. They fought
hard for us. For what? To die alone somewhere?"

Little Rock Roads

CHAPTER
20

A Message from the Grave

F ather Emmett helped fund a Cheyenne oral history project during
the 1970s. Cheyenne speakers tape recorded elders talking about
memories of pre-reservation life, battles with the U. S. Cavalry and
other tribes, horsemanship, courtship and raising children, humorous
stories, life stories, rules of behavior for chiefs and their wives,
religious beliefs, early reservation period and land allotment, religion,
school experiences, medicinal plants and the Cheyenne woman's
viewpoint on numerous subjects.

Many recordings had not been translated or transcribed into English
due to lack of funding and time. By September of 1995, Father had the
time and personal funding to complete the project he had envisioned
twenty-five years before. Bisco Spotted Wolf agreed to translate the
tapes and since he had known most of the people interviewed on the
recordings, his help was invaluable. The plan was to transcribe the
recordings for use in Cheyenne history classes at Chief Dull Knife
College and in reservation schools.[319]

Working with a transcriber, Bisco translated the first tape, an early
1970s chief's meeting. In what proved an eerie coincidence, the chiefs
discussed Father Emmett. All of the chiefs on the tape recording had
been dead for years, including Father's old friend and Cheyenne mentor,
Charlie Sitting Man Jr. Bisco had known all of the chiefs and could tell
who was speaking. The irony of translating the first tape and finding
out it contained a message for Father Emmett, surprised Bisco and he
gave the transcription to Father.

The taped conversation was between Charlie Sitting Man Jr., Charles White Dirt, former Keeper of the Sacred Hat Bundle, Grover Wolf Voice, traditional flute maker and Jim Medicine Bird, a tribal historian and grandson of Ice, a famous medicine man. Their discussion involved the serious plight of the Northern Cheyenne elderly. Sitting Man said that many elders, despite illness, refused to go to the doctor because they didn't want to end up in a nursing home 100 miles away from family and friends. Tribal members had few telephones, money or gasoline to visit their elders. When an older person with hearing and sight problems went to an elderly home and couldn't speak English well, he had a frustrating time telling nurses what he needed, even when it came to simple things like asking for drinking water, turning over in bed, or opening a curtain to see the sun. The aged person felt abandoned, depressed and stopped eating. It didn't take long before he lost hope and faded away. The slightest infection took him to the spirit world.

In the middle of their discussion, Charlie Sitting Man said: ". . . the old die alone and come back in a bag – a bag of bones! We need an elderly home on this reservation. We should sit down with Father Emmett and tell him. He will help us!"[320] When Father Emmett read the translation of the chief's conversation and then listened to the tape, it hit him hard. "The hair stood up on the back of my neck," he said. The chiefs had been right. Nearly every one of them had ended up in exactly the place they had dreaded – nursing homes far from their reservation. "It was like the old chiefs were calling me from their graves," Father told Bisco.

That night the recorded voices touched Father's soul. As he said his nightly prayers, an idea came to him. These revelations often came to him during prayer and he had to write them down. Charlie Sitting Man's message, taped twenty-two years earlier, pulled Father out of retirement. He decided to raise funds for an assisted living center, a home where Cheyenne elders could feel safe with 24-hour staff attention in warm, safe, comfortable surroundings close to their families.

The September nights were getting colder. Reservation elders suffered without enough heat, food and transportation during the frigid winter months. Some had frozen to death trying to walk to town for groceries. That night, Father Emmett renewed the solemn vow that he had made over 40 years before. The next morning he founded a non-profit organization called Soaring Eagle, a Public Charity. His friends were flabbergasted. "You're retired for heaven's sake," Connie reminded him. "Don't overdo it!"

For years Father had raised money for Indian children, but this new direction meant more research and a lot more effort to find donors. He had to rebuild his donor base and use his own personal savings from his consultant job to do it. Father began to travel a great deal, leaving Fergie with Viola. Concerned about his shortness of breath, people tried to get him to slow down, but he'd only frown and say, "Stop nagging me!"

Soaring Eagle's first project was the construction of the Heritage Living Center on a hill above Ashland. Father walked the hills overlooking the Tongue River Valley, searching for just the right location. He wanted the building to look out over the Cheyenne homelands. In short, he wanted an ideal spot. One morning as he walked with Fergie, he spied a picturesque meadow in the distance surrounded by prairie rose bushes and pines. A small herd of deer grazed nearby. The minute Father saw it, he knew. He hurried up the hill, heart pounding all the way to the top. And there it was – a panoramic view of the Tongue River Valley. He picked up Fergie. "This is the place Ferguson. We found it!"

The beautiful acreage belonged to Alice Snodgrass Huller, a good friend and former elementary teacher and principal at St. Labre Indian School. Negotiations for the land purchase began. As was his custom, Father focused his entire attention on the new project and began the tedious and expensive appeal process. He needed to raise $5 million dollars to build the facility, with an endowment that would keep the charity running long after his death. Occasionally, the project got a little overwhelming but an encouraging letter from a donor or from a Cheyenne tribal member elevated his spirit. On November 30, 1997, Rick Robinson, Director of the Boys & Girls Club of the Northern Cheyenne Nation, wrote: "Dear Father Emmett, . . . I thank you for your years of work and effort. Ha Ho! God Bless, Rick[321]

Nothing started Father's adrenaline pumping faster than words of confidence from a Cheyenne like Rick Robinson. Another letter came from respected Cheyenne historian, artist and journalist, Donald Hollowbreast, who began donating from his meager funds. Hollowbreast advised Father to build the Heritage Living Center entrance facing east. The old-time Cheyenne lodges faced east and

Hollowbreast knew that Father Emmett would take his advice.[322]

Building the assisted living center was a difficult undertaking. For one thing it meant taking out a loan. In all of his years at St. Labre, he had never needed a bank loan because donors had generously responded to his appeals. All of the buildings were paid for long before they were completed. Now he realized that the more money he raised for the Heritage Living Center, the smaller the loan would have to be, but the real question was – who would give a large loan to a 70 year-old "beggar priest" with heart problems? On December 26, 1997, Billings Gazette writer Dan Burkhart interviewed Father about his project. Dan asked him why the assisted living facility was needed and Father gave him an example:

> A Northern Cheyenne named Harold Fisher . . . got old but he still liked to drive into town. He couldn't afford an engine heater so during the winter when it was freezing cold, he would get up every now and then in the middle of the night and go outside to start his car. He wanted to make sure the engine didn't freeze up on him, because he had to go to his dialysis treatments. One morning, they found Harold . . .
> He had gone out to run the engine but he didn't make it back. Harold froze to death. That's why we need an assisted living facility . . . These elders need help. It's a crime that elders have to suffer and die like Harold – all alone out in the cold.[323]

Horrified at Harold's passing, Father Emmett focused all the more on the Heritage Living Center. When people told him he had to slow down, he sometimes took time for simple pleasures. Not long after daybreak, it was not unusual to find him in his garden singing "DUM de dum dum" in his pajamas and slippers. People up at sunrise might have been startled to see him in his garden, puttering among the cabbages and tomatoes, Fergie at his heels. He had to make sure that his tomatoes were the biggest. Second best wasn't good enough. Luckily, he wasn't in the produce business. With his new charity in full swing, his retirement years had meaning now and Father had all but forgotten the anguish of the past five years.

Viola was also enjoying her later years, especially during the summer and fall when she threw out her line in many a calm lake or rushing stream on weekly fishing trips. She had always taken great pleasure in being outdoors. Early in September, 1998, she and a friend had driven to Crazy Head Springs to pick wild plums and chokecherries on the reservation. Far down on the creek, surrounded by high red hills, stands of aspens and plum trees heavy with fruit, she never gave a thought about the occasional bears rumored to be in the area. To Viola's delight, the plums had ripened and fallen to the ground so it wasn't much work picking them up. They drove home with baskets full of fruit, past the deep, clear pools and natural springs where fish were jumping. Viola didn't know that it would be her last hike in the Cheyenne hills.

On September 10th, Father flew to Bishop Eldon Schuster's funeral in Great Falls. That evening, he planned to fly back to Billings to meet Viola and several friends to see a play at the Alberta Bair Theatre. At the same time, Viola got ready to drive to Billings so that she could shop and visit before meeting Father.

On her way, Vi stopped at the Ashland Post Office to pick up her mail. The local mail wasn't in the boxes yet, so she had a few minutes to chat with friends. Ten minutes later, horrible news swept from one side of the reservation to the other. A cement truck had run Viola down in front of the post office!

As she lay twisted on the pavement, a crowd of people gathered around her. Some stood while others knelt next to the nurse who had helped them for 41 years. Viola's friends, Jeanne Haugan, Faith Tall Whiteman and Lorraine Robinson were on their knees beside her. Not far away, Joseph Haugan, a Cheyenne, prayed with his open Bible.

Although Viola was conscious, her left leg stuck out at an awkward angle, completely mangled. The right leg was crushed. Large, black tread marks crossed over her thighs and lower abdomen, her right hand oozed blood. Not a minute after the accident, a call had gone out for an ambulance, but the ambulance crew had left on emergency to another location on the reservation. Due to Ashland's isolated location, it took hours before the ambulance finally got there. Viola never lost consciousness during the excruciating wait, but her face had turned the color of cold pine ash. People on the street cried and prayed, but there was nothing that anyone could do for her. For most of them, it was the longest and most agonizing wait they had ever experienced in their lives.

Some said Vi had seen the truck and screamed "Stop! Stop!" Others said she never saw what hit her. A crew had been working on the side of the post office to pave a drive-through and there were no pedestrian barriers. As she walked around the front of a parked cement truck, the driver suddenly gunned the engine and drove forward to turn onto the highway. As he turned, the driver felt a bump and he thought he'd hit a rock. After a second bump, he glanced in his rear view mirror and was horrified to see Viola's crumpled body. It looked as though she had been run over twice, first by a large front tire and then again by a back tire, but no one seemed to know for sure. Only the tread marks across her clothing told the tale. The driver was beside himself with remorse and had to stand and watch as Viola's life ebbed away.

Friends provided shade to keep Viola from the glaring sun until the ambulance finally arrived. Doctors in Lame Deer stabilized her until the St. Vincent Hospital helicopter (Help Flight) team picked her up and flew approximately 100 miles west to St. Vincent's Hospital in Billings. By then, she was in searing pain. When he heard of the accident, Father caught a quick flight back to Billings and was waiting for Vi when she got to the hospital. She had lost a lot of blood and the pain was unbearable. He didn't want to scare his old nurse by giving her Last Rites, but he gave her Absolution. Father had once been airlifted to Billings by helicopter after a heart attack, so he knew, like others who live in southeastern Montana, that if a person has an accident, or a serious, life threatening condition, the Help Flight helicopter is the only hope of getting to a well-equipped hospital.

Late that afternoon, a doctor left the Intensive Care Unit to talk to Father Emmett. Many of Viola's friends had driven to Billings and were with Father in the waiting room. The doctor explained that Viola's left leg had been amputated and they wanted to amputate her right leg as well. During the operation, her stomach had bloated with blood and fluids. They had drained the fluid and removed her gall bladder, but when they had tried to close the incision, the swelling was so great, the wound could not be closed. Despite a plastic bandage over the gaping wound, infection was likely. "I must tell you Father Emmett," the doctor said, "Viola will not look like the person you know. But if you want to see her, it's best you go in now. Due to her age and condition, we feel that she has less than one hour to live."

Father's body slumped. Visibly agitated, he asked to see her immediately. Viola's Cheyenne friends, Butch and his wife Lena (Whitedirt) Sooktis, had already prayed with Fr. Emmett and all of those in the packed waiting room. In a poignant moment, Butch had placed his hand on Father's bowed head. The crisis had brought Cheyennes, non-Indians, Crow/Korean, Mexicans and Laotian-Americans together in grief. The same thing had happened in Ashland. People who had never talked to each other because of racism, fear, or ignorance, now felt the need to reach out and comfort one another, regardless of race. One woman said that she had not been able to pray for years but when she leaned over Viola in the road, a rush of faith and love shot through her body as she prayed.

Suddenly the color of one's skin meant nothing. They were all human, all mortal, and their common feelings were exposed. In her pain, Viola had brought the community together. It was exactly what she would have wanted. But the question everyone asked was, "Why Viola? Why did the person who had helped so many people over the years have to suffer such a terrible accident?

Silently, Vi's friends filed into the Intensive Care Unit. They stood by her misshapen body, swelled as if she weighed 300 pounds, a monster covered with bloody bandages, her lips bloated like a giant sucker fish. Father stood over her, trying to give the Last Rights. Tears streamed down his face and fell on the pages of the open prayer book. Sobs fumbled the words. He anointed her forehead and prayed: "May the Lord in His love and mercy, help you with the grace of the Holy Spirit . . ."

His hands trembled. He was about to lose his faithful nurse and friend, the person who had supported him and his work since 1957. In those tragic moments between life and death, Father remembered that Viola had volunteered at St. Labre for many years without payment for her services, including the many times she had nursed him back to health. He wanted to tell her how proud he had been of her, but Vi was in a silent coma from which none thought she could possibly survive.

Lena Sooktis called her brother, Gilbert Whitedirt, Keeper of the Sacred Hat Bundle of the Northern Cheyenne Tribe. She told him that doctors were saying that Viola had only one hour to live. Not impressed, Gilbert told her, "The doctors are not Maheo (God). It is not up to them. Keep praying and don't pay attention." That night, Whitedirt and others had special prayers for Viola in a sweatlodge ceremony. Butch Sooktis walked the high rim rocks overlooking the city of Billings, just as his ancestors had done, to request help from "Maheo" the One Above.

Not long afterward, Gilbert Whitedirt had a dream. He saw Viola in a peaceful green meadow, sleeping among the wildflowers. She was surrounded by Indian angels, their translucent wings pulsating above her. A Cheyenne Holy Man bent down close to Vi. He placed a gentle, healing hand on her forehead. The angels produced an intense energy together, while their wings glowed and vibrated above her.

The dream made him feel sure that Viola would live. Gilbert was right. She lived a week, then two. She hung on through several serious infections and irregular heartbeats. Six weeks and eight operations later, Viola was still unconscious, still holding on. Due to the morphine drip, she held mysterious conversations with invisible spirits above her bed. One day she woke up, looked down and saw that she had only one leg, and the other so badly damaged, she might lose it as well.

Vi was miraculously alive, but Father Emmett's secure and dignified routine had fallen apart. Schedules no longer stabilized his life. He didn't say Mass every morning but he tried very hard to take care of Viola's relatives who had come in shifts from Minnesota. Her devoted sisters, brothers, nieces and nephews all needed a place to stay and food to eat. Father made them all comfortable, drove them to and from the hospital several times a day, cooked for them, washed clothes and tried to raise funds for the Heritage Living Center – all at the same time. His face took on a haggard, sad appearance. Sorrow had carved a silence in his heart.

While Vi lay in a semi-conscious state, Father believed, as Gilbert Whitedirt did, that she would live. It wasn't if she would live, it was where she would live – Viola would have to remain close to the hospital. A nursing home was out of the question. A wheelchair wouldn't fit into Father's Billings office. There had to be another alternative. One day Father went out looking for a house and found one for sale a few blocks from his office. Within days he had moved all the furniture from his old office to the new house.

Ninety days after the accident, Viola came home from the hospital. She found that she could see two lovely aspen trees outside her window, but that was all she could do. It is said that from tragedy comes growth. People noticed a definite change in Fr. Emmett after Vi's accident. Most successful men have healthy egos and Father Emmett was no exception. But after the tragedy, a big part of Father Emmett's ego went out for a long walk. The accident had been a humbling experience for him.

Friends noticed that he rarely drove over the speed limit, a miracle in itself, considering he had gotten a speeding ticket two months earlier for driving 112 mph. The emotional barrier he had built around his heart cracked open and feelings came tumbling out. He remembered his commitment to his old friend.

The laughing, cheerful person Vi had been, the healthy, outdoorsy woman who loved to fish and walk in the hills – that woman had been crushed under the huge tires of a cement truck. She had experienced a devastating physical and mental accident made worse because of the independent person she had been. The carefree woman with few problems who could get up and go anywhere, anytime she liked – that woman was gone. Now she couldn't lift her arm without pain. No longer bursting with energy and a shadow of her former self, she had no appetite and barely enough strength to sit up. But Vi could still pray. She never stopped praying.

Viola Campeau was 76 years old. She had survived death, but was handicapped for life. How was Father going to take care of an invalid, a woman who needed help all day and at night? It was certainly on her mind. One way or another, life would be different now – radically different.

The year 1999 went by in a blur. Father Emmett ran himself ragged trying to take care of himself, Viola's many needs, his independent consulting business and the Soaring Eagle charity. His religious faith, his 12-step sobriety program and Chelation Therapy kept him going.

At 6:15 a.m. every morning he climbed a flight of stairs to the kitchen, then climbed five more stairs to bring Viola a banana and coffee in bed. All day long he went up and down the stairs, huffing and puffing, bringing the food he had carefully prepared, collecting the dishes and taking them down to be washed and put away. When she could come to the table on the main floor, he pushed her in a wheelchair down each stair and then pulled her back up the stairs when she wanted to go to bed. He washed, dried and ironed their clothes and when they went out for a drive, he sometimes lifted her into the car and then folded and put her wheelchair into the trunk. Compassion filled his heart.

But Father's closest friends asked each other, "Who is taking care of Fr. Emmett? He took excellent care of Vi but like other caregivers, he got tired, and cranky, especially when he was exhausted or didn't feel well. Nevertheless, he persevered and turned out to be a superb caregiver. Now, instead of giving dinner prayers with the staccato speed of a tobacco auctioneer, he prayed with thoughtful deliberation. It was his turn to pay back and he more than lived up to the bargain. In doing so, he grew closer to God, closer than he had ever been before.

By 1999, Fergie could no longer jump up on her ottoman or go up the stairs by herself. One day on her usual walk, Fergie lay down on the sidewalk and refused to go any further. It wasn't until they got back to the house that Father realized that Fergie had suffered a heart attack. For a couple of months he watched over her but she got progressively weaker. Putting her to sleep was the only humane thing to do. The day he took Fergie in, he cried so hard in the car that he almost had an accident. For the next three weeks he cried at the slightest thought of her. Vi decided to buy Father Emmett another West Highland puppy just like Fergie for his birthday. He named the new puppy Fergie II. Taking care of a very active puppy, on top of Father's other duties, proved exhausting, but little Fergie was worth the trouble.

In mid-August, 2000, Father Emmett became frustrated and impatient. He grew irritable with Viola and his staff. Those who knew him well saw that something was very wrong. For days he hid the fact that he was in constant pain, but he finally admitted it. Father couldn't sleep but he had brushed it off as indigestion. He called Dr. Edward Malters and the doctor told him to come in for tests. Afterwards, when Father went home to prepare lunch the doctor called: "Father Emmett, you'd better come back to the hospital right away. It's more serious than I originally thought. You have an aneurysm."

In the hospital that night, Father knew that he was in trouble but as usual, he made light of it. He took pain medication and nurses told him to stay as motionless as possible. They sand bagged his body to keep him from moving. Although Father knew what could happen if the aneurysm leaked or burst, he still joked around as if nothing was wrong. The nurses had a hard time keeping him quiet. To make matters more difficult, the anesthesia administered during the angiogram made him groggy and he wanted to tell jokes and move around. That night, Connie called Father: "Well Emmett" he said, "God has brought you this far – He won't drop you on your ass now!" Notified in New Jersey about Father Emmett's condition, Cooky became distraught: "If he dies," she said, "90% of me will die with him." Cooky felt helpless so far away. She decided to come to Billings to take care of him.

Father wasn't thinking about death. Most people who have had a Near Death Experience do not fear death. In fact, they know that death is the most glorious moment of life. Early the next morning, Butch Sooktis came early to pray in Cheyenne before Father went into surgery. Dolly Not Afraid, a Chippewa neighbor, came to say a Christian prayer with him. The last faces he saw before he went into surgery were Indian faces.

Many of Father Emmett's friends were in the waiting room during the surgery. The hours dragged on with no word about how the surgery was going. Then, after more than four hours, a nurse reported that Father Emmett had survived. Dr. Barry Winton, a brilliant surgeon, had removed multiple aneurysms.[324]

Seven days later Father came home from the hospital. Cooky flew in from New Jersey to take care of him for a month. The bond that had always existed between them was further strengthened when, for the first time, they discussed Mary McGarvey. Father told Cooky that he had always loved her adopted mother. When he was stronger, they took a short walk. Soon Cooky had Father walking a block, and then two. One evening they watched a multi-layered Montana sunset with rays of sunlight shooting downward through gold and red clouds. A few regrets were mentioned and some tears shed, but it was a meaningful, memorable time for them both.

After Cooky returned to New Jersey, Father immediately went back to work. Within a week he flew to Minneapolis on a business trip, but before he left, he went in to see his physician and the doctor expressed amazement at his remarkable recovery. The mischievous priest sat on the edge of his bed like a jet preparing to take off. Dr. Malters grinned. "You're a lucky man, Father Emmett," he chuckled. "God still must have important work for you to do."

Heart attacks, quadruple bypass surgeries, multiple aneurysms – nothing stopped Fr. Emmett. The push now was to get the Heritage Living Center built, one way or the other. Father had applied for a huge loan, but he had to wait 8 months for the bank to make a decision. Those eight months did not go by in a flash. Every day was hard. He'd built million dollar school buildings with donated money that he already had or knew he was going to get, but now he felt butterflies in his stomach having to face a bank loan officer. In June of 2001, First Interstate Bank in Billings informed him that Soaring Eagle had been approved for the loan.

Father planned the Heritage Living Center groundbreaking ceremony
for June 15, 2001, but a week before the ceremony, rain poured down
in torrents with no end in sight. Too many spring rains in Montana can
cause lovely green meadows to turn into sinkholes of gumbo mud that
none dare cross, so everybody watched the skies – everybody except
Father Emmett. As usual, his prayers for a beautiful day were answered
when the rain stopped and the thirsty meadow left the soil just right for
the groundbreaking.

On the morning of the ceremony, Bisco Spotted Wolf was the first
Cheyenne to arrive. Before long, a cortège of old pickups and cars
drove up and parked. The elderly passengers sat quietly in the cars and
spoke in hushed tones. When lunch was served, they were helped to
their chairs. After a delicious lunch of beef stew, fry bread and
traditional berry pudding, the ceremony began. Four Northern
Cheyenne chiefs, each facing a different direction, stood guard at
willow posts marking the four directions. The poles stood about 50
yards apart. Chief Bisco Spotted Wolf took his place at the eastern
willow, with the white prayer cloth fluttering in the wind. The Bundle
Keeper for the Elk Horn Scraper's Society, Joe Fox Sr., stood at the
southern willow with the red cloth. Chief John Russell, a principal chief
of the Northern Cheyenne Council of 44, took his place at the western
point with the yellow prayer cloth and Gilbert Whitedirt, a member of
the Elk Horn Scraper Society and former Keeper of the Sacred Hat
Bundle, guarded the northern pole wound with black prayer cloth.

Prayer leader, Charles "Butch" Sooktis, also a member of the ancient
Elk Horn Scraper Society, stood in the center of the circle offering the
opening prayer to Maheo to bless the earth on which the Heritage
Living Center would stand. He then motioned for all the point men to
bring the four colored prayer cloths to the center of the circle.

Gilbert Whitedirt lit the coals and offered cedar smoke as Butch prayed.
They passed the cloths through the rising smoke. Next, the assembled
chiefs and Father Emmett were called to the center and each of them
in turn was blessed with the smoked prayer cloths.

Geri Small, the first woman President of the Northern Cheyenne Tribe,
was blessed with cedar smoke. The honor to turn over the first spade of
dirt went to Bisco Spotted Wolf, after which each point man turned over

a shovel full of earth.

Only one thing went wrong at the groundbreaking ceremony. Father Emmett had ordered 6 or 7 port-a-potties placed at convenient locations for the comfort of elders who couldn't get around without help. The company didn't show up until after the ceremony. People had to wander off into the trees once in awhile. When the port-a-potty crew finally arrived, Father ambushed them at the pass. Nobody actually saw the confrontation, but it must have been an extremely unpleasant experience.

For the next year, Father spent many days on the hill watching the walls and the roof of the Heritage Living Center going up. The warmth of summer days turned to the red and gold leaves of autumn. A high windstorm tore down part of the roof but it was quickly repaired. An unusually warm December meant that construction continued throughout the winter. On August 31st, 2002, Northern Cheyenne elders celebrated the opening of the Heritage Living Center with a poignant dedication ceremony. Many faithful donors, like 86 year-old Carl Williams, traveled thousands of miles to attend. Carl's two nephews brought him from California because it was Carl's one wish to see the completed Heritage Living Center. At the luncheon served for the hundreds who attended the ceremony, Carl told Father Emmett, "This is beyond my belief! The building is first-class in every respect."[325] Donors from all over the country met each other for the first time and they bonded in their shared pride in the fulfillment of the "old chiefs' dream." Conrad Sump and Paul Morigi were there as well. They had helped build the Center and the joy they felt on that special day healed every wound.

Soon, Northern Cheyenne elders moved into the Heritage Living Center, 46,239 square feet of gracious living space with 250 windows, each with a breathtaking view of the Tongue River Valley, the pine-covered foothills and meadows of wildflowers, prairie rose bushes and sage.

With round-the-clock care, nutritious meals and warm rooms, their winters spent in safety, the elders were nevertheless cautious about moving into the "miracle on the hill" above Ashland. After all the poverty they had suffered in their lives, it seemed too good to be true. The new Admissions and Activities Director, Dewanda Little Coyote, made them feel welcome and when they moved in, the quality of their lives rose beyond their highest expectations. Soon they developed living patterns along tribal lines and laughter and teasing filled the hallways. The elder women, night owls and card sharks among them, began the evening "T.A." card game. The television was of no interest in comparison. Knurled, arthritic fingers deftly dealt the cards and the old gambling spirit returned in earnest. Sometimes bingo or hand games brought on boisterous singing, laughing and hand drumming. Some people say that Indians are not competitive. One look at the evening card games, the elders eyeing each other, expertly holding their cards, soon dispelled that myth. Nightly games at the pool table on the second floor engaged the men who ignored their health problems when a rival was at hand.

Elders and staff people benefited from having intimate window corners in which to take in the sweep of forest pines shimmering in the sunlight. One night, Madonna Bordeaux, a Lakota staff member, was eating her lunch on the midnight shift. All the lights were off in the Night Hawk Room, a TV/recreation center with large windows all around. She and her sister Anna Antelope were enjoying their break, eating sandwiches. Suddenly, they heard a strange noise at the window. Madonna sat bolt upright but Anna took off running down the hall. A face with large eyes stared straight at Madonna through the window. Neither one blinked. A mule deer calmly licked frost on the glass, its nose pressed against the window. The doe and 15 others seemed interested in what kind of sandwich Madonna was eating. They knew they were safe on the center grounds munching grass, as safe as the elders who enjoyed their company at dawn and during the last golden rays of evening sunlight.[326]

Stories like this were enjoyed by one and all at the Heritage Living Center and by the children in the Montessori School and Child Day Care. As time went on, elders integrated Cheyenne language, art and traditional story-telling into the Montessori classroom. On hand to give parenting advice to teenage parents, residents visited great, great grandchildren in the complex. At times the children made cookies for delighted residents and in spring they planted flowers and vegetables, the harvest of which was shared with residents and family members.[327]

While the Heritage Living Center was an unqualified success, the September 11, 2001 terrorist attack in New York left a gaping hole in the economy. Americans sent hard-earned money to help thousands of terrorist victims, while job layoffs and business failures threatened the economy. The plight of charities across the nation continued and by the end of 2002, Soaring Eagle's donations had dropped 44% lower than the previous year. Father Emmett lay awake at night worrying about the monthly mortgage payments.

Father landed in the hospital in early December, 2002, with his heart pounding so hard that he felt it would jump out of his chest. Doctors were unable to stabilize his pulse and blood pressure. With Jamie Olson, the Heritage Living Center's Administrator and Sam Widdicombe, Maintenance Safety Coordinator, present in Father's room, a doctor came in to tell Father Emmett that unless he underwent a delicate medical procedure, he might not make it.[328] The process meant stopping the heart, jolting an electric current through it and then jump-starting the heart again.

Exhausted, Father was too tired to joke with the nurses. He immediately began dictating a letter to donors, saying how much he loved them and appreciated what they had allowed him to do for the Northern Cheyenne. He asked them to continue helping his charity, even if he didn't make it through the surgery. Father hugged his staff and they left the room and went directly to the hospital chapel to pray for his recovery. Kneeling in prayer, tears trickling down his face, Sam Widdicombe prayed: "God, if you will allow Father Emmett to live, I will give up chew! (chewing tobacco) Less than an hour later, a Sister came to tell them that Father Emmett's heart had recovered and his pulse was fine. When Father later found out that Sam had promised to stop chewing, he made Sam live up to his promise.[329]

Father had survived yet another close call at the age of 77. His doctors warned him that if he didn't slow down and seriously focus his mind on recovery, he wouldn't make it. They recommended that he move into the Heritage Living Center and refrain from cooking, cleaning, lifting and driving. He was not to go up and down stairs and not to attend long meetings. No overdoing it. Father never dreamt that he would end up living in the Heritage Living Center. Viola moved into her own apartment at the Center and was happy to see that many of the staff had been her students at St. Labre, where she had cared for them. Now they were caring for her. Father too, was surrounded by those who loved him. With everyone's best added together, the Heritage Living Center took on a special warmth and luster. In this healing atmosphere, Father finally let others take control.

It wasn't easy for a powerful man to accept the fact that his body was in decline, especially in an institution he had built. It took grace and humility to yield his place to others. It had been Father's nature to serve alone, with secret insights and plans, maneuvering and oiling the machinery he had designed. But now things were different. Still shy, sometimes indifferent, kind yet impatient, imaginative, daring, clever, and at times almost ruthless, one of his traits never declined – his charisma. He is especially pleased when donors visit so that he can show them what their generosity has created.

⊷⊶ ⋝◊⋜ ⊷⊶

The Northern Cheyenne tribe now has a bank, a fully accredited junior college, a new tribal office building, new clinic and high school. Although poverty and poor health still worry the Cheyenne people, their living conditions have improved compared to the Third World poverty that Father first encountered when he came to the reservation in 1954.

But today, there exists a different and dangerous enemy – a devastating drug and alcohol problem, not unlike conditions in inner cities and in wealthy suburbs across the nation. Crank and cocaine have invaded the reservation. In dress, speech, actions, clothing and hair styles, many young people mimic rap singers they see on television. Using that image, drug pushers share free drugs until teenagers are addicted. Once hooked, they have to pay cash. Pushing drugs, stealing and burglarizing homes are ways to afford their addictions. Suddenly, teenagers have pagers and cell phones and are stealing their grandmothers' diabetic syringes to shoot cocaine. Elders lucky enough to get social security, now face young family members desperate for drug money. Crank addicts give birth to crank babies and young parents leave their children with already overburdened grandparents.

Consequently, drug abuse has left elders the most vulnerable and the poorest segment of the reservation population. Tribal leaders are well aware of these problems and they are taking steps to rid the reservation of drugs. But the Northern Cheyenne people have faced severe challenges before. Over the years they experienced scores of corrupt agents, criminal government neglect, coal exploitation, hungry land speculators, medical epidemics, bootleggers, racial and religious persecution. How did they survive?

They have always been a cautious people, not quick to befriend or to hate. They watch, listen and wait, instead of "popping off" at the slightest aggravation. They know how to use humor and laughter to heal. Most important of all, they know how to pray. The drug problem will be solved, not just by help from outside forces, but by the strength and determination of tribal leaders from within. Their religious faith in "Maheo," Creator God, will sustain them.

In the meantime, elders must be protected. The Heritage Living Center provides that urgent need. Rosie Eaglefeathers moved into the center and at first she was very shy. That didn't last long. Soon she was laughing and enjoying the delicious food and the nightly T.A. card games. Then Rosie's son, Clifford Long Sioux, joined the staff. After many years of struggle, Rosie enjoys her peaceful life, no longer worried about people stealing money, high fuel bills and winter's ice and snow. Her golden years will be spent in comfort and safety.

Like many other Cheyennes, Rosie had close relatives who were killed in the Ft. Robinson Outbreak in 1879. Other relatives survived a U.S. Army attack on Chief Dull Knife's village on the Red Fork of the Powder River. The nearly naked people ran for their lives in the snow, scaling a slippery cliff nearly 800 feet high. Eleven babies froze to death the day of the attack. Survivors listened and watched from the cliff top as troopers shot over 700 horses to death in screaming agony.

Although years have passed, the Cheyennes have not forgotten these tragic memories. But they know that Father Emmett and Soaring Eagle's caring donors have built the Heritage Living Center especially for Cheyenne elders. This has caused a profound healing of past wrongs committed against the tribe. Rosie's son Clifford is thankful that his mother and other elders can live independently, yet medical help is just a few steps away. Impressed with the bi-cultural atmosphere, he calls the center a "reconciliation of the races."

Father Emmett's determined effort on behalf of the Northern Cheyennes has resulted in a remarkable record of success in educational advancement, industrial development, architectural achievement and fund raising, the scope of which is unequaled in the history of the 20th century Catholic Church in the American west.

Surrounded by Cheyennes, Father Emmett's physical, mental and spiritual wounds have healed at the Heritage Living Center. He is recovering from illnesses that would have brought down the average man, but not the renegade who still walks in the hills, often looking back, imagining that he is not alone. A short distance behind he feels the presence of the old chiefs, some in full headdress, eagle feathers flowing in the wind. Father Emmett knows in his heart that after 50 years, the last 22 years sober, he has fulfilled the vow he made before God to help the Northern Cheyenne people. Someday, it will be time to join the chiefs in his journey to the next camp. When Father leans into the wind, he can almost hear them singing the Chief's last Journey Song:

Creator God, I am with Him.

Creator God, I am with Him.

Creator God, I am with Him.[330]

Endnotes

CHAPTER 1

1 St. Francis of Assisi founded the Order of Friars Minor in 1206. From this group, three others developed, the Friars Minor, the Friars Minor Conventual and the Friars Minor Capuchin. Priests and brothers of the Capuchin Order are working as cloistered monks, parish priests, teachers, foreign missionaries and chaplains in many parts of the world. They labor in every type of apostolic work. The initials O.F.M. Cap., which follow a Capuchin friar's name, stands for Order of Friars Minor Capuchin. A portion of this information was taken from Sandal Prints, Volume VI, No. 6, November – December 1957, published by Capuchin Friars, Detroit, Michigan. For brevity, the Capuchin initials are omitted in the text of this book.

Father Marion Roessler, O.F.M., Cap was born in Jefferson, Wisconsin, March 30, 1904 and passed away in 1991. Father Marion was Director and Pastor of St. Labre Mission from 1947 to 1955, when he was forced to leave due to severe emphysema. During his tenure at St. Labre, the school was on the verge of closing due to lack of funds. Although he left St. Labre, the successful direct mail campaign that he began, continues to the present day.

Father Marion greatly appreciated Northern Cheyenne culture and language. He began tape recording elders, many of whom had survived the Battle of the Little Bighorn. It is believed that many of his tapes were destroyed in a flood during the 1960s. For more information on Father Marion, see Sister Eustella M. Bush (O.S.F.) Unpublished book, *Sand, Sage, and Struggle*, pp 201- 211. Hereinafter: Bush, *Sand, Sage, and Struggle.*

2 See Father Marion's unpublished essay entitled "An Appreciation of the Northern Cheyenne Indian" by Father Marion Roessler, O.F.M. Cap. In the essay he says: ". . . Their frustration result(ed) from the stern measures taken against the Indians who participated (in the Custer Battle), particularly against the Northern Cheyennes, . . . up to the present day, they have not been able to live down the depressing psychological impact caused by these measures."
SEHP Collection, Billings, MT

3   Interview with Cheyenne tribal member Rubie Sooktis – 5/1996
     See also George Bird Grinnell Collection, Benjamin Clarke's interview with Mrs.
     Black Bear, Southwest Museum, Los Angeles, CA

4   Ibid, George Bird Grinnell Collection. See also Orlan J. Svingen's excellent book,
     The Northern Cheyenne Indian Reservation 1877-1900. Niwot, CO: University
     Press of Colorado, 1993. Hereinafter: Svingen, Northern Cheyenne

5   Soaring Eagle Heritage Project Collection, Billings, Montana. Hereinafter: SEHP
     Collection

     We the undersigned this day agree to give and to hold as long as the Mission stand
     by the Sisters of St. Labre Mission the 41 acres of land of Tongue River
     Reservation East of the Mission joining their meadow, and all the land on (the
     Southeast side inside the Mission fence 13 acres of said reservation. Should at any
     time the Mission be closed this land shall be returned to the Indians, Signed This
     day of Our Lord, Jan. 21, 1918.

Eugene Yellowhair	Woodenleg	Iron Teeth
Little Eagle	Charles Crawling	Charley White Shield
Raymond Sharpnose	William Red Bird	P. David Yellow Hair
Isadore White Wolf	White Frog	Joe Walkseasy
George Crook	High White Moon	Arthur Woodenthigh
Henry White Wolf	Yellownose	Willis Chasing Bear
Alfred Sponge	Mrs. George Crook	Pat Tallwhiteman
Oliver Yellow Eyes	Mrs. Yellownose	

6   Bush, Sand, Sage, and Struggle, 47-54, Letter from Sister Ignatius to Mother
     Amadeus, December, 23, 1884.

7   Ibid. 48-49

8   Passim. Bush, Sand, Sage, and Struggle

9   The Meriam Commission, headed by Lewis B. Meriam, documented the
     substandard health conditions due to governmental inefficiency and lack of
     adequate funding on the Northern Cheyenne Reservation. The report described
     conditions as "murderous neglect." See National Library of Medicine. "The
     Meriam Commission and Health Care Reform (1926-1945)." National Archives,
     Washington, D.C.

10   SEHP Collection. "Peyote Information, History and Ceremonies." During the
     1930s and early 1940s, Father Bede Scully, O.FM. Cap., began a zealous attack on
     Cheyennes who were using peyote in their religious ceremonies. He enlisted the
     help of Catholic Cheyenne spies to inform on Cheyenne Church members who
     had been praying with peyote since the 1890s. When he found that faithful
     Catholic Catechist, Henry Standing Elk, was also a member of the Native
     American Church, (Peyote Church) he berated Standing Elk in public and wrote
     libelous letters to the Commissioner of Indian Affairs, the Bishop of Montana and
     the United States Senate. He included his report, "Peyote, with Particular
     Reference to the Northern Cheyenne Indians of the Tongue River Reservation,"
     which was widely circulated and which condemned Standing Elk. After receiving
     a letter from John Collier, then Commissioner of Indian Affairs, saying that the

Cheyennes had the right to use peyote, Father Scully tried another tactic. He made each Cheyenne Catholic Church member sign the following pledge:

" . . . I hereby RENOUNCE the PEYOTE RELIGION and Cult and Practices and the NATIVE AMERICAN CHURCH. This solemn promise must be signed by all Catholics before they make Easter Communion.

If the Indian does not sign, he or she cannot receive the sacraments of confession and communion . . . cannot have their children baptized in the Catholic religion . . . cannot be buried from the Catholic Church or in a grave that is blessed by the Priest of God."

Henry Standing Elk did not sign the pledge. Those Cheyenne people who signed the pledge ignored the threats and continued to attend both peyote meetings and Catholic services. Angered, Father Scully wrote a scathing report, circulated nationally entitled: "Specific Report of Cases – showing the Peyote Practice as the CHIEF HINDRANCE to the progress of the Faith among the Cheyenne." (This Statement on Peyote was presented to the Ecclesiastical Superiors June, 1939.) In this account he accused Henry Standing Elk as being a "medicine man" in the Native American Church. Standing Elk, who had dutifully served as a Catholic Catechist for 15 years or more, wrote Father Scully a letter telling him that he would worship as he pleased. In the early 1940s, Father Bede Scully, now despised by many Cheyennes, left the reservation and never returned.

11 Father Patrick Berther O.F.M Cap. was born in Madison, Wisconsin on May 18,1902. He served a huge rural area of eastern Montana for 60 years in various churches and became a legendary figure. He died on 1/10/01. One of the best known stories about Father Pat concerned his love of fishing. One day he was fishing on the banks of the Tongue River when a rattlesnake bit him. He continued to fish the afternoon away until he caught his limit. Only then did he go to the doctor. Father Emmett was very fond of Father Pat and called him "the old cockroach."

12 Bush. *Sand, Sage, and Struggle*. 133-139. Letter from Father Van der Velden to his brother in October 1897, "The whites were after my life; my death was resolved upon and only because I took the part of the Indians." Father Van der Velden received three death threats from white ranchers and left the Mission after 12 years of continuous struggle, his health broken. See also *Cabins and Campfires in Southeastern Montana* by Gene Philbrick. Worland, Wyoming: Worland Press, 1973.

13 Interview with Sister Phyllis M. Hoffmann S.D.S, 2/4/1996.

CHAPTER 2

14 Hamlin Garland is quoted in "Boy Life on the Prairie" in Charles Round's book, *Wisconsin Authors and Their Works*, (Madison: Parker Educational Company. 1918. 5.

15 Interview with Catherine Hoffmann Yost, La Crosse, Wisconsin, 10/2/1997. (Catherine was Father Emmett's paternal aunt.) See also Michael Kronenwetter's book, *Wisconsin Heartland: The Story of Wausau & Marathon County*. Midland,

WI: Pendell Publishing Company, 1884.

[16] Ibid. Yost

[17] Ibid. Yost

[18] Interview with Marion Placke, (Father Herbert Hoffmann's housekeeper) Hazelgreen, WI, 1/8/1998. Ibid, Yost.

[19] Newspaper articles on deaths:

La Crosse Tribune:

" Death Car Speeds Off in Darkness" – December 11, 1921
"Little Andrew Hoffmann Dies During Night" – December 13, 1921
" Police Continue Hunt For Driver of Death Car" – December 15, 1921
" Two Arrested For Double Tragedy" – December 18, 1921

CHAPTER 3

[20] Fetterman, John. ed. *Life in Rural America*. Washington, DC: National Geographic Society, 1974. See also Kronenwetter, Michael. *Wisconsin Heartland, The Story of Wausau & Marathon County 1914-1940*, Midland, MI: Pendell Publishing Co., 1984. See Nesbit, Robert C. *The History of Wisconsin*, Vol. 5. Madison: WI: State Historical Society of Wisconsin, 1985. Also Straub, A.G. The *History of Marathon, Wis. 1857-1957*. Marathon: Marathon Times, 1957. Also *This Fabulous Century, 1930-1940*. Vol. 5, Alexandria: Time-Life Books. 1969.

[21] Interview with Sister Phyllis M. Hoffmann S.D S. 2/4/1996

[22] Interview with Father Emmett's sisters, Dorothy and Marilyn. 7/15/1996

[23] Interview with Sister Phyllis M. Hoffmann S.D.S. 2/4/1997. All of the Hoffmann children adored their father.

[24] Ibid.

[25] Uys, Errol Lincoln. *Riding the Rails*. NY: TV Books L.L.C., 1999. See also: Baker, Bob. *Wisconsin Rails*. Racine, WI: Wisconsin Chapter NRHS. 1995.

[26] Unpublished Master's Thesis, Kung, Tim Yuan Shiao. "Spilt Milk: Diary Farmer Rhetoric and Actions During the Wisconsin Milk Strikes of 1933," University of Wisconsin, 1996.

Jacobs, Herbert. "The Wisconsin Milk Strike." Wisconsin Magazine of History 35 (Autumn 1951): 30-35.; Wausau Times, February 15, 1933. "Dairymen Strike." See also: Wausau Times, "One Thousand Guardsmen Called Out" April 27, 1933; Wausau Times "Union Organizers Rally" May 18, 1933. See the Bibliography for more articles on this event.

[20] Marathon Times, "Milk Strike Is Cause of Suicide Near Marathon," May 18, 1933.

CHAPTER 4

28 Butter, Jon and Harry S. Stout. *Religion In American History: A Reader*.
New York: Oxford University Press, 1998. See also Myers, Gustavus, *History of
Bigotry in the United States*. New York: Capricorn Books, 1960. See also
Coughlin, Father. *His Facts and Arguments*. n.p. New York: 1939.

29 *This Fabulous Century, 1930-1940*, Vol. 5. Alexandria: Time-Life Books,
1969, 24.

CHAPTER 5

30 Interview with Father Chester Poppa O.F.M. Cap., 6/8/1996

31 Interview with Father Chester Poppa O.F.M. Cap, 8/14/1998

32 Interview with Catherine Hoffmann Yost, 10/2/1997

33 Interview with Father Emmett Hoffmann, 4/1/1996

34 Adams, Michael C. C. *The Best War Ever: America and World War II*. Baltimore:
Johns Hopkins University Press, 1994. See also Ambrose, Stephen E. *Citizen
Soldiers*. New York: Simon & Schuster, See also Alperovitz, Gar. *The Decision to
Use the Atomic Bomb and the Architecture of an American Myth*. New York:
Knopf, 1995.

35 Goldstein, Donald and Harry J. Maihafer. *The Korean War: Story & Photographs*.
Dulles, Virginia: Brassey's Inc., 2000. See also Batson, Denzil. *We Called It War!
The Untold Story of the Combat Infantry in Korea*. Leawood, Kansas: Leathers
Publishers, 1999.

CHAPTER 6

36 Chief Clarence "Bisco" Spotted Wolf has a long and honorable heritage.
Whistling Elk, his great-grandfather, was a famed medicine man of the Northern
Cheyennes. Bisco's grandfather, Spotted Wolf, (1846-1896) was one of the bravest
of the old-time warriors. He fought in the Beecher Island Battle and the Fetterman
fight near old Ft. Kearney. In 1867, Spotted Wolf and his band of warriors
wrecked a Union Pacific train, the only known incident of its kind in frontier
history. In 1876, Spotted Wolf led the Cheyennes against General George Crook at
the Battle of the Rosebud, along with Crazy Horse, who led the Lakota. One week
later, Spotted Wolf, a Kit Fox warrior, his sons, White Shield, Yellow Nose and
White Elk fought the forces of Lt. Col. George Armstrong Custer at the Battle of
the Little Bighorn on June 25, 1876.

During that battle his son Yellow Nose captured the 7th U.S. Cavalry guidon,
Spotted Wolf and another of his sons captured two matching "Custer six-shooters."
Tribal historian and author John Stands In Timber said that Spotted Wolf lost an
eye in hand-to-hand combat. For his valor during the Custer fight, the elder
Spotted Wolf was made a chief by his tribe on the day following the battle. Chief
Spotted Wolf's Sharp's carbine can be seen in the Bighorn Battlefield Museum.

Chief Spotted Wolf's youngest son, Patrick, was born in 1887. When Pat was 9 years old, his father died and he watched as the old man was laid to rest in a traditional Cheyenne rimrock burial.

Pat was educated at St. Labre Mission and later married Jean Walters. The couple had 8 children, one of whom was Clarence or "Bisco" as he came to be known. Patrick served as tribal councilman for his tribe and he was the director of the Cheyenne Indian Livestock Association and Steer Enterprise for many years. John Stands In Timber, author and noted Cheyenne historian, called Pat "the best rider and roper on the reservation."

Pat's son, Clarence "Bisco" Spotted Wolf was born in 1925. He attended school at St. Labre Mission and Lame Deer Public School and served as a tribal councilman in the 1950s. In 1964, Bisco was a champion rodeo team roper. After his father's death, he became a Chief of the Northern Cheyenne Council of 44. Bisco worked at St. Labre Indian School for more than 35 years. He and his wife Adeline, retired in 2002. Bisco is currently the director of the Soaring Eagle Heritage Project and also serves on the Board of Directors of Soaring Eagle, a Public Charity.

During the summer of 2001, Bisco met a man with a similar heritage, Kenneth Custer, a descendant of Lt. Col. George Armstrong Custer's family. The two men, born of cultures that fought each other without mercy on the western plains, formed a bond of friendship that may well last the rest of their lives. The history of the Northern Cheyenne Tribe reflects a proud heritage. The Spotted Wolfs were among those who fought for their people and who ultimately left a legacy of sacrifice and bravery. From Chief Spotted Wolf, who fought alongside his friend Crazy Horse to victory against General Crook and Lt. Col. Custer, to his grandson Bisco, who has come full circle by offering his hand in friendship to the descendant of a mortal foe.

[37]   Anonymous Cheyenne elder

[38]   Father Peter Powell. Sweet Medicine, Volume I, page 66

[39]   See "President Nixon Presents A New Indian Doctrine. The President's Message to Congress July 8, 1970." Indian Record. August 1970:

As recently as August of 1953, in House Concurrent Resolution 108, the Congress declared that termination was the long-range goal of its Indian policies . . . This policy of forced termination is wrong, in my judgment . . . I am asking Congress to pass a new Concurrent Resolution which would expressly renounce, repudiate and repeal the termination policy as expressed in HRC 108 of the 83rd Congress. This resolution would explicitly affirm the integrity and right to continued existence for all Indian Tribes and Alaska Native Governments, recognizing that cultural plurism is a source of national strength . . .

[40]   Letter from Father Marion Roessler O.F.M. Cap. To donor Harry John, December, 1956:

Since the government has allowed our Cheyenne Indians to purchase liquor in any place off the Indian reservation, our Cheyenne Indian WOMEN have followed their husbands in taking to drink. As a result, many Indian parents are becoming more and more incompetent to take care of their children, and the Indian court is having to take many Indian children away from them, – at least until the Indian parents stop drinking, and prove competent to again have the care of their children.

See also an article in the Forsyth Independent Press "Indian Institute Hears Justice Issue warning on Pending (liquor) legislation." April 6, 1953. Also see Peters, Sunny. *Hi Cheyennes,* Bozeman, Montana: Color World Printers, 1992. Ms Peters didn't see alcohol and drug abuse on the Northern Cheyenne Reservation during her years as a nurse in the first 35 years of the century. She was helpful in eradicating tuberculosis on the reservation by personally helping tribal members get chest x-rays.

SEHP Collection - Tape #028B Jim Medicine Bird: "In 1954 everything changed for us. Everybody enjoyed visiting and traveling before that. It was really good them days. Enjoyable. Nobody brought in liquor up to that time. Life before 1954 was good. Then white people turned us loose."

SEHP Collection – Tape #153 – Comment by Clarence "Bisco" Spotted Wolf:

"Everything was quiet before World War II. After the war is when men came home from the war and started drinking. There were no fancy foods, no electricity, no running water, few old cars, old clothing, old dirt roads – not like they had it when they were in the army and overseas. They were used to good living. So it got to them and they didn't have anything to look forward to. They started drinking. Them old days – we were pretty careful in our lives. But that other lifestyle hit us. Hurry up, always hurry up. Maybe it's the kids that brought this fast life on. The chiefs used to talk to the young and old during the Depression. The younger generations don't understand when you talk to them in Indian. I don't know why they want to go the white way instead of keeping the Indian language. Maybe they would understand what is said to them in Indian better than in English if they could speak our language."

Interview with Joe Fox Sr. 6/12/96 "I didn't drink until I came back from the war. I got used to having clean clothes, driving in cars – I just took it for granted. When I came home I really saw the poverty for the first time. I never noticed we were poor before I left for the service. I got depressed because I didn't see how things could change. I couldn't get a decent job and provide for my family. I finally got over that when I went back to my Indian religion, but it took some time. Those were hard times for everybody."

CHAPTER 7

41 Miles City Star, May 19, 1935, "Capuchin Fathers Are Welcomed"

42 Reno Charette, a Crow, was among the little children who had dared to walk on the grass. She remembered seeing Father Emmett descending on the screeching nun. After Father told the children they could walk and sit down in the grass, Reno leaned back in the grass and raised her arms up and down like a "snow angel." She had never felt grass before and she thought it was wonderful. Interview with Reno Charette, 6/4/ 2003.

[43] Bush, *Sand, Sage, and Struggle*, p. 207: Quote from Father Marion Roessler in a 1954 appeal letter to donors: "I have been here at St. Labre for seven years, constantly traveling the length and breadth of these 444,837 acres of desolate reservation. I have been in the dilapidated tepees and . . . huts of these people, at their bedside when they were dying of tuberculosis or the ravages of other diseases caused partially by undernourishment."

See also Kramer S.S.F., Sister Giswalda. "Memoirs of a Missionary, St. Labre's Mission, August 19, 1933. Northern Cheyenne Indian Reservation, Ashland, Montana," The School Sisters of St. Francis Achives, Milwaukee, Wisconsin, Hereinafter "Memoirs of a Missionary." SEHP Collection.

[44] "Montana Catholic Register" March 22, 1973.

[45] "Memoirs of a Missionary," Journal entry August 22, 1933.

[46] Interview with Eddie Foote, 10/18/95

[47] Interview with Leo Dohn Jr., 5/3/2001

[48] Letter from Leo Dohn Sr. to Father Marion Roessler, January 24, 1953: " I am happy indeed that your Christmas letter fell into my hands . . . I found time to read it immediately and was greatly impressed with your work and future plans . . . I prefer to think this was all providential. Your letter belongs to this chain of circumstances."

Letter to Father Marion Roessler from Leo Dohn Sr. , January 29, 1953: "There is something about your appeal that has aroused my enthusiasm and fired my imagination . . . You seem to have the vision to develop a substantial Indian program. If it is the will of God, you will succeed. We will spare no human effort." Leo Dohn Sr. spent the rest of his life raising funds for the benefit of Northern Cheyenne and Crow children at St. Labre Indian School.

Father Emmett Hoffmann began writing St. Labre appeal letters to donors in 1954, although the letters bore Father Marion's signature.

[49] "The Race of Sorrows," April 1957, Vol. 2., Number 2.

[50] Bush. *Sand, Sage, and Struggle*, p. 210

[51] Interview with Father Emmett Hoffmann, 2/14/96

CHAPTER 8

[52] Interview with Thelma Two Two, 6/18/96, Ashland, MT

[53] SEHP Collection, Tape #138 Catherine Bull Coming

[54] "Race of Sorrows" January 1958, Vol. 3, Number 1.

[55] John Woodenleg's quote in the Billings Gazette, "Cheyennes said gaining," 11-15-72

56 Bisco Spotted Wolf ran his own ranch while he worked at St. Labre Indian School for over 35 years, retiring in 2002.

57 SEHP Collection. Bisco Spotted Wolf's comments can be found in this collection.

58 Mary McGarvey's unpublished Memoirs, page 1, Courtesy Carol Ann Kunkel Collection, Hereinafter McGarvey Memoirs.

59 Ibid. page 1. "I wished it were possible to become a foster parent."

60 Ibid. page 2. "Altho I was truly frightened by my forthcoming experience, at the same time, I was a bit proud & happy that finally I had committed myself to do something worthwhile . . ."

61 Ibid. page 2.

62 Ibid. page 2.

63 Ibid. page 4

64 Interview with Jane Talbert Wagner, 6/12/96

65 Father Emmett's conversation with his father, Edward Hoffmann 6/57

66 McGarvey Memoirs, page 6.

67 Ibid. page 6.

68 Interview with Bisco Spotted Wolf 8/12/96

69 Vivienne Wilbur passed away in May of 2003. She is remembered for her organizational skills and incredible sense of humor

70 Letter from Father Emmett to Rev. J. B. Tennally, Bureau of Catholic Missions, 7/18/56. SEHP Collection

71 McGarvey Memoirs, page 4.

72 Interview with Vivienne Wilbur 8/2/97

73 Interview with Jane Talbert Wagner, 6/12/96

74 Interview with Father Emmett Hoffmann, 8/15/97

75 Ibid.

76 Ibid.

77 Ibid. 5/4/97

CHAPTER 9

78 Petter, Dr. Rudolph. *Mission Memoirs. n.d. n.p.* The Petter family lived in Vevey, Switzerland. When Rudolph was a boy, he sat bolt upright in bed one night after hearing the village bell. He told his brother, "I hear the call of God. From now on I shall devote my life to His service." Not long afterward, his brother woke him up and told him, "I just had a dream and I saw you in America preaching to some Indians."

Dr. Petter came to the U.S. in 1890. His first wife died in 1916 and his second wife was Bertha (Kinsinger). Dr. Petter and his family moved to Montana in 1896. Dr. Petter was a talented linguist, speaking French, German, Latin, Greek and Hebrew. The Petters were Mennonite missionaries on the Northern Cheyenne Reservation and founded what became the Petter Memorial Mennonite Church. Dr. Petter studied the Northern Cheyenne language and translated the Bible into Cheyenne and wrote a Cheyenne Dictionary before he passed away in 1947. Mrs. Petter, faithful wife, teacher, printer, nurse, author and community leader, lived to a very old age.

79 McGarvey Memoirs. Page 6.

80 Interview with Bisco Spotted Wolf 7/12/98

81 Interview with Teddy Woodenthigh 7/14/98

82 McGarvey Memoirs. Page 8.

83 Interview with Jane Talbert Wagner 6/12/96

84 McGarvey Memoirs. Page 18

85 McGarvey Memoirs. Page 10

86 Interview with Jane Talbert Wagner 6/12/96

87 McGarvey Memoirs. Page 11

88 Interview with Father Emmett Hoffmann 6/10/97: "I was always paranoid about being seen. So if we'd go out to eat, the three of us, I'd make sure it was far away. She never got used to that. I'd say, "I'm sorry, but I'm doing something that I'm not supposed to be doing." Once I was sitting in a restaurant with Cooky and Mary. Five priests came in and sat down at another table. We got up and left. The waitress didn't know what the hell was going on. I literally ran out. That was painful."

89 Interview with Rubie Sooktis, direct descendant of Chief Dull Knife, 6/24/98. Her father, Charles Sooktis Sr., a former Sacred Hatkeeper, planned the first pow wow at St. Labre with David Strange Owl Sr., Father Emmett and several others.

90 McGarvey Memoirs. Page 13.

91 Interview with Father Emmett Hoffmann 6/10/96

[92] Ibid

[93] McGarvey Memoirs. Page 17

[94] Interview with Fr. Emmett Hoffmann 2/12/97

[95] Interview with Carol Ann Kunkel 12/22/98

[96] Interview with Teddy Woodenthigh 7/14/98

[97] Arthur Woodenthigh's obituary appeared in the "Race of Sorrows," Vol.7, No. 1, March 1962.

[98] McGarvey Memoirs. Page 18

[99] Interview with Bisco Spotted Wolf, 10/14/98. "Xavier and his new wife were getting ready to go with Mary and Fr. Emmett to the courthouse to sign the papers so Mary could adopt Cooky. I was standing near the car and I could tell that there was some kind of argument going on in the car. Xavier's wife didn't want to go. Father Emmett put a stop to the argument and they went on their way."

[100] McGarvey Memoirs. Page 19

[101] Interview with Carol Ann Kunkel 12/22/99

[102] Interview with Jane Talbert Wagner 6/12/96

[103] Interview with Carol Ann Kunkel 12/22/99

[104] Interview with Jane Talbert Wagner 6/22/99

CHAPTER 10

[105] SEHP Collection – Northern Cheyenne Tribal Resolution No. 1128

[106] Interview with Viola Campeau 3/12/97

[107] Viola Campeau's private collection – St. Labre scrapbooks for the years 1957-1965.

[108] Dr. Ross Lemire graduated from the University of Montana and Creighton College School of Medicine. He specialized in Internal Medicine. Dr. Lemire worked for many years at St. Vincent Hospital in Billings, MT. His advice cured many children at St. Labre and probably saved many lives.

[109] Passim. Svingen, Orland J. The Northern Cheyenne Indian Reservation 1877-1900. Niwot, CO: University Press of Colorado, 1993. See also Chapter 1, Endnote 9

[110] Taken from "To The Friends Of Our Beloved Deceased Fintan Schaub, Fintan's Death and Burial." Fintan Schaub worked faithfully for the Capuchins for more than 70 years and at St. Labre Mission for more than 30 years without any pay

except room and board. Fintan was born on September 29, 1883 at Mt. Calvary, Wisconsin, close to the Capuchin monastery. His father worked for the priests. When Fintan was three years old his mother died. By the age of five Fintan was helping the priests serve Holy Mass. He often sang the song, "Ave Maria" in church. When he was 12, he left home for Milwaukee to learn a trade and the English language. He learned the tinning and plumbing trades, which served him well in the years to come. He then established his own shop. When cameras first came out, Fintan purchased a camera and began taking photographs and later moving pictures.

He loved doing unusual things in order to give pleasure to others. He could yodel very well and he often climbed to a high place in town to yodel early in the morning to wake people up. He was often called out to help neighbors and on such a trip during the winter, his truck hit a telephone pole. Doctors said he would be paralyzed for life. During his recovery he told God that if he were allowed to recover from his injuries he would devote the rest of his life to the Capuchins. It wasn't long before he was well and on October 4, 1932, he arrived at St. Labre Mission in Montana to begin his life's work. His main work at the Mission was to keep the boilers and plumbing running smoothly. He often shoveled coal all during the night. He also raised chickens and turkeys, flowers and vegetables and baked bread. During the Great Depression when gardens dried up, Fintan's enormous vegetables won ribbons at the Montana State Fair. His gardens fed all the children and staff at St. Labre for many years and he sold produce to help fund the Mission.

Fintan seemed miraculous. He had premonitions that saved barns from burning and people from being hurt. He kept a barrel of water in the garden that never needed to be refilled after many people drank from it and used it for watering the trees and flowers around the Mission during the hot 1930s. St. Labre became an oasis of beauty because of Fintan's hard work. Fintan died on July 12, 1966. To this day he is missed by the elder Cheyennes and community friends who regarded him as a beloved friend to all. SEHP Collection

[111] "Race of Sorrows," March 1959. St. Labre's 75th Anniversary Issue.

[112] Father Emmett was constantly constructing, cleaning or saving money for yet another repair. He used every inch of space to its full potential and worried constantly about overcrowding in the dorms. This was a critical health issue during measles, cholera, diphtheria and hepatitis outbreaks. When children slept close to one another, diseases spread rapidly throughout the dorms. For this reason, he built more spacious dorms and classrooms, dining hall and kitchens.

CHAPTER 11

[113] Interview with Viola Campeau 8/12/97

[114] Interview with Jane Talbert Wagner 6/12/96

[115] Ibid.

[116] Interview with Richard Thomas, Father Emmett's flight instructor. 12/8/2000
"I kept asking Father if he was studying because there was an awful lot of reading

to it. Then one day I asked him, "Are you ready for the written test?" He said, "Oh Yeah, Yeah." The test was 3 hours long. Two weeks later the test results came back. I saw him walking along, kind of drooping. He was so sure he had aced that test! Then he got with the program and he took it again the following month. This time he passed. Father Emmett was a very good pilot."

117 Interview with Viola Campeau, 7/12/97. The fire destroyed St. Xavier Mission on the Crow Reservation on February 26, 1968.

118 Interview with Warren Vest. 4/7/2003 Edward Daly was born in Chicago on November 20, 1922. When his father died during the Depression, young Daly had to fend for himself. He was drafted after Pearl Harbor and served the entire war in the Pacific theater. He bought World Airways in 1950. In 1956, the Hungarian Revolution began, with some 180,000 refugees fleeing into neighboring countries. World Airways received a contract to fly refugee flights to Austria. Daly personally visited the refugee camps and made 14 trans-Atlantic crossings, in what would foreshadow World's humanitarian missions in Vietnam. More than any other airline, World played a major role in America's involvement in the Vietnam conflict. During the conflict, World provided airlift for military personnel and material across the Pacific. World started Rest and Rehabilitation (R&R) flights for battle weary troops from Vietnam to Japan, and Australia. Daly often made trips to Vietnam to help spread Christmas cheer to those in Saigon. Daly, the humanitarian, ignored official advice to get World out of Vietnam in 1975 due to the deteriorating situation. He flew two 727s to Da Nang in hopes of rescuing women and children. When the first plane landed, with Daly aboard, thousands of people rushed the plane and clambered aboard. Daly stood at the air-stairs using his fists and the butt of a pistol to knock off the Vietnamese soldiers trying to climb aboard the already overloaded plane. With the runway full of people racing toward the airplane, Daly took off from a taxiway of about 5,000 feet in length. Despite being hit by a grenade, several bullet holes and striking a pole on take-off, the aircraft made it up into the sky. When they landed at Saigon, the crew realized that they had carried between 330 and 338 passengers – including about 60 in the cargo and eight hidden in the landing gear wells.

Despite the success of the "Last Flight From Da Nang" and the worldwide media exposure, Daly was depressed that of the hundreds of souls aboard, only eleven women and children were among them. As the North Vietnamese closed in on Saigon, Daly flew another flight – this time back to the U.S. with 218 Vietnamese refugees – including 57 orphans for whom he took personal responsibility. On January 21, 1984, Edward J, Daly died at the age of 61. Father Emmett liked Ed Daly and thought of him as a brave, intelligent and generous man. For more information see "World's Colorful Past" by Jeff S. Johnson in the Sept./Oct. issue of Airliners. See also *Operation Babylift: The Last Flights out of Saigon* by Cherie Clark.

119 Northern Cheyenne Tribal Council Resolution No. 98. SEHP Collection

120 Interview with Fr. Emmett Hoffmann 8/8/96

121 Ibid. Mary told her family that she and Cooky were moving back to New Jersey because of Cooky's health problems. Mary did not mention in her memoirs why they left St. Labre.

[122] Interview with Fr. Emmett Hoffmann 8/8/96

[123] Interview with anonymous Capuchin priest.

[124] Billings Gazette, March 6, 1957, "Cheyenne Who Saw Chief Joseph Surrender, Dies in V.A. Hospital"

[125] Interview with Clarence "Bisco" Spotted Wolf, 1/25/99

[126] Viola got hepatitis one year and it took her 6 weeks to recuperate. Luckily, Father Emmett didn't catch any of the diseases.

[127] After this quote appeared in the New York Times in 1962, Robert Kennedy came to the reservation to see the conditions for himself. He was shocked by the poverty.

[128] Billings Gazette, "Northern Cheyennes Make Good" 4/5/62

[129] Ibid

CHAPTER 12

[130] Interview with Carole Ann Kunkel 3/7/98

[131] Interview with James Stone, Yankton Sioux, Marty, SD 5/12/79.

[132] Interview with Jane Talbert Wagner 6/12/96

[133] Interview with Carol Ann Kunkel 3/5/98

[134] Interview with Fr. Emmett Hoffmann 4/12/98

[135] Interview with Carol Ann Kunkel 3/5/98

[136] Ibid.

[137] Fr. Emmett Hoffmann's letter of recommendation for Mary McGarvey written June 10, 1964: "I am happy to supply this letter of recommendation for Mary McGarvey who was employed at St. Labre Indian Mission and School from August 1955 to May 1964 . . . Her daughter , Carol Ann, is now 10 years old . . . Miss McGarvey is a most dependable, reliable and honest person and would be an asset to any employer . . . I might add that since Miss McGarvey left our employment I have hired three people to do the work she did."

[138] Letter from Fr. Emmett to Cooky, 6/3/64. Mary stopped writing to Father Emmett after she left St. Labre, perhaps to try and forget him. He wrote to Mary but she did not respond so he wrote to Cooky.

[139] June 1964 "Race of Sorrows." By June Father was very lonely.

[140] Letter from Fr. Emmett to Cooky, 12/2/64

141 "Race of Sorrows," July 1965, Vol.1, No.2.

142 "Race of Sorrows," July 1965, Vol.1, No.2.

143 Letter to Cooky from Fr. Emmett, 3/24/65.

144 Letter to Mary from Fr. Emmett, 9/25/65

145 Ibid

146 Mr. Dohn was very conservative about other people's appearance but not his own. His hat had nicotine stains on it from moving it back and forth on his head when he talked. He had many friends among the Italian priests. They knew he had a heart of gold despite his rough exterior.

147 Father Emmett's postcard to Cooky and Mary from Rome, Italy 11/8/65.

148 Billings Gazette, December 31, 1963, "Bright Future For Morning Star People." See also The Christian Science Monitor, January 8,1964

149 Tribal Chairman John Woodenleg's letter to several newspapers was printed in the Congressional Record, February 21, 1966 at the request of Senator Lee Metcalf, D-Montana. See also Billings Gazette, March 18, 1966, "Probe Asked." Also Billings Gazette, March 26,1966, "Negotiation May Solve Tribulations of Tribe."

150 Ten page letter from Fr. Emmett to Senator Mike Mansfield, May 20, 1966. See also Letter from the Commissioner of Indian Affairs, U.S. Department of the Interior, Robert Bennett, July 22, 1966 to Senator Mike Mansfield: "First, we wish to say that . . . the good work of St. Labre in education and welfare . . . has always been beneficial and so recognized by the Bureau of Indian Affairs on all levels." SEHP Collection

151 Letter to Father Emmett from Senator Mike Mansfield written on June 1, 1966 and another written on July 25, 1966, SEHP Collection

152 Billings Gazette, July 28, 1966. Red Scrapbook entry, no title. SEHP Collection. Also in letter from Commissioner of Indian Affairs, Robert Bennett, to Father Emmett, July 22, 1966.

153 SEHP Collection – Father Emmett Hoffmann's collection of photographs

154 The housing, inside and out, was well maintained by a crew that kept the plumbing in good condition, the yards clean and the houses painted. Although a manager kept the housing and the rules in order, Father Emmett kept an eye on the housing maintenance and roads.

155 Dohn's statement was echoed in an interview with Lee Eckman, Manager of the Northern Cheyenne Pine Saw Mill, by Fr. Emmett's long-time employee, Vivienne Wilbur and by many donors over the years.

CHAPTER 13

[156] Kunhardt, Philip B. ed. *Life, The First Fifty Years 1936-1986*. Boston: Little, Brown & Company 1986. p. 213

[157] Nixon, Richard. *United States Foreign Policy for the 1970s*. NY: Bantam, 1970. See also "Morning Star People" Vol.10. No. 3. September 1973, "According to 1971 Pentagon statistics, over 42,000 Indians fought and served in Southeast Asia during the Viet Nam War."

[158] Butler, Jon and Harry S. Stout. *Religion in American History: A Reader.* New York: Oxford University Press, 1998. Also: Ferraro, Barbara, and Patricia Hussey and Jane O'Reilly. *No Turning Back*. New York: Poseidon Press, 1990. Hebblethwaite, Peter. *Paul VI*. Mahwah, NJ: Paulist Press, 1993. See also: Levi, Virgilio and Christine Allison. *John Paul II*. New York: William Morrow & Company, 1999. Also: Ryan Penelope J. *Practicing Catholic: The Search for a Livable Catholicism*. New York: Henry Holt and Company, 1998. Also: Abbott, Walter M. S.J. and Rev. Joseph Gallagher, M.S.G.R., eds. *The Documents of Vatican II*. New York: The American Press, 1966, Hereinafter *Documents of Vatican II*.

[159] Davidson, James D. "Generations have different views of the church, Vatican II is the dividing line," National Catholic Reporter, October 29, 1999. p. 18.

[160] Ibid.

[161] Ibid.

[162] Interview with Bisco Spotted Wolf, 8/12/97, "The priests acted a little confused."

[163] *Documents of Vatican II*, p. 662

[164] "The Race of Sorrows," December 1971, Vol. 17, No. 4. "For many years I have thought about this future date when the Chapel could be completed. You will recall how I begged you for years. It has been 16 years since I first contemplated this project. I can't fully express the joy that fills my heart."

[165] Interview with Viola Campeau, 6/17/97. "Father Jochim had trouble giving the last Mass in the old chapel. All the Indians were crying and he didn't think he could continue."

[166] "Race of Sorrows," December, 1971, Vol.17. No. 4. "The exterior of the new St. Labre Chapel gives the appearance of a giant stone tepee. The cross seems to be carried on the back of the chapel . . . the stained glass windows form an arrow pointing to the heavens. The colors of the glass are drawn from the many colors of Grandmother Earth."

[167] Interview with Fr. Emmett Hoffmann. 8/12/97

[168] Interview with Fr. Larry Abler, O.F.M. Cap. 2/11/2000. Father Larry was born on August 4, 1938 at St. Cloud, Wisconsin. He spent over 12 years working at St. Labre Mission and on the Crow Reservation at St. Xavier. Father raised the funds and oversaw the construction of the new Solanus Casey Center in Detroit,

Michigan. He is currently the Pastor of St. Joseph's Parish in Appleton, Wisconsin.

169 Letter from Fr. Emmett to Cooky, September 29, 1966. "Be sure to tell your mother that I think of her always . . . I will never be able to thank your mother enough for everything that she has done for me and St. Labre. The spirit of St. Labre today is reflected in so many ways in the ideas your mother had in years gone by. It wasn't possible to do all the things we dreamt of immediately, but today they are becoming a reality."

170 Suicide quote in Capuchin Newsletter called "Sandal Prints,". Vol. XVIII, No. 1, November-December, 1969. The photograph that accompanies the quote shows a haggard looking priest with furrowed brow, dark circles under his eyes and smoking.

171 One woman donor often called in the middle of the night to play the piano for Fr. Emmett. He listened patiently at 2:30 a.m. He always answered the phone thinking it might be an emergency and didn't have the heart to tell the woman not to call.

172 "The Morning Star People," December, 1966, Vol. 2, No 4.

173 Letter from Father Emmett to Mary, n.d. Carol Ann Kunkel Collection.

174 Interview with Fr. Larry Abler, 2/11/2000

175 Interview with Tony Foote 9/12/95
Interview with Larry Kostelecky 11/8/2000
Interview with Viola Campeau 8/2/97

176 Interview with anonymous Northern Cheyenne tribal member, 8/3/97

177 Interview with Father Larry Abler, 2/11/2000

178 Undated pamphlet called "A New Era for the American Indians" in SEHP Collection.

179 Undated article in Scrapbook entitled "Cheyenne History" SEHP Collection. Passim, Bush, *Sand, Sage, and Struggle*

180 In one of the sweatlodge ceremonies some hippies came in. They took peyote and threw up. This disgusted Father Emmett. He thought they should not have been allowed into the spiritual ceremony because they were just curious and not serious about praying.

181 Interview with Fr. Emmett Hoffmann, 7/5/1999

182 Ibid Chapter 1., Endnote 10

CHAPTER 14

183 Interview with Carol Ann Kunkel 12/22/98

184 Letter From Father Emmett to Cooky, 2/11/1968

185 Interview with Conrad Sump 2/18/99. Conrad Sump was born on the coldest day in New York City history, February 9, 1934. It was 15 degrees below zero. Both his parents were from Northern Germany. His father operated a deli and owned several other businesses. In 1960, "Connie" as friends called him, graduated from New York University with an MBA in accounting. He met his lovely future wife, Ruth Henning, when his roommate introduced his sister. The Sumps have two children, Conrad Jr., an attorney and a daughter, Linda Spang, a counselor. Connie said of his early years at St. Labre: "I rode by the seat of my pants in those days. I admired what Fr. Emmett was doing." Father Emmett liked the brash New Yorker from the start. "He analyzed everything. He always asked me, "'How much sticks to the ribs?'" He disliked adding machines because he thought it ruined young accountants. Connie always knew how much we needed for every project."

186 Interview with Conrad Sump 2/4/99; Interview with Father Larry Abler 2/11/2000; Interview with Paul Morigi 7/18/98 and 5/4/2003. Paul settled in New York City in 1945, after World War II. He and his wife, Muriel, had two children. Paul has worked for the prestigious firm of Morgan Stanley for many years and founded his own company. On 9-11, when terrorists attacked the World Trade Center, Paul was 30 blocks away. If he had still been at his old address, Number One Wall Street - just two blocks from the World Trade Center, he might not have made it out alive.

For 35 years Paul Morigi has been like a brother to Father Emmett. He advised Father on investments and continues to do so to the present day. Father, Connie and Paul were a team and together they worked tirelessly to make St. Labre Indian School one of the finest private schools in the country.

187 Interview with Conrad Sump 2/4/99; Interview with Father Larry Abler 2/11/2000. This irritating habit made people feel that they were not important enough to command his full attention. When a person brought this to his attention, he scoffed, saying, "I can do more than one thing at a time."

188 Interview with Virginia Toews 6/23/2000. Virginia was the Executive Director of the Northern Cheyenne Housing Authority in Lame Deer from 1963 until 1986. Her husband John was artist Denver Horn's good friend. After they retired, John and Virginia moved to Billings. In the early 1990s, John had a massive stroke that left him paralyzed and unable to speak. Virginia worked and had a caregiver take care of John. Five years later, Virginia was at work when the caregiver called and told her to come at once. When Virginia reached her husband's side (he had not spoken a word for three years), he was talking to someone in his room. Every so often she could hear a burst of laughter. John was gesturing with his paralyzed arm and having a spirited conversation with thin air. There was nobody else in the room. "John," who are you talking to?" Virginia asked. "Oh, it was Denver Horn." John told his shocked wife. "He came to thank me for all that I'd done for him over the years. He said he'd see me again soon." Virginia tried to ask her husband another question, but he had drifted back into his silent, paralyzed state. That afternoon, Virginia read the terrible news that Denver Horn had died in a house fire at about the same time that John had been talking to him! A couple of days later, John quietly passed away. Virginia was comforted by the thought that Denver Horn, her husband's old friend, had come to take John home to a far better place.

189 Letter from Fr. Emmett to Mary and Cooky, 7/4/68.

190 "The Morning Star People," September 1968, Vol. 5, No. 3. "For the first time in the 84 year history of the St. Labre Indian School, a layman has assumed the position of Superintendent. Mr. Kostelecky, a native of Dickenson, North Dakota, has had twelve years of teaching experience with the Cheyenne Indians." In an interview with Mr. Kostelecky in the same article he said, "There is a very definite conflict between the values of the white man and the Indian. In our education of the Indian we have thought only of conformity with our own ideals and values and have emphasized the same. In this process, the very rich Indian heritage is ignored and even destroyed. The end result has been confusion and conflict by the time the Indian youth reaches the junior high school level." Kostelecky dedicated his administration to helping each child to develop his full and true potential.

Interview with Larry Kostelecky 3/16/99. Larry began teaching on the Northern Cheyenne Reservation in 1956. For 8 years he taught at Lame Deer Public School. In 1964, he transferred to St. Labre as head of the mathematics department. Larry's wife Cindy was the medical x-ray technician for the Department of Health, Education and Welfare in Lame Deer.

191 Ibid.

192 Letter from Father Emmett to Cooky, 8/26/74

193 Letter from Father Emmett to Mary and Cooky, 5/12/74

194 Letter from Father Emmett to Cooky, 11/5/72

195 Letters from Fr. Emmett to Cooky, 9/7/73 and 12/12/73

196 Mary's poem in her Memoir dedicated to Cooky. n.d., Carol Ann Kunkel Collection

197 Letter from Father Emmett to Cooky, 2/12/74.

198 Interview with Carol Ann Kunkel, 3/4/98

199 Ibid.

200 Ibid.

201 Interview with Carol Ann Kunkel, 8/23/98

202 Interview with Carol Ann Kunkel, 9/14/98

203 Interview with Carol Ann Kunkel, 10/12/98

204 Ibid.

205 Ibid.

206 Interview with Carol Anne Kunkel, 4/4/99

207 Interview with Fr. Emmett Hoffmann 10/2/96

CHAPTER 15

[208] Passim. Bowlby, John. *Attachment and Loss*. New York: The Perseus Book Group,1983.

[209] There were between 40 and 50 children in the Cheyenne Home in 1975. After Mary McGarvey left St. Labre in the late 1960s, Jasper and Becky Tallwhiteman became the housemother and father. The children loved them. Becky worked until she passed away suddenly in 1984 at the age of 67. She "grandmothered" hundreds of children.

[210] Oursler, Fulton, *Father Flanagan of Boys Town*. New York: Doubleday. 1949

[211] Father Emmett often called Father Gilbert Hemauer, O.F.M. CAP., "the idea man." Father Gil founded the Tekakwitha National Center in 1977. At that time there were only 1 or 2 native clergy representing the Catholic Church in America. Dissatisfied with the meager representation, Father Gil hoped to develop a unified native presence, voice and leadership in the church. By the 1980s there were 20 American Indian priests. Through Father Gil's efforts, Pope John Paul attended the 1984 Tekakwitha Conference in Phoenix, Arizona. Thousands of Indians and non-Indians attended the conference. Father Emmett assisted Father Gil is this enormous project.

[212] Interview with Father Larry Abler, 2/11/2000

[213] Viola Campeau's Journal, January 28, 1975

[214] Interview with Sister Phyllis Hoffmann S.D.S. 2/4/96. Father Emmett had never heard of a Near Death Experience before he experienced one himself.

[215] Passim. Moody, MD, Raymond A. Jr., *Life After Life*. New York: Bantom Books, 1988. See also: Brinkley, Dannion with Paul Perry. *Saved By The Light*. NY: Villard Books, 1994.

[216] Viola Campeau's Journal, March 7, 1975. "The next morning after Father's surgery I went to see him and he was sitting up in a chair eating breakfast! I expected the worst but he was his old self. I stayed in his room. He was worried that I wouldn't hear him if he cried out for help. I got a rod so that if he got sick in the night, he could poke me to wake me up. He was a very good patient, never demanding."

[217] Interview with Father Larry Abler, 2/11/2000

[218] "The Morning Star People," July 1975, Vol. 12. No. 3.

[219] Interview with Conrad Sump Sr. 2/4/99

[220] Ibid.

[221] Letter to Cooky from Father Emmett, 11/6/75

[222] Letter to Cooky from Father Emmett, 3/12/75

223 Viola Campeau was the only medical help at St. Labre, the town of Ashland and the surrounding area. When she took off her hearing aid at night, she could not hear a sound. This meant that late at night the people were as isolated from medical help as she was from the ringing of a telephone or frantic pounding at her door. She would often lose sleep worrying that someone might need urgent help in a life or death crisis and she wouldn't be able to hear emergency calls.

One evening Vi heard on the nightly news about Hearing Dog, Inc. in Colorado. The organization trained dogs for the hearing impaired. Vi knew this was the answer to her problem. The employees at St. Labre raised $2,800 to pay for the hearing-dog training. On July 15, 1980 a small, gentle-eyed dog named Charmin arrived at Viola's house. Charmin was trained for burglar alert, smoke alarm, alarm clock, door knock and telephone ring. When he heard one of these at night, Charmin jumped up against Vi, waking her up.

Viola talked Tom Asay, a Montana legislator, into introducing a bill that would protect the right of the hearing impaired to have their dogs in public restaurants, airplanes and parks. The bill passed but not before Vi and Charmin were almost kicked out of the Old Faithful Inn at Yellowstone Park. Then she was stopped from boarding a plane in Texas and it took some time before the airlines finally allowed them to board. Montana Governor Ted Swinden found out about the incidents and helped Vi lobby for U.S. Senate legislation. Her letter writing campaign paid off when Vi and Charmin were invited to Helena to witness the signing of House Bill 91. Another victory came when the United States Department of the Interior finally "revised Title 36, Code of Federal Regulations (CFR) Section 2.15, to provide for hearing ear dogs to accompany hearing-impaired persons visiting any unit of the National Park Service. Charmin lived for many years and was a faithful, devoted friend.

224 Interview with Leo Dohn Jr., 2/11/2000

225 Ibid.

226 Billings Gazette article, "Guild Factory to Close", February 6, 1977.

227 Interview with Conrad Sump Sr. 12/10/96

228 "The Morning Star People," St. Labre Indian School , June 1977, Vol.14., No. 2.

229 Interview with Conrad Sump Sr. 12/10/96
Interview with Carol Ann Kunkel 2/4/99

CHAPTER 16

230 Interview with Carol Ann Kunkel, 12/22/99

231 Clarke, Gerald. *Capote: A Biography*. New York: Simon and Schuster. 1998

232 Ibid.

233 Ibid.

234 Woodward, Bob and Bernstein, Carl. *All the President's Men.* NY:Simon & Schuster, 1974. See also Hougan, Jim. *Secret Agenda: Watergate, Deep Throat, and the CIA.* NY: Random House, 1984.

235 It didn't take long for the tribe to find out that they had gotten a raw deal. By the 1970s, Tribal President Alan Rowland wanted out of the contracts and he worked night and day to that end. He was so persistent that coal company executives began calling him "the Indian equivalent of John Wayne." Rowland wasn't about to be pushed around by big coal companies. During his tenure a massive anti-coal campaign with anonymous flyers, posters and cartoons were distributed in every reservation district showing Indians lined up to enter the gaping, open-mouth of a skull called "coal black death." Another poster depicted a reservation cabin high up on top of a narrow piece of land with a bulldozer digging a big hole around its base. The publicity worked – tribal members took notice and turned against the coal companies. Rowland investigated the coal leases and found that permits issued by the BIA involved gross violations of the law. The Secretary of the Interior issued a decision virtually stopping the coal companies from proceeding without further consent of the tribe. The final decision came just days before Peabody Coal Company, the largest strip mining operator, was to begin a $700,000 mining investment on 16,000 acres of leased reservation land. Throughout the investigation, Father Emmett backed Alan (Chuggy") Rowland's stand against the unfair coal leases. Father and Rowland were great friends.

See "Coal rush – A boom or a last stand?" Billings Gazette, October 1, 1972.
  "BIA answers complaints over coal by Indians," Billings Gazette, December, 14, 1973
  "King Coal Arises" Billings Gazette, March 17, 1874
  "Cheyenne Tribe fears coal effects," Billings Gazette, April 21, 1974
  "Alan Rowland looking for trouble," Billings Gazette, January 28, 1977

236 Tom Gardner was the Community Action Director for his tribe. His viewpoints were serialized in "The Morning Star People" newsletters. His undated article "A Cheyenne Tragedy" can be found in a red Scrapbook entitled "Coal Scrapbook – 1974" and the blue "Coal scrapbook," page 13, SEHP Collection.

237 Ibid.

238 Interview with Conrad Sump Sr. 2/4/99

239 Interview with Sister Phyllis Hoffmann S.D.S. 2/4/96. Father Emmett dreaded this visit because he had to face his mother. She had thoroughly disapproved of his taking a sabbatical, which made him feel guilty, a perpetual guilt that never left him. He felt that whatever he did, he could never really please her.

240 Interview with Carol Ann Kunkel 12/22/99.

241 Ibid.

242 Interview with Conrad Sump Sr., 8/12/2000

243 Ibid. 8/12/2000

244 Ibid.

245 Summer 1996 interviews with Father Emmett Hoffmann's sisters in Wisconsin;
Sister Phyllis Hoffmann, Dorothy Karlen and Marilyn Mondrowski.

Father Emmett accompanied the author on this trip to his old home, a dairy farm
outside Marathon, Wisconsin. The farm is owned by the Krautkramer family, the
people who bought the farm at auction. The buildings still appear clean and well
cared for. Father walked to the barn his grandfather had carefully constructed, the
scene of many of his childhood memories. He opened the back barn door to show
me a clear view of Rib Mountain. Today most farmers in the area grow ginseng, a
cash crop. Father showed me the taverns and stores in Marathon, the site of the old
mercantile and the shoemaker's shop where he spent many happy hours with the
old cobbler, Mr. Urban, one of the only places where the boy felt comfortable and
relaxed. Mr. Urban's leather apron, the tap tapping of his hands as he artfully
placed small nails in leather shoes he had made or repaired and most of all his
understanding nature and soft spoken gentleness mesmerized the child and gave
him a certain peace.

Finally we drove up to the Catholic cemetery on the hill above Marathon. Father
Emmett became silent and deeply reflective as he stood at the foot of his mother
and father's graves. His grandfather George and wife Anna's graves were not as
well trimmed, weeds growing up here and there. "I want to be buried with the
Cheyenne" he said quietly and turned to walk back to the car.

246 Interview with Father Emmett Hoffmann 8/4/99

CHAPTER 17

247 Northern Cheyenne Tribal News. Vol. 1, March 1981.

248 Ibid.

249 The Ashland Story, October 12, 1983.

250 "The Morning Star People," September 1984, Vol. 21, No. 4.

251 Interview with Conrad Sump Sr. 2/4/99

252 Giago, Tim, Lakota founder and editor of "Indian Country Today" is the author of
several books. He writes a syndicated column, "Notes From Indian Country." This
article appeared nationally in 1998: "Retribution for Catholic sins is near."

Also: Interview with the anonymous Lakota daughter of a Jesuit priest. 1996. Her
mother attended a Catholic boarding school in South Dakota during the 1940s.
One of the priests at the school began a sexual affair with the teenager and she
became pregnant. When the priest found out, he arranged for her to leave. She was
sent to a maternity home in the south, where she gave birth to a daughter. The
nuns tried to make her give up custody of her baby but she refused. She ran away
and returned to her parents home to raise her daughter. The girl grew up and
graduated from college. She is bitter about her father and feels that her mother's
life was ruined by a sexual predator within the Catholic Church.

253 Interview with anonymous Southern Cheyenne spiritual leader.

254 Interview with Leo Dohn Jr. 2/11/2000.

255 Interview with Tony Foote, St. Labre Indian School comptroller, 9/9/96. Tony remembers meeting Father when he was walking home from school with his cousins. Father stopped to give them a ride. They were driving along when Tony spotted a deer in the trees. "Stop the car Father!" he shouted. Alarmed, Father Emmett screeched to a halt. Father was aghast. The boys opened the car doors and they jumped out and ran after the deer. Within 5 minutes they had chased down the deer, killed it and put it into the trunk of the Mission car. It was like looking at a scene happening in 1800. He couldn't believe how quickly they had surrounded and brought down the deer.

Also see Tony Foote's letter of recommendation for Father Emmett, written to the Montana Jefferson Award Committee, August 12, 1994. "He is not only our hero," Tony wrote, "he is everyone's friend." SEHP Collection.

256 Interview with Lee Eckman, Manager of the Northern Cheyenne Pine Company, 8/2/96. Lee was an excellent manager and friend.

257 Interview with Daniel Foote, 6/12/2003. Eddie Foote was a rodeo bareback rider, a Sundancer, a Native American Church member and member of the Elk Horn Scraper Society. His Indian name was Hotomo or Buffalo. He was married to Regina Tall White Man for 44 years. Father Emmett loved his practical jokes and his humorous way of looking at life. He worked at St. Labre for many years and passed away on February 20, 1997 of throat cancer. His funeral was the largest ever held at St. Labre Mission.

258 Interview with Robert Bement, 3-25/2003. Robert graduated from St. Labre Indian School in 1965. He attended Western Montana College and North Dakota State School of Science, earning his Graphic Arts Degree in 1973. He has been the master printer at St Labre for 37 years. It is the first and only job he has had and he is still there. Over the years, Robert worked for 10 CEOs and 8 Development Directors at the school. He married Deloras Garcia, whom he calls "the love of my life" in 1996.

259 Jennette Brey recommendation letter for Father Emmett, January 11, 1985. SEHP Collection.

260 Interview with 40-year St. Labre employee, Patsy Brey, 4/16/2001.

261 Interview with Deloras Little Coyote 4/16/2001

262 Interview with Chief Jimmie D. Little Coyote a week before his death on October 20, 1995. Jimmie loved to tell the story of shooting out a stained glass window at St. Labre with a bean shooter and never getting caught. He laughed when he said, "I was always getting into trouble with the Sisters and priests when I was a kid. I got my ear pulled a lot by Father Emmett. In fact, it's Father Emmett's fault that one of my ears is higher than the other!"

Interview with Father Emmett about his relationship with Jimmie's daughter Dewanda Little Coyote, 1/12/96. Dewanda is now the the Admissions and

Activities Director at the Heritage Living Center in Ashland, Montana. Dewanda has two children, Cordell James (C.J.) and Shawn. Cordell is the youngest chief in the Northern Cheyenne Council of 44. Dewanda is the great granddaughter, the granddaughter and the daughter of chiefs and now her son takes his rightful place as chief. She is devoted to Father Emmett and vice versa.

263 Interview with Mary Jo Fox, 6/25/96

264 Interview with Lee Eckman 3/6/96

265 Interview with Mary Jo Fox 6/25/96

266 Ibid. On Mary Jo's last day at work she was standing in the doorway to Father's office when one of the younger priests she called, "The Weasel," walked by. She was ready to give him a piece of her mind but Father Emmett stopped her with one word. "Don't" he said. She left without telling the priest what she thought of him.

267 Big Horn County News. n.d. White Scrapbook in SEHP Collection.

268 Ibid.

269 Interview with Father Emmett Hoffmann 4/15/97

270 Father Emmett has always considered Father Pascal Siler O.F.M. Cap., a special friend. Fr. Pascal was born on August 17, 1933 in Merrill, Michigan. Now with 44 years in the priesthood, Fr. Siler remembers 5 years of missionary work in Saudi Arabia. He was there with permission from King Ryhad. He had services in 50 communities but in August of 1985 he was seized without warning and imprisoned for "proselytizing" Fr. Pascal was no extremist but they took him to prison without allowing him to see a lawyer. The first 6 days he saw no one. He was interrogated for 14 days. Two other Saudis were also in prison and they cried when they found out he was a priest. He slept on a carpet with a blanket and was well fed. Faith sustained him. "It was a prayerful experience," he said. Just as suddenly as he was arrested, he was deported. When he returned to the United States, he served in an inner city parish in Detroit and then came to the Northern Cheyenne Reservation in 1973 and stayed until 1980. He returned later and has spent a total of 18 years with the Cheyenne people. He is still the parish priest at St. Labre Indian School.

271 Interview with Tony Foote 8/12/95

272 Father Emmett's letter to benefactors of St. Labre, February 1988. SEHP Collection

CHAPTER 18

273 Interview with Father Dennis Druggan, O.F.M. Cap. 3/17/2003

274 Billings Gazette, "Gestapo tactics upset director," May 15, 1991

275 Billings Gazette, "St. Labre Home Abuse Rumored," May 22, 1991.

276 Billings Gazette – "BIA, U.S. attorney mum on St. Labre" May 16, 1991

277 Interview with Father Dennis Druggan O.F.M. Cap. 3/17/2003

278 Ibid.

279 Inteview with Viola Campeau. 5/12/96

280 nterview with Father Dennis Druggan O.F.M. Cap. 3/17/2003

281 Both Southern and Northern Cheyenne tribal members who wish to remain anonymous. 1997-1998

282 Interview with Father Emmett Hoffmann 4/5/99

283 Interview with Conrad Sump Sr. 2/3/2001 and 4/18/2003

284 Interview with Dr. Ross Lemire 2/2/2001 and 4/8/2003

285 Ruether, Rosemary. "Crisis and Challenges of Catholics Today." *America* (March 1, 1986): 152-158.

286 Interview with Father Emmett Hoffmann 9/7/97

287 Milwaukee Journal, December 20, 1992, "8 men tell of sex abuse by friars," Many articles appeared in 1992 and 1993 with Ken Reinhardt's photograph relating to the molestation of young men, while at the same time Reinhardt was going for Father's jugular vein in Ashland, Montana.

288 Ibid.

289 Ibid.

290 The Reporter, Fond Du Lac, Wisconsin, "Over and Over," December 20, 1992. Victim Michael Rocklin described 50 sexual encounters with a teacher and principal at St. Lawrence Seminary.

291 Father Emmett Hoffmann's journal, 12/18/97

292 Bernardin, Joseph Cardinal. *The Gift of Peace*. Chicago: Loyola Press, 1997, page 22-23. Hereinafter Bernardin.

293 Bernardin, pages 36-38

294 Letter from Father Emmett to Bishop Anthony M. Milone DD, 2/19/93.

295 Ibid.

296 Text of speech for the dedication of the Father Emmett Hoffmann Soaring Eagle Center, "The Morning Star People," July 1993, Vol.31, No.3. SEHP Collection

297 Interview with Conrad Sump Sr. 12/10/96

[298] Interview with Conrad Sump Sr. 12/10/96

[299] Billings Gazette, "Hoffmann Leaves St. Labre," November 22, 1993. See also "Hoffmann to quit St. Labre Unless . . . " November 13, 1993.

[300] Father Emmett's appeal letter to donors on November 22, 1993

[301] Television News coverage taken by Vivienne Wilbur of protestors marching at St. Labre. KTVQ NEWS clips - October and November 1993. SEHP Collection

[302] Ibid.

[303] Letter from Father Emmett to Provincial Minister, Rev. Anthony Scannell OFM, Cap., November 17, 1994.

[304] 1 John 3:15

CHAPTER 19

[305] Walker, Morton D.P.M. *The Chelation Answer*. Atlanta: Second Opinion Publishing, 1994. Also: Brecher, Harold and Arline. *Forty Something Forever, A Consumer's Guide to Chelation Therapy*. Herndon, Virginia: Healthsavers Press, 1992.

[306] Father Emmett often refers to himself as a "renegade," hence the title of this book.

[307] Appreciation Award for Outstanding Achievements – 1954 – 1994, from the staff of St. Labre. SEHLC Collection

[308] Letter from Vivienne Wilbur to the St. Labre Educational Association, 6/17/93 Vivienne worked a total of 64 years for St. Labre.

[309] Interview with Bula Brey 10/18/96. Bula has worked at St. Labre Indian School for over 40 years.

[310] Letter from Father Emmett to Father Gil Hemauer O.F.M. Cap. February 22, 1995.

[311] Interview with Conrad Sump Sr. 8/9/98

[312] Interviews with Paul Morigi 10/7/1999 and 5/12/2003. Interviewed about the St. Labre complaint, Mr. Morigi said, "It destroyed me. All my work seemed for nothing."

[313] Interview with Conrad Sump Sr. 4/12/98

[314] Interview with Conrad Sump Sr. 8/5/99

[315] Interview with Tony Foote 11/6/95

[316] Ibid.

[317] Interview with a Capuchin priest who will remain anonymous. 9/14/97.

318 Final Report of John Mudd, legal mediator, sent to all parties on May 9, 1996. SEHP Collection

CHAPTER 20

319 In 1997, Father Emmett (out of his own pocket), hired Clarence "Bisco" Spotted Wolf to translate Cheyenne tape recordings. The author agreed to transcribe the recordings gratis. It has been a labor of love and taken 6 years of part-time work to complete and transcribe 100 tapes – a monumental, tedious task taking thousands of hours. Assistants Ingrid Angel Duke and Jamie Porter are putting the transcriptions on computer with a grant from Soaring Eagle, a Public Charity.

320 Tape #105, Heritage Translation Project, SEHP Collection

321 Rick Robinson founded the Boys and Girls Club of the Northern Cheyenne Nation in 1994. By 1997, the membership had skyrocketed to more than 900 youth aged 5-18. Tim Burke, writing for *YOUTH TODAY,* said that number reflected "over 40 percent of the entire 2,200 residents of Lame Deer and 20 percent of the reservation's total population of 4,800." The club building was donated by St. Labre Indian School and later the club affiliated with the Boys and Girls Club of America. "The club was born out of tragedy," Burke writes. Drunk and on drugs, a teenager, Danny Lamewoman, was murdered by his best friend in 1993. Another teenager, the son of a tribal leader, died soon afterward in an auto accident brought on by the use of alcohol.

Rick Robinson was appalled and vowed to do something about the rise in youth drug and alcohol abuse, violence and crime. Rick himself had survived a troubled youth. He began to drink when he was a very young boy. When Rick felt wretched about himself and reached the lowest point in his life, he wondered if life was worth living. Skeptical about religion, he decided that if there really was a God, he would ask for a sign. Although he knew the chapel door was always locked at night, Rick turned the door knob and the door opened for him. The chapel at St. Labre sat empty, save for a votive candle flickering at the altar. Rick looked up at the crucified Christ and asked "Maheo," God the Creator, to give him sobriety and peace. Suddenly, Rick was filled with a moving spiritual experience - an epiphany – so great that it filled his heart and changed his life forever. From that time on, he took control of his life. He went to college, married, started a family and decided to devote his life to the youth of his tribe, a true story of suffering, forgiveness, survival and great courage in the face of many obstacles that would have brought down anyone who had not felt God's grace.

This 21st century warrior has battled red tape, tribal politics, ignorance and downright evil people to provide a safe environment for thousands of Cheyenne children. The Boys and Girls Club was incorporated in 1996 as a non-profit organization and today, "Robinson pursues a clear-eyed mission of straightforward youth work, providing activities, challenge and positive adult leadership to make a difference in the lives of the reservation's young. A devout Christian, he refuses to wallow in any kind of victim mentality and is determined to work from the bottom up to build a more caring society."

See Burke, Tim. "New Indian Youth Club Runs the Gamut." *YOUTH TODAY,* reprinted by "1996 Trends in Indian Health, available from HHS Indian Health

Service, Office of Health Programs, Rockville, MD 20857.

322 Sooktis, Rubie. ed., Cheyenne News, A Collection of Articles by Donald Hollowbreast, Lame Deer, Montana: Morning Star Memorial Foundation, 2001. Donald Hollowbreast's 42 years as a journalist for the Northern Cheyenne Reservation and surrounding communities preserved Cheyenne history and culture. His writings were the teachings of a Cheyenne elder. His column "The Lame Deer News" also appeared in the Rosebud County News for many years. He gathered Cheyenne stories using sign language and a pen and note pad because Donald was profoundly deaf.

Hollowbreast lived in the remote village of Birney without access to a store, a post office or a police station. Here in 1959, without running water or electricity, Don Hollowbreast put out his first newspaper, "The Birney Arrow," which he humbly called "an erstwhile publication." In many ways, Hollowbreast took the place of the old-time Cheyenne crier, who rode from village to village announcing the news every morning.. The newspaper helped Cheyenne people to read and to care about their culture, genealogy and customs. Donald Hollowbreast's death on June 26, 2001 was much more than the death of an artist, historian and respected journalist – it was the passing of a Cheyenne who overcame deafness to communicate with the ages.

323 Burhart, Dan. "Still Soaring" Billings Gazette, December 26, 1997

324 Fr. Emmett's surgical report, written by Barry Winton, M.D. Thanks to Dr. Winton's expert surgical skills, the surgery was successful.

325 Interviews with donor Carl Williams, 8/31/2002 and 9/6/2002

326 Interview with Madonna Bordeaux, 4/17/2003

327 Kimmie Olson, the teacher at the Heritage Living Center Montessori School, studied at the Caspari Montessori Institute International, Inc. in Livingston, Montana. Before coming to the Center, Kimmie served her country in the U.S. Army Communications Command. She was employed at St. Labre Indian School, Cheyenne Homes, for 8 years as a houseparent, working with troubled Indian youth from ages 5-18. She then worked for the Missoula Youth Home as Youth Care Worker and House Manager for 3 years. She returned to Ashland when Father Emmett asked her to become Director of the Montessori School. Kimmie and her husband Jamie have two children, Corrine and Logan.

Mary Jane Robinson is the Director of the Child Day Care and Nursery. Previously, she worked at St. Labre Indian School for 8 years as a 1st grade teaching assistant and for many years she was a substitute teacher in the Head Start Program, besides ranching full time.

328 Jamie Olson is the Administrator of the Heritage Living Center. He served his country in the United States Army, 82nd Airborne Division and worked for 8 years at St. Labre Indian School as a Cheyenne Home houseparent, supervising youth aged 5-18. Jamie owned and operated the Rise and Shine Dairy Distributing business in Missoula for four years until Father Emmett asked him to return to southeastern Montana to run the Heritage Living Center.

329 Sam F. Widdicombe worked at St. Labre Indian School for 7 years in the print shop and in the maintenance department. He is currently the Maintenance Safety Coordinator for the Heritage Living Center.

330 Chief Johnny Russell Jr., a member of the Northern Cheyenne Council of 44, quietly passed by us on his way to the next camp on May 10, 2003. His tragic loss at the age of 57 leaves a shocked and grieving tribe. He'heenoohvoKomasaestse (White Black Bird) was born February 21, 1946. He grew up in the Busby area and graduated from Busby High School in 1964. John graduated from Haskell Indian School, where he received an AA degree in auto mechanics and later served his country in Vietnam in the U.S. Army during the fierce fighting of what came to be known as the Tet offensive.

He was a former school board chairman, served on the Northern Cheyenne Council and at the time of his passing he was the Northern Cheyenne Food Distribution Director. John was a traditional Cheyenne who served as a spiritual leader, a member of the Hereditary Chiefs' Society, Native American Church, Northern Cheyenne Honor Guard and participated in Sweatlodge ceremonies. He also participated in Sundances and followed the pow wow circuit with a drum group called the C & A Singers.

John enthusiastically supported the Heritage Living Center and took part in the Dedication and Grand Opening Ceremonies. He was asked for a chief's song that represented a life of service to others and Johnny responded with a song that he said summed up Father Emmett's journey through life with the Cheyenne people.

Bibliography

BOOKS

Aadland, Dan. *Women and Warriors of the Plains*. New York: Macmillan, 1996.

Abbott, Walter M.S.J., and Gallagher, Rev. Joseph MSGR., eds. and trans. *The Documents of Vatican II*. New York: The America Press, 1966.

Adams, Michael C.C. *The Best War Ever: America and World War II*. Baltimore: Johns Hopkins University Press, 1994.

Alland, Alexander Sr. *Jacob A. Riis: Photographer & Citizen*. New York: Aperture Foundation, 1973.

Ambrose, Stephen E. *Citizen Soldiers*. New York: Simon and Schuster, 1997.

American Bible Society. *Good News Bible*. New York: American Bible Society, 1979.

Anderson, Sherwood. *Home Town*. New York: Alliance Book Corporation, 1940.

Armstrong, Regis R. ed. and trans. *The Constitutions of the Capuchin Friars Minor*. 1990.

Arrow, St. Labre Indian School Year Book, 1977-1989.

Baker, Bob. *Wisconsin Rails*. Racine, Wisconsin: Wisconsin Chapter NRHS, 1995.

Barnhouse, Ruth T. *Clergy and the Sexual Revolution*. Washington DC.: Alban Institute, 1987.

Batson, Denzil. *We Called it War!* Leawood, Kansas: Leathers Publications, 1999.

Bernardin, Joseph Cardinal. *The Gift of Peace*. Chicago: Loyola Press, 1997.

Bernstein, Carl and Bob Woodward. *All the Presidents Men.* 2d ed. NY: Touchstone Books, 1994.

Berry, Jason. *Lead Us Not Into Temptation.* New York: Doubleday, 1992.

Berthrong, Donald J. *The Cheyenne and Arapaho Ordeal.* Norman, OK.: University of Oklahoma Press, 1976.

Bittle, Celestine N. *A Romance of Lady Poverty.* New York: The Bruce Publishing Company, 1933.

Blegen, Theodore C., ed. *Land of Their Choice, the Immigrants Write Home.* Minneapolis: University of Minneapolis Press, 1955.

Bosworth, Allan R. *America's Concentration Camps.* New York: W. W. Norton & Company, 1967.

Bowlby, John. *Attachment and Loss.* New York: The Perseus Book Group, 1983.

Brantl, George. *Catholicism.* New York: George Braziller, 1962.

Brecher, Harold and Arline. *Forty Something Forever: A Consumer's Guide to Chelation Therapy.* Herndon, Virginia: Healthsavers Press, 1992.

Brinkley, Dannion with Paul Perry. *Saved by the Light.* New York: Villard Books, 1994.

Broadus, Margaret Bailey. *Through the Rosebuds.* Englewood, CO.: Caruso Associates, 1987.

Briggs, Kenneth A. *Holy Siege: The Year that Shook Catholic America.* San Francisco: HarperCollins, 1992.

Bryan, William L. Jr. *Montana's Indians: Yesterday and Today.* 2d ed. Helena, MT.: American & World Geographic Publishing, 1996.

Burns, James MacGregor. *Roosevelt: The Lion and the Fox.* New York: Harcourt Brace Jovanovich, Inc., 1956.

Butler, Jon and Harry S. Stout. *Religion in American History: A Reader.* New York: Oxford University Press, 1998.

Caldwell, Taylor. *Grandmother and the Priests.* Garden City, NY.: Doubleday, 1963.

Capps, Benjamin. *The Old West: The Great Chiefs.* Alexandria, VA.: Time-Life Books, 1975.

Carriker, Robert C. *Father Peter John De Smet: Jesuit in the West.* Norman, OK.: University of Oklahoma Press, 1995.

Carson, Mary Eisenman. *Blackrobe for the Yankton Sioux.* Chamberlain, SD.: Tipi Press, 1989.

Chase, Ilka. *New York 22*. Chicago: Sears Readers Club, 1951.

Chief, St. Labre Mission High School Year Book, 1953.

Churchill, Winston S. *Memoirs of the Second World War*. 1959. Reprint. Boston: Houghton Mifflin Company, 1987.

Clarke, Gerald. *Capote: A Biography*. New York: Simon and Schuster, 1988.

Colton, Joel. *Twentieth Century*. New York: Time-Life Books, 1968.

Cornelius, Nellie Benson. *Indian Trails*. Ashland, MT.: Mission Press, 1993.

Coughlin, Father. *His "Facts" and Arguments*. New York: Publisher s.n., 1939.

Daws, Gavan. *Holy Man: Father Damien of Molokai*. New York: Harper and Row Publishers, 1973.

Dees, Morris. *Gathering Storm*. New York: Harper Collins Publishers, 1996.

Delaney, John J. *Dictionary of Saints*. New York: Doubleday, 1980.

Deloria, Vine Jr. *Red Earth White Lies*. New York: Scribner, 1995.

Delury, George E., ed. *The World Almanac & Book of Facts*. New York: Newspaper Enterprise Association, Inc., 1977.

Derum, James Patrick. *The Porter of Saint Bonaventure's*. Detroit: The Fidelity Press, 1968.

Dorsey, George A. *The Cheyenne*. Fairfield, WA.: Ye Galleon Press, 1975.

Dunlay, Thomas W. *Wolves for the Blue Soldiers*. Lincoln, NE.: University of Nebraska Press, 1982.

Everett, Susanne. *Lost Berlin*. New York: Gallery Books. W. H. Smith Publishers, Inc., 1979.

Exley, Richard. *Dangers, Toils & Snares*. Sisters, OR.: Multnomah, 1994.

Fedullo, Mick. *Light of the Feather*. New York: William Morrow and Company, 1992.

Ferraro, Barbara, and Patricia Hussey, and Jane O'reilly. *No Turning Back*. New York: Poseidon Press, 1990.

Fetterman, John, ed. *Life in Rural America*. Washington, DC.: National Geographic Society, 1974.

Fischer, James A. *Priests*. New York: Dodd, Mead & Company, 1987.

Forbis, William H. *The Old West: The Cowboys*. New York: Time-Life Books, 1973.

Fortune, Marie M. *Is Nothing Sacred*. NY: Harper & Row, 1989.

Fowler, George. *Dance of a Fallen Monk*. New York: Addison Wesley Publishing Company, 1995.

Frazier, Thomas R. *The Underside of American History*. 3d ed. New York: Harcourt Brace Jovanovich, Inc., 1978.

Friel, John C., and Linda D. Friel. *Adult Children : the Secrets of Dysfunctional Families*. Deerfield Beach, FL.: Health Communications, Inc., 1988.

Fulmer, Genie Philbrick. *Cabins and Campfires in Southeastern Montana*. Worland, WY.: Worland Press, 1973.

Gannon, Robert I. *The Cardinal Spellman Story*. Garden City, NY.: Doubleday & Company, Inc., 1962.

Gerard, James W. *My Four Years in Germany*. n.p.: George H. Doran Company, 1917.

Giago, Tim. *The Aboriginal Sin*. San Francisco: Indian Historian Press, 1978.

Gillard, David. *Industrial Revolution and the New Wealth*. New York: The Hamlyn Publishing Group Ltd., 1970.

Girandola, Father Anthony. *The Most Defiant Priest*. New York: Crown Publishers, 1968.

Glenmore, Josephine Stands in Timber, and Wayne Leman. *Cheyenne Topical Dictionary*. Busby, MT.: Cheyenne Translation Project, 1984.

Goldstein, Donald and Harry J. Maihafer. *The Korean War: Story and Photographs.* Dulles, Virginia: Brassey's Inc., 2000.

Goulden, Joseph C. *The Best Years: 1945-1950*. New York: Atheneum, 1976.

Gramick, Jeannine, and Pat Furey, eds. *The Vatican and Homosexuality*. New York: Crossroad Publishing Company, 1988.

Grinnell, George Bird. *By Cheyenne Campfires*. Yale University Press.,1962. Reprint. Lincoln, NE.: University of Nebraska Press, 1971.

———. *The Cheyenne Indians*. 2 vols. Yale University Press. 1923. Reprint. 2d. ed. New York: Cooper Square Publishers, 1962.

———. *The Fighting Cheyennes*. 1915. Reprint. Norman OK.: University of Oklahoma Press, 1956.

Gutman, Judith, Mara. *Lewis W. Hine and the American Social Conscience*. New York: Walken and Company, 1967.

Hagan, William T. *Indian Police and Judges: Experiment in Acculturation and Control*. Yale University Press. 1966. Reprint. Lincoln, NE.: University of Nebraska Press, 1980.

Hallowell, Edward M.. M.D. and John J. Ratey, M.D. *Driven to Distraction: Recognizing and Coping with Attention Deficit Disorder from Childhood through Adulthood.* New York: Simon & Schuster, 1994.

Hardorff, Richard G., ed. *Cheyenne Memories of the Custer Fight.* Lincoln, NE.: University of Nebraska Press, 1995.

Harrington, Michael. *The Other America.* Baltimore: Penguin Books, 1962.

Hebblethwaite, Peter. *Paul VI.* Mahwah, NJ.: Paulist Press, 1993.

Hedin, Raymond. *Married to the Church.* Indianapolis: Indiana University Press, 1995.

Hofstadter, Richard. *The Age of Reform.* New York: Vintage Books, 1955.

Holiday, eds. *Europe in Color.* Philadelphia: The Curtis Publishing Company, 1957.

Holland, Jack, and John Monroe. *The Order of Rome.* Boston: The Boston Publishing Company, Inc., 1986.

Hopkins, Nancy M. *The Congregation is also a Victim.* Washington, DC.: Alban Institute,1992.

Hougan, Jim. *Secret Agenda: Watergate, Deep throat, and the CIA.* NY: Random House, 1984.

Hurley, Jack F. *Portrait of a Decade.* Baton Rouge, LA.: Louisiana State Press, 1972.

Iverson, Peter., ed. *The Plains Indians of the Twentieth Century.* Norman, OK.: University of Oklahoma Press, 1985.

————. *When Indians became cowboys.* Norman, OK.: University of Oklahoma Press, 1994.

Johansen, Bruce E. and Donald A. Grinde, Jr. *The Encyclopedia of Native American Biography.* New York: Henry Holt and Company, Inc., 1997.

Jones, Douglas C. *The Treaty of the Medicine Lodge.* Norman, OK.: University of Oklahoma Press, 1966.

Kane, Harnett T. *The Ursulines, Nuns of Adventure.* New York: Vision Books, n.d.

Kinnaird, Clark, ed. *It Happened in 1945.* New York: Duell, Sloan and Pearce, 1946.

Knauer, Kelly. *Time 70th Anniversary Celebration: 1923-1993.* New York: Time Books, 1994.

Kubler-Ross, Elisabeth. *The Wheel of Life.* New York: Scribner, 1997.

Kunhardt, Philip B., ed. *Life the First Fifty Years: 1936-1986.* Boston: Little, Brown and Company, 1986.

Kraman, Sister Carlan O.S.F. *A Portrait of Saint Labre Indian Mission Through One Hundred Years.* Ashland, MT.: Mission Press, 1984.

Kronenwetter, Michael. *Wisconsin Heartland: The Story of Wausau and Marathon County.* Midland, MO.: Pendell Publishing company, 1984.

Kurtz, Ernest. *Not-God: A History of Alcoholics Anonymous.* Center City, MN.: Hazelden Educational Materials, 1979.

Kushner, Harold S. *When Bad Things Happen to Good People.* New York: Avon Books, 1981.

La Flesche, Francis. *The Middle Five: Indian Schoolboys of the Omaha Tribe.* The Regents of the University of Wisconsin., 1963. Reprint. Lincoln, NE.: University of Nebraska Press, 1978.

Lau, Alfred. *Deutschland 1683 - 1983.* Bielefeld, Germany: Univers-Verlag, 1983.

Lauro, Joseph M. and Arthur Orrmont. *Action Priest, The Story of father Joe Lauro.* New York: William Morrow, 1971.

Lehnartz, Klaus, and Allan R. Talbot. *New York in the Sixties.* New York: Dover Publications, 1978.

Leman, Wayne., ed. *We Are Going Back Home*: *Cheyenne History and Stories.* Busby, MT.: Algonquian and Iroquoian Linguistics, 1987.

Levi, Virgilio and Christine Allison. *John Paul II.* New York: William Morrow & Company, 1999.

Long, Luman H., ed. *The World Almanac and Book of Facts 1972.* New York: Newspaper Enterprise Association, Inc., 1971.

Longo, Gabriel. *Spoiled Priest.* University Books, Inc., 1966.

Low, Ann Marie. *Dust Bowl Diary.* Lincoln, NE.: University of Nebraska Press, 1984.

Marcus, Sheldon. *Father Coughlin.* Boston: Little, Brown and Company, 1973.

Marquis, Thomas B. *The Cheyennes of Montana.* Algonac, MI.: Reference Publications, Inc., 1978.

McBride, Sister Genevieve, O.S.U. *The Bird Tail.* New York: Vantage Press, 1974.

McCarthy, Mary. *Memories of a Catholic Girlhood.* New York: Harcourt, Brace and Company, 1957.

McCullough, Colleen. *The Thorn Birds.* New York: Avon Books, 1977.

McGeady, Sister Mary Rose. *God's Lost Children.* New York: Covenant House, 1991.

Miles Nelson A. *Personal Recollections & Observations of General Nelson A. Miles:* 2 vols. 1896. Reprint. Lincoln, NE.: University of Nebraska Press, 1992.

Monahan, James. *Before I Sleep...The Last Days of Dr. Tom Dooley.* New York: Farrar, Straus and Cudahy, 1961.

Moody, Raymond A., Jr. *Life After Life.* New York: Bantom Books, 1988.

Moore, John H. *The Cheyenne.* Cambridge: Blackwell Publishers Inc., 1996.

Mulvey, Deb. *We Had Everything But Money.* New York: Crescent Books, 1995.

Moquin, Wayne., ed. *Great Documents in American Indian History.* Praeger., 1973. Reprint. New York: Da Capo Press, 1995.

Murphy, Annie, and Peter De Rosa. *Forbidden Fruit.* Boston: Little, Brown and Company, 1993.

Myers, Gustavus. *History of Bigotry in the United States.* New York: Capricorn Books, 1960.

National Clergy Conference on Alcoholism. *Alcoholism a Source Book for the Priest.* Indianapolis: NCCA, 1960.

National Geographic Society. *Life in Rural America.* National Geographic Society, 1974.

Neeser, Fr. Regis, Capuchin. *Cheyenne Dictionary & Grammar.* Unpublished manuscript.

Nesbit, Robert C. *The History of Wisconsin. Vol. III, 1873-1893.* Madison, Wisconsin: Wisconsin State Historical Society, 1985.

Nesbit, Robert C. *The History of Wisconsin. Vol. V, 1914-1940.* Madison, Wisconsin: Wisconsin State Historical Society, 1985.

Nevin, David. *The Old West: The Soldiers.* New York: Time-Life Books, 1973.

Nixon, Richard. *United States Foreign Policy for the 1970's.* New York: Bantam, 1970.

Official Catalog of the Province of St. Joseph of the Capuchin-Franciscan Order. Detroit: Provincial Publications, 1987.

Oursler, Fulton. *Father Flanagan of Boys Town.* NY: Doubleday, 1949.

Palladino, L.B. S. J. *Indian and White in the Northwest: A History of Catholicity in Montana, 1831-1891.* Lancaster, P.A.: Wickersham Publishing Company, 1922.

Pederson, Jane Marie. *Between Memory and Reality: Family and Community in Rural Wisconsin, 1870-1970.* Madison, WI.: University of Wisconsin Press, 1992.

Peters, Robert. *Crunching Gravel, A Wisconsin Boyhood in the Thirties.* Madison, Wisconsin: University of Wisconsin Press, 1988.

Peters, Sunny. *Hi Cheyennes.* Bozeman, MT.: Color World Printers, 1992.

Powell, Peter J. *People of the Sacred Mountain: A History of the Northern Cheyenne Chiefs and Warrior Societies, 1830-1879.* 2 vols. San Francisco: Harper and Row, 1981.

Powell, Peter J. *Sweet Medicine.* 2 vols. Norman, OK.: University of Oklahoma Press, 1969

Price, Con. *Memories of Old Montana.* Hollywood: The Highland Press, 1945.

Quinn, Peter. *Banished Children of Eve.* New York: Penguin Books, 1994.

Rice, David. *Shattered Vows.* New York: William Morrow and Company, Inc., 1990.

Richardson, Lemont Kingsford. *Wisconsin R.E.A.: the Struggle to Extend Electricity to Rural Wisconsin.* Madison, WI, 1961.

Rosebud County History. *They Came And They Stayed.* Forsyth, MT.: Rosebud County History, 1977.

Rediger, G. Lloyd. *Ministry & Sexuality.* Philadelphia: Westminster Press, 1990.

Rounds, Charles. *Wisconsin Authors and Their Works.* Madison, Wisconsin: Parker Educational Company, 1918.

Ryan, Penelope J. *Practicing Catholic: The Search for a Livable Catholicism.* New York: Henry Holt and Company, 1998.

Sanders, Helen Feitzgerald., and William K. Bertsche, Jr., eds. *X. Berdler: Vigilante.* Norman, OK.: University of Oklahoma Press, 1957.

Sandoz, Mari. *Cheyenne Autumn.* Mc Graw-Hill., 1953. Reprint. Lincoln, NE.: University of Nebraska Press, 1992.

Schwartz, Warren J. *The Last Contrary.* Sioux Falls, SD.: The Center for Western Studies, 1988.

Seger, John H. *Early Days Among the Cheyenne & Arapahoe Indians.* Norman, OK.: University of Oklahoma Press, 1956.

Shapiro, William E., ed. *The New Book of Knowledge Annual 1970.* New York: Grolier, 1970.

Shannon, David A., ed. *The Great Depression.* Englewood Cliffs, NJ.: Prentice-Hall, 1960.

Sheed, F. J., ed. *Saints Are Not Sad.* New York: Sheed and Ward, Inc., 1949.

Small, Lawrence F., ed. *Religion in Montana.* Billings, MT.: Rocky Mountain College, 1992.

Stands in Timber, John., and Liberty, Margot. *Cheyenne Memories.* Yale University Press., 1967. Reprint. Lincoln, NE.: University of Nebraska Press, 1972.

Steinbeck, John. *The Grapes of Wrath*. 1939. Reprint. Harmondsworth, UK.: Penguin, 1976.

Straub, A.G. *The History of Marathon, Wisconsin 1857-1957*. Marathon, Wisconsin: Marathon Times, 1957.

Stuart, Granville. *Pioneering in Montana: The Making of a State 1864-1887*. Edited by Paul C. Phillips. The Arthur H. Clark Company, 1925.

Svingen, Orlan J. *The Northern Cheyenne Indian Reservation 1877-1900*. Niwot, CO.: University Press of Colorado,1993.

Terkel, Studs. *Hard Times: An Oral History of the Great Depression*. New York: Random House, Pantheon Books, Inc.,1970.

Time-Life Books, eds. *The American Indians: Cycles of Life*. Richmond, VA.: Time-Life Books, 1994.

Time-Life Books, eds. *This Fabulous Century. Vol. 5, 1930-1940*. Alexandria, Virginia: Time-Life Books, 1969.

Uys, Errol Lincoln. *Riding the Rails: Teenagers on the Move During the Great Depression*. New York: TV Books, L.L.C., 1999.

Vaughn, J.W. *The Reynolds Campaign on Powder River*. Norman, OK.: University of Oklahoma press, 1961.

———. *With Crook at the Rosebud*. Harrisburg, PA.: The Stackpole Company, 1956.

Walker, Morton D.P.M. *The Chelation Answer*. Atlanta: Second Opinion Publishing, 1994.

Washington, D.C. rev. ed., New York: Crescent Books, 1986.

Weaver, Kenneth L. *Reflections on Tribal Governance in Montana*. Bozeman, MT.: Montana State University, 1990.

Welsh, Douglas. *The USA In World War I*. New York: Galahad Books, 1982.

Weist, Tom. *A History of the Cheyenne People*. rev. ed., Billings, MT.: Montana Council for Indian Education, 1984.

Whitaker, Julian M., MD. *Reversing Heart Disease*. NY: Warner Books, 1985.

White, E. B. *Here is New York*. New York: Harper & Brothers Publishers, 1949.

Whitfield, Charles L. *Healing the Child Within*. Deerfield Beach, FL.: Health Communications, Inc., 1987.

Wilson, Joan Hoff., ed. *The Twenties: The Critical Issues*. Boston: Little, Brown and Company, 1972.

Witkin, Georgia Lanoil, Ph.D. *The Male Stress Syndrome* New York: Newmarket Press, 1986.

Woititz, Janet G. *Adult Children of Alcoholics.* Pompano Beach, FL.: Health Communications, Inc., 1983.

NEWSPAPER SOURCES

The Ashland Story (local Ashland, MT newspaper)
October 12, 1983 n.t.

Billings Gazette

"Cheyenne, Who Saw Chief Joseph Surrender, Dies in V.A. Hospital"
March 6, 1957

"Ashland Mission Director Sues U.S. for Postage"
n.d., 1962

"Northern Cheyennes Make Good"
April 5, 1962

"Indian Housing Program Pushed"
February 24, 1962

"Cheyenne Get Industry Chance"
August 24, 1962

"Indian Sanitation Drive Pushed"
February 2, 1963

"Better Housing on Reservation a Benefit to Crow Family"
October 25, 1963

"Mrs. Petter Looks Back on Years of Service, Friendship with Cheyennes"
November 21, 1963

"Cheyennes Set Job Records"
November 30, 1963

"Bertha Petter, Missionary to Cheyenne Indians Looking Ahead at 91"
December 29, 1963

"Bright Future for Morning Star People"
December 31, 1963

"Tribe Plans to Maintain Proud History"
January 1, 1964

"Self-Help to House Indians"
February 16, 1964

Billings Gazette

"Northern Cheyennes Wait Loan Approval"
April 16, 1964

"Ashland Factory in New Plant"
December 25, 1964

"Cheyennes Dedicate Ashland Plant"
February 20, 1965

"All the Indians Want to Be Chiefs"
October 9, 1965

"Cheyennes' Crafts Plant Laying Off 50 Workers"
March 18, 1966

"Cheyennes Troubled by New Homes"
March 18, 1966

"Probe Asked"
March 18, 1966

"Negotiation May Solve Tribulations of Tribe"
March 26, 1966

"BIA Put on Notice"
April 10, 1966

"Why Not Share?"
May 3, 1966

"Christmas on Reservation"
July 1966

"Indians Adapting Well To Light Industry Skills"
July 26, 1966

"Indian Health Moves Upward"
September 27, 1966

"Shepherd of the Morning Star"
April 23, 1967

"Off the Reservation is Trouble"
July 9, 1969

"Life's Rough for Welfare Indians"
March 15, 1970

"Carbon Monoxide Danger Facing Some Cheyennes"
April 15, 1970

272

Billings Gazette

"Study Reveals Indians Most Disadvantaged Group"
November 19, 1970

"Indian Housing Progresses"
January 20, 1971

"Indian Housing Funds Approved"
June 19, 1971

"Coal Rush – a Boom or a Last Stand?"
October 1, 1972

"BIA Answers Complaints Over Coal by Indians"
December 14, 1973

"King Coal Arises"
March 17, 1974

"Cheyenne Tribe Fears Bad Effects"
April 21, 1974

"Alan Rowland Looking for Trouble"
January 28, 1977

"Soon the Music Ends; Guild Factory to Close"
February 6, 1977

"BIA, U.S. Attorney Mum on St. Labre"
May 16, 1991

"St. Labre Home Abuse Rumored"
May 22, 1991

"Hoffmann Leaves St. Labre"
November 12, 1993

"Hoffmann to Quit St. Labre Unless..."
November 13, 1993

"Historian Studies St. Labre Priest"
November 28, 1997

"Still Soaring, Priest Devotes Life to Helping Northern Cheyennes" 1997

"Miracle on the Hill"
December 21, 2002

Christian Science Monitor

"Cheyennes Chalk Up Gains"
January 8, 1964

Denver Post

"Tribe Disputes Poverty tale"
March 15, 1966

Forsyth Independent

"Ashland Plastics Plant to Close"
January 13, 1977

Hardin Tribune Herald

"Heat Bills High, No Water, Sewer in New Cheyenne Reservation Housing"
March 17,1966

"Cheyennes Fear Possible Closing of Ashland Plant"
March 17, 1966

Indian Country Today

"Notes From Indian Country – Retribution for Catholic Sins is Near"
1998 n.d.

La Crosse Tribune

"Death Car Speeds off in Darkness"
December 11, 1921

"Little Andrew Hoffmann Dies During Night"
December 13, 1921

"Police Continue Hunt for Driver of Death Car"
December 15, 1921

"Two Arrested for Double Tragedy"
December 18, 1921

Michigan Catholic

"Indian Spokesman Hits Schools for Indians"
December 28, 1967

Milwaukee Journal

"Catholic Children's Home Investigated for Sex Abuse"
May 20, 1991

Milwaukee Journal

"Sex Abuse Charges Investigated"
May 21, 1991

"8 Men Tell of Sex Abuse by Friars"
December 20, 1992

National Catholic Reporter

"No Turning Back"
November 12, 1999

New York Times

"For the Indian: Squalor in the Great Society Despite Antipoverty Program"
March 13, 1966

"American Indians' Self-Help"
March 15, 1966

Reporter (Fond Du Lac, Wisconsin)

"Sex Molestations Cited, a Seminary County Investigates St. Lawrence Teacher"
December 20, 1992

Seattle Times

"False memories common, study says"
February 16, 1997

Toledo Blade

"Nurse Credited in Curbing of TB Among Indians"
November 3, 1963

Wausau Pilot

"Milk Strike In State Not Felt In Wausau, Say Local Dairymen"
February 16, 1933

"Highlights In Milk Strike Situation"
May 18, 1933

"Milk Pool Head Fails to Appear at Strike Meeting"
May 18, 1933

"Milk Strike in This County Free From Violence"
May 18, 1933

"Milk Strike is Cause of Suicide Near Marathon"
May 18, 1933

Wausau Pilot

"Milk Strike Ends In Agreement to Arbitrate Issues"
May 25, 1933

"Strike Pickets Released Under $250 Bail Bonds"
May 25, 1933

"Milk Pool Agrees To Join Farm Holiday Strike"
October 26, 1933

"Strike Picket Taken Into Custody Today"
October 26, 1933

"County Holiday Group Ignores Order Terminating Farm Strike"
November 2, 1933

"Local Dairy Plants Receive Milk Supplies"
November 2, 1933

"Farmers Strike Assumes Watchful Waiting Attitude"
November 9, 1933

"County Board in Midst of Annual Session This Week"
November 16, 1933

"Farm Strike Sympathizers Invade the City"
November 16, 1933

"Result of State Wide Strike Vote To Decide Issue"
November 16, 1933

"County Board Authorizes Poll In Farm Strike"
November 23, 1933

"County Tax Is Jumped $206,544.67 This Year"
November 23, 1933

"Nearly 900 Men Obtain Work In Marathon County"
November 30, 1933

"Strike Vote Is Over Two To One Against Issue"
November 30, 1933

JOURNAL AND MAGAZINE ARTICLES

Berry, Jason. "Listening to the Survivors: Voices of People of God." *America* (November 13, 1993):4-9.

Buckley, William F. "The Church's Newest Cross, Pedophiliac Priests." *National Review* (April 26, 1993):63.

276

Burke, Tim. "New Indian Youth Club Runs the Gamut." *Youth Today,* reprinted by "1996 Trends in Indian Health," H.H. Indian Health Service Office of Health Programs. Rockville, MD 20857.

Cannon, Angie and Jeffery L. Sheler. "Catholics in Crisis: With continued revelations of sex abuse scandals and cover-ups, the faithful look to the church for change" *U.S. News and World Report* (April 1, 2002)

Castelli, Jim. "Abuse of Faith: How to Understand the Crime of Priest Pedophilia." *U.S. Catholic* (September 1993):6-15.

Chua Eoan, Howard G. "After the Fall: Catholic Church Lags Behind in Forging a Policy on Priestly Pedophilia." *Time* (May 9, 1994):56-58.

Clark, Donald C. "Sexual Abuse in the Church: the Law Steps In." *The Christian Century* (April 14, 1993):396-398.

Connors, Canice. "The Moment After Suffering: Lessons from the Pedophilia Scandal." *Commonweal* (October 21, 1994):14-17.

Cooper White, Pamela. "Soul Stealing: Power Relations in Pastoral Sexual Abuse." *The Christian Century* (February 20, 1991):196-199.

Curran, Dolores. "If it weren't for Vatican II: The Catholic Experience, then and now." *Catholic Digest* (October 2001):69-77.

Dreese, John J. "The Other Victims of Priest Pedophilia." *Commonweal* (April 22, 1994):11-14.

Freund, Kurt. "Phallometric Diagnosis of Pedophilia." *Journal of Consulting and Clinical Psychology* (February 1989):100-105.

Hall, Gordon C. "Validity of Physiological Measures of Pedophilic Sexual Arousal." *Journal of Consulting and Clinical Psychology* (February 1988):118-122.

Jacobs, Herbert. "The Wisconsin Milk Strike." *Wisconsin Magazine of History* 35(Autumn1951):30-35.

Jordan Lake, Joy. "Conduct Unbecoming a Preacher." *Christianity Today* (February 10, 1992):26-30.

Komonchak, Joseph A. "The Most Important Religious Event of the Century." *Catholic Digest* (October 2001):61-68.

n.a. "I Live Happily: A German Immigrant in Territorial Wisconsin." *Wisconsin Magazine of History* (Spring 1957):254-259.

McGeary, Johanna. "Can The Church Be Saved?" *Time* (April 1, 2002)

Miller, Lisa and David France. "Sins of the Fathers." *Newsweek* (March 4, 2002)

Ruether, Rosemary. "Crises and Challenges of Catholics Today." *America* (March 1, 1986):152-158

Sheler, Jeffery L. "The Unpardonable Sin." *U.S. News & World Report* (November 16, 1992):94-96.

Sullivan, Andrew. "They Still Don't Get It: How can a church that judges so many faithful cover up its own offenses?" *Time* (March 4, 2002)

Wall, James M. "There ought to be a Law." *The Christian Century* (May 4, 1994): 459-460.

UNPUBLISHED SOURCES

Bush, Sister Mary Eustella O.S.F. *Sand, Sage, and Struggle*. Unpublished book, 1973, SEHP Collection, Billings, Montana.

Kramer, Sister Giswalda. "Memoirs of a Missionary," School Sisters of St. Francis, School Archives, Milwaukee, Wisconsin.

Kung, Tim Yuan Shiao. "Spilt Milk: Dairy farmer Rhetoric and Actions During the Wisconsin Milk Strikes of 1933." Master's thesis, University of Wisconsin, 1996.

McGarvey, Mary. "Memoirs." Carole A. Kunkel Collection, Bayonne, New Jersey.

n.a. "To The Friends of Our Beloved Deceased, Fintan Schaub." SEHP Collection, Billings, Montana.

n.a. "A Chronological Narrative of the Northern Cheyennes 1876-1942." Prepared for the Northern Cheyenne Tribe and Montana State Historical Project by the Historic Project Resource and Data Department, Northern Cheyenne Planning Office, September 7, 1982. Lame Deer, Montana.

Sacred Heart, Sister. "A History of the Northern Cheyenne." 1885, Ursuline Archives, Great Falls, MT.

Name Index